The Micro
Millennium

By the same author

MIND IN CHAINS (ed.)

MIND AT BAY (ed.)

CULTS OF UNREASON

PSYCHOLOGY: A DICTIONARY OF THE MIND,
BRAIN AND BEHAVIOUR

The Micro
Millennium

Christopher Evans

THE VIKING PRESS · NEW YORK

1981

Copyright © 1979 by Christopher Evans
All rights reserved
First published in 1980 by The Viking Press
625 Madison Avenue, New York, N.Y. 10022
Published in Great Britain as *The Mighty Micro*

LIBRARY OF CONGRESS CATALOGING IN PUBLICATION DATA
Evans, Christopher Richie.
The micro millennium.
Includes index.
1. Computers and civilization.
2. Micro-computers. I. Title.
QA76.9.C66E9   001.6′4   79-23459
ISBN 0-670-47400-2

Printed in the United States of America
Set in Plantin

CONTENTS

CONTENTS

INTRODUCTION

The Computer Revolution

THIS BOOK IS about the future. Not some distant future which we and our descendants can blissfully ignore, but one which is imminent and whose progress can be plotted with some degree of precision. It is a future which will involve a transformation of world society at all kinds of levels, and while taking place slowly at first, will gather pace with sudden force. It's a future which is largely moulded by a single, startling development in technology whose impact is just beginning to be felt. The piece of technology I'm talking about is, of course, the computer.

Computers will be frequently mentioned in this book, and while most people avoid reading or thinking about them on the grounds that they are simply too complex to understand, no technological knowledge or insight is going to be necessary to follow the arguments presented. I have gone briefly into the history of computers, however, partly because it is a fascinating area largely unknown to most people, but also because a knowledge of their evolution from their earliest beginnings to the present day helps one to understand the nature of their inevitable development in the future. Part One is therefore Computers Past. Part Two is Computers Present, where I look at the present state of computer technology and consider some of the colossal pressures that are already driving computer evolution on an upward spiral. The remaining parts are devoted to the future—the short term, medium term and long term, and it is a measure of how fast things are moving that I will take my long-term predictions no further ahead than the year 2000—now only twenty-one years away. It is in this section—where I have also devoted a chapter to the nature of intelligence, its significance in animals and men, and its ultimate realization in machines—that we will be talking about the world transformed.

Threats or promises that the world is about to be transformed are by no means uncommon, and the human race as a whole—wisely—pays little attention to them and goes about its business planning, if it bothers to plan at all, to face the crisis, catastrophe or new millennium when it actually materializes. In fact, events that are radical enough to overcome the huge social, economic and psychological inertia of the earth's population tend to be extremely rare. Even global wars affect only a small percentage to any significant degree, and the same is true of famines, floods, earthquakes, and just about anything else you can think of. But there have been global trends which have had enduring, if rather long-term, significance. The discovery of navigational techniques is one example, and the invention of printing another. More recent, more far-reaching, and more rapid in the speed with which it unleashed its effects was the Industrial Revolution.

It is almost impossible to overestimate the extent and significance of this turning point in human affairs, which arose because man found means to supplement and amplify the power of his muscles with machinery. Suddenly it became possible to perform feats of literally superhuman strength, to perform tasks of endless duration without the need for rest. No country on earth remained untouched by the effects of this change, and those, like Britain, which were involved in its innovative stages became globally wealthy and powerful.

There are four important features of the Industrial Revolution which need to be identified and considered, for they will turn out to be extremely significant for the next great turning point which mankind is rapidly approaching—the Computer Revolution. The first of these concerns the scale and scope of change: the Revolution brought immense shifts in all aspects of human society, affecting the individual, his family, his neighbours, his domestic and working environment, his clothes, his food, his leisure time, his political and religious ideals, his education, his social attitudes, his life-span, even the manner of his birth and death. The second feature is that these changes took place with great rapidity, remoulding the face of our society in less than a hundred years. Thirdly, once the process of the Revolution was fully under way, its dynamic growth was remorseless, and no power, no man or combination of men, could set it back against its course. Any efforts made to soften its impact and direct its strength into areas that might offer lasting benefit to mankind rather than simply increasing universal affluence were of minor import.

Finally, and perhaps the most interesting of the four points, hardly anyone—certainly no one who could do anything about it—foresaw its momentous coming. Only the gallantly misguided Luddites, who feared a loss of affluence from the coming of the machines, seemed to have any glimmering of insight into what was about to happen.

I have spelt out these points rather formally because they have very direct bearing on the Computer Revolution, in which we move from the amplification and emancipation of the power of muscles to the amplification and emancipation of the power of the brain. As with the Industrial Revolution it will have an overwhelming and comprehensive impact, affecting every human being on earth in every aspect of his or her life. Again, paralleling its predecessor, it will run at a gallop, though its time course will be shorter and its force may well be spent not in 150 years, but in twenty-five. Thirdly—again note the parallel—once the Revolution is under way it will be unstoppable, for reasons which we will consider in detail.

But there is an essential point of difference: whereas the Victorian machine age began, surged into motion and, indeed, almost ran its course before most people were aware of what had happened, we of the closing years of the 1970s have the gift of foresight, the ability to contemplate—if not for long—the amazing change that man is about to force upon himself. This book is an attempt to predict the nature of the change, and to signal its imminence and inevitability. There may be very little time left for us to prepare ourselves for the future—but any time is better than none at all.

Part One

THE PAST

CHAPTER ONE

The Weavers of Numbers

IN ONE SENSE computers have had a brief history—not much more than twenty-five years. In another sense their use stretches back in time to the first occasion when Man picked up a few small stones, or scratched marks in the earth as a kind of memory aid. What he was doing was using a physical unit or set of units to represent numbers or quantities, and the essence of computers is just this: a number or a quantity can be represented by a *physical thing*, whether it is a pebble, a bead on a wire, a mark on a bit of paper, a mechanical gear wheel, an electrical relay, a vacuum tube or a sub-microscopic area of magnetized material. Once numbers can be expressed in this way, it becomes possible to manipulate them or change their state and cause them to represent different numbers or quantities. This, in turn, means that it becomes possible to construct a machine to perform these manipulations. The important point to grasp—and it is all one needs to know about the physical make-up of computers to understand and follow the rest of this book—is that while numbers are abstract in one sense, they are really all expressible as physical units or chunks and that provided one chooses the right kind of physical chunk, it is possible to calculate with them and to store them over time.

A crude example of storage and calculation is the speedometer on a motor car. Here the mileage is expressed by a row of numbers in a window, and these reflect the positions of a set of interlocking cogs behind them. These cogs (each of which has ten teeth) record tenths of miles, miles, tens of miles, and so on. No doubt this will all seem maddeningly obvious, but we will press on at this simple level: as the car's wheels turn they cause the first of the cog-wheels to turn, and a sequence of "tenths-of-mile" units is displayed in the window; a complete revolution is made each

THE MICRO MILLENNIUM

time a mile has been covered. As each revolution is completed, a lever on the side of the first cog hits one of the teeth on the mile-recording cog next to it, causing *it* to turn through a tenth of a revolution, and the appropriate "mile" number is displayed in the window. After ten such blows it too has revolved completely and taps the ten-mile cog next to it, and so on. The lever which passes the message from one cog to another is of course the equivalent of the "carry" in paper-and-pencil arithmetic.

What we have been describing is a very simple mechanical calculator which has (a) counted distances in decimal units, (b) added tenths-of-miles to make miles, miles to make tens-of-miles, and (c) displayed its "answer" in a way that a human can read. Strictly speaking this is a mechanical "adder"—it can't multiply or divide, though it could "subtract" if you decided to drive the car in reverse. When the car is stationary, the speedometer "remembers" the mileage it has covered.

It would be wrong to give the impression that these metallic clankings represent the mode of operation of modern computers, but the example of the speedometer will do to introduce the central concept of machines counting numbers and doing something with them; and that, as I have said, is all that has to be grasped.

Clearly there were calculators before the invention of the car speedometer. The most commonly cited example of a primitive device is the abacus, which has been around for about five thousand years. The abacus is a collection of beads on a series of rods or wires, and the position of the beads in relation to one or other end of the frame denotes their number. The different levels of the frame denote different parts of the sum to be calculated, and computation is performed by moving the beads back and forth according to a set of rules. People get to be very nimble at operating the abacus, and its use has only recently died out in Japan.

Part of the spur to develop devices like the abacus—there were several different types of them being used all over the world at one time—was the difficulty people experienced in doing "pencil-and-paper" calculations. Try to imagine a method of multiplying the following Roman numerals:

CCXXXII times XLVIII

The problem is even worse in ancient Chinese notation, but when translated into Arabic numerals, the sum becomes 232 times 48 and the whole thing takes on a different complexion. This is not simply because we are more familiar with Arabic numerals; they actually are far easier to perform written calculations with, and those societies which adopted them when they first came on the scene—which included all Europe west of Russia—not only freed themselves from having to use the abacus for every non-trivial calculation, but also opened the way for their scholars to delve into levels of mathematics beyond the scope of those stuck with more primitive notational methods.

But even Arabic numbers don't make for effortless calculating. As medieval societies became more complex and dependent upon extensive economic exchanges, so the routine calculations that had to be churned out grew and grew. Most of this was sheer drudgery, and too much for the average individual who, by the way, was more or less totally innumerate. Even educated people were not taught rudimentary mathematics in their basic schooling, and though some businessmen attempted to master huge sets of tables—up to 24 times 24 for example—a better solution was to hire professional "mathematicians" to do the routine number-crunching. But it was impossible to work for more than an hour or so at a stretch without fatigue and error creeping in, and it is not surprising that the invention of the slide-rule in the latter half of the seventeenth century was greeted with shouts of joy.

The slide-rule, which had an active life of over three centuries before it was ingloriously consigned to the scrap-heap in the mid-1970s on the appearance of pocket calculators, was an invention which sprang naturally out of the discovery of logarithms by the Scotsman, John Napier.

Logarithms, as most schoolchildren know—or at least used to know, because logarithms as calculation aids are also being whisked away on the winds of history—are tables of numbers which greatly simplify routine multiplication and division. For every positive number, Napier discovered, there exists another number (called its logarithm), and the relationship between them is such that the multiplication of any two numbers is achieved by *adding* their logarithms. Division is achieved by *subtracting* their logarithms. The drawback is that you have to convert the numbers to their appropriate logs by looking them up in a table and, after you have done the sum, reconvert it to "real" numbers by looking it up in an "anti-log" table. But the process is still far simpler than routine multiplication and division.

Since logarithms are, as it were, compressed versions of their original numbers, people realized that by converting these into lengths on a scale or ruler, multiplication and division could be done by simply adding or subtracting the two lengths on the scale. From this point the concept of the slide-rule more or less springs to mind, and with it the notion of a machine as a calculation aid. Curiously, Napier himself doesn't seem to have thought of it. But he did have another clever idea, which was to lay out multiplication tables on the faces of a set of rotatable wooden cylinders; you turned the appropriate cylinders (there was one for each of the ten digits) and added or subtracted whatever numbers came up on the exposed faces. The set was mounted nicely in a wooden box with instructions on the lid, and became known as Napier's Bones. The types of calculations you could perform with them were really extremely trivial—the kind of thing anyone can do in their heads now—and the fact that they were invented at all and sold in quite large numbers is a testimony to the poor state of the mathematical education of the time.

The first true machine capable of performing arithmetical functions appeared about a quarter of a century after logarithms, and it made no use of Napier's discovery whatsoever. Its inventor was Blaise Pascal, the son of a French tax collector. He was a mathematical prodigy who made a tremendous mark on seventeenth-century science and philosophy, and while still in his teens he generated the design for his mechanical adder—probably moved by observing his father labouring away into the night on the financial calculations which were his bread and butter. Today it looks pretty unimpressive, a set of interlocking cogs and wheels on various axles, but it *was* the world's first calculating machine. You set up the numbers you wanted to add by literally dialling them, which caused the cogs and wheels inside to rotate appropriately. When you'd finished dialling in the last number, the result—which of course merely expressed the new positions of the wheels inside—was displayed in a little window. It was called the Pascaline, and everyone was suitably amazed. A machine that could add! It could subtract too, incidentally, though you had to make an adjustment inside to make it "count backwards". With a bit more effort it could multiply by a series of repeated additions, or divide by repeated subtractions, which is the way that most mechanical calculators operated until quite recently.

The cleverness of the device lay in the fact that Pascal had realized how a machine could tackle the task of "carrying", a problem which had to be solved if one was going to compute numbers larger than ten, and the principle is the same as that used in the speedometer. The Pascaline was in essence foolproof and, as it would undoubtedly take the drudgery out of much routine calculation, a number of units were constructed and marketed. But few, if any, buyers were found. The reasons were simple and are often encountered today in computerizing some modern business organizations. No one doubted that the Pascalines would work: the fact was that the clerks and accountants employed by the potential customers of the machines were afraid that if many of the things were purchased they would be out of a job. This attitude is interesting as a precursor of much of the present resistance to automation and computerization, but it is not actually the most important factor.

It is a basic tenet of capitalism that profitability is the first thing to strive for, and if the businessmen had felt that Pascal's invention would save them significant sums of money they would have bought it in vast numbers and cheerfully sacked all the clerks and accountants. But a Pascaline was rather an expensive instrument to buy and, while its running costs were zero, its repair and maintenance would not be cheap. Against this, the clerks and accountants were extremely cheap and, of course, they did the whole job while the mechanical adder only did a part of it. The sole justification for a Pascaline would to be to make life a bit easier for the drudge accountants, and why waste money on them? So the brilliant invention was a flop economically, if not scientifically.

Businessmen may have rejected the world's first mechanical calculator, but men of science were less able to do so, and one of the first people to inspect one in operation and have a really good think about it, was Gottfried Leibnitz. Born in Saxony in 1646, just after Pascal had put together the first of his adders, Leibnitz was another child prodigy who, after the fashion of his kind, was writing Greek and Latin verse by the time he was ten, and had moved on to the principles of formal logic in his early teens. He quickly saw that the great weakness of the Pascaline was that the tasks of multiplication and division were tackled by it in a most laborious fashion, and that any really useful mechanical calculator would have to work on a different principle.

Leibnitz solved the problem by introducing a new kind of multiplier wheel, which was stepped with nine teeth of different lengths. It was a brilliant idea and it really worked, and the chances are that if you pull apart one of the electro-mechanical calculators of the 1960s, now gathering dust in the corners of many schools and research laboratories, you will see how well his invention survived three hundred years. There is no doubt that it markedly speeded up all kinds of routine calculation, unlike Pascal's device which merely made them a bit easier, and if Leibnitz had pushed ahead with manufacturing his machine it might well have caught on. But by then he was bored with the project and moved on to other things. Included among the "other things" were developing the notation of differential calculus, and he also flirted, in a way that is most tantalizing to the historian who is obliged to wonder what would have happened if the flirtation had flowered into passion, with binary arithmetic.

Most human calculating is done according to the principles of decimal arithmetic. We begin counting from zero through to nine, and then start all over again prefacing the same ten digits with a 1, later with a 2, 3, 4 and so on. In other words we employ a maximum of ten symbols, including zero, and form any and every number out of permutations of these symbols. This may seem to be labouring the obvious, but it is necessary to do so because most people think that this is the "natural" or the only way to count. But what is special about ten? Why not an octal (based on eight) system for example? Using this we would have only eight symbols and would count 0,1,2,3,4,5,6,7,   10,11,12,13,14,15,16, 17,   20, etc. This emphasizes that, though we currently count in tens, it is just one of a very large number of ways in which arithmetical systems can be built up. This fact is one of which all mathematicians are fully aware, and indeed were aware in the time of Leibnitz and Pascal, but most of them were convinced of the virtues of the decimal system and could see no obvious reason for changing it. For a period, Leibnitz began to take a more than passing interest in a system of counting which is one of the oldest known to man—the binary system. Here only two basic numbers are used, 0 and 1. There are no 3s, 4s, 5s, etc. Even so it is possible to express any number that can be expressed in the decimal—or any other system for that matter—using just these two symbols. It is worth looking at this briefly because it helps one to grasp the basic principle of operation of all modern computers.

Binary arithmetic starts off quite straightforwardly, 0 being written 0 and 1 being written 1. But from there it moves rapidly away from conventional decimal notation. 2, for example, is 10, while 3 is 11 and 4 is 100. Remember that in the octal system there is no special symbol for 8, and after 7 the next number you write is 10. The same applies in binary, the only difference being that you get to the mathematical turning point, if it can be put that way, after two numerals instead of eight. Now things get even stranger. There is no symbol for 5, so instead you write 101. 6 is 110; 7, 111 and 8 is 1000. 9 is 1001; 10, 1010; 11, 1011 and 12, 1100. For 13 we have 1101 and 14, 1110, and 15 is 1111. At 16 the number lengthens once again and we have 10000 while 17 is 10001 and so on. This may look a bit complicated and perhaps a bit mad, but the important thing to grasp is that with this system, you can do mathematical calculations using only *two* types of symbols, whereas, of course, in a decimal system you need ten. This may not be much of an advantage to human beings, and the long numbers which build up using binary notation are difficult to comprehend at a glance. But for calculating machines, mechanical, electronic or otherwise, nothing, just nothing, can be so convenient or appropriate as a binary system.

The reasons for this are obvious if you consider the interior of even Pascal's simple calculator. Every single number up to ten had to be represented in his device by a tooth on a cog-wheel, and thus every cog-wheel had to have ten teeth. The same applied to other cog-wheels coping with the 10s, the 100s, the 1000s and so on, making for a mass of interconnecting gears, an increase in complexity, and a corresponding probability of mechanical error with every increase in the size of the device.

Now, as I have said, there was a brief period in his life when Leibnitz turned his tremendous intellectual powers to bear on the utility and the potential of binary arithmetic, becoming fascinated with its elegance, economy and simplicity. How, one wonders, would the future of calculating machines have progressed if he had spotted that instead of all those interlocking gears there could have been a series of on-off binary levers or sprung switches, simple to design, cheap to build, easy to assemble and enormously reliable? Giant steam-driven computers in the nineteenth century perhaps? The beginning of the Industrial Revolution fifty years ahead of its time and in Germany instead of Britain? One can go on guessing endlessly, but there is little point in it for Leibnitz's brain did not integrate the two areas of possibility.

And so the eighteenth century, full of economic and political upheaval, but relatively uneventful in terms of the advance of automatic calculating machines, came to a close. In its last decade, however, Charles Babbage, who is generally considered to have invented (so far as it is possible to establish the source of an invention) the computer, was born.

Babbage, an inventor and a mathematician of eminence, was born in England in 1791. He was, like many of the scholars of the time, a man of considerable inherited wealth, which he ultimately spent in the mad, gallant enterprise which was to become his life's work. In the early nineteenth century the growing complexity of life was already beginning to make itself felt and more and more people made their living solely by performing calculations and compiling numerical data of all kinds. Among the most arduous and error-prone tasks was the compilation of log tables, and Babbage was forever spotting trivial errors in them. According to his own account it was pondering the time-wasting and desperately routine nature of log calculations which led him to conceive that a machine ought to be able to do this kind of thing far more easily and accurately. Before long, the basic scheme for such a machine began to assemble itself in his mind, and in 1821 he was sufficiently confident of what he was doing to announce to the Royal Astronomical Society that he would build a pilot model and demonstrate it before them. The machine would work, he indicated, "on the method of differences", and he gave convincing details as to how it would go about its business. We don't need to explain exactly how it worked, but it could solve polynomial equations by calculating successive differences between sets of numbers. He showed it to the assembled Society in 1822, and the presentation was so well received that his paper "Observations on the Application of Machinery to the Computation of Mathematical Tables" was awarded the Society's gold medal—its first. Thus enthused, Babbage set out to build a full-scale working version.

Even the sketchiest glance at Babbage's plans reveals that it was a very ambitious scheme indeed. The basic principles of calculation—cogs and wheels again—were no different from anything that had been built before. But it was very much bigger and very much more complicated, and, with his limitless optimism, Babbage had determined that it should not only calculate tables, but also print them out on paper at the end. He even applied for support from the British Government who awarded him a grant of £1500. A workshop was built on Babbage's estate, skilled workmen hired and construction got under way.

The main task was the turning up on special lathes, and to the highest possible tolerances, of the hundreds of rods, wheels, ratchets and gears which would constitute the Difference Engine's working parts. And it was here that big snags appeared. The little unit which he had built for the Astronomical Society was a demonstration piece. Minor irregularities in its components might lead to slack in the system, but this would be too insignificant to cause jamming or inhibit its overall function. But in the Difference Engine proper, any series of minor imperfections tended to compound, leading to great internal shakings and seizures. Babbage tightened up the manufacturing specification, and urged his workers to greater and greater care. There was an improvement, but not enough to match the overall complexity of the system. Undaunted by his first setbacks, perhaps stubbornly so, he lashed his mechanics in a vain attempt to make them perform better than the tools and materials of the time would allow, and applied to the Government for more and more money. They obliged up to a total of £17,000 and then decided that enough was enough; the project went into suspended animation in 1833. Now if Babbage had been a sensible man—which he wasn't—this is the moment when he would have sat back and surveyed the tons of brass and pewter cog-wheels, sprockets and other knick-knacks and faced up to the fact that he was a hundred years ahead of his time—which he was. But instead, his restless mind began to consider an even more ambitious scheme. And at that moment the concept of the computer was born.

Although the Difference Engine was of an order of magnitude more advanced than anything that had been attempted in the past, it was still basically capable of doing just one job—solving polynomial equations. And this it achieved by going through a fixed set of movements, one set of wheels inducing the turning of another set, one lever raising another and so on, all in a more or less predictable sequence. The system in other words was what would now be called a special-purpose computer. It had one job it could do, and that was all it lived for.

Pondering this, Babbage saw that it was far from the whole story. A machine which could perform calculations of one kind could, in all probability, perform any kind of calculation—a hunch which was to be demonstrated mathematically over a century later by another British genius, Alan Turing. A radical and exciting concept now emerged. Why not make a single machine which didn't have a fixed purpose, but which could tackle a whole variety of tasks as and when the owner wanted it to? It might be a lot more complicated than the Difference Engine, and a lot more expensive to build, but it would be a whole lot more useful. The "obvious" thought must have been to see the new machine as a composite of lots of other machines, part "a" coming into being for task "a", and part "b" for task "b", but all of them using, say, a common input mechanism and a common link to the printer or other output device. But Babbage rejected the obvious, and in doing so achieved his magnificent insight. The machine's design should be such that its internal parts could be employed in a great variety of different ways, so that when a particular task was being tackled, a unique sequence of internal activity would be set up, with each different task being tied to unique internal "patterns of action". All that was needed was a clever idea for telling the machine which of the infinite variety of "patterns of action" were to be employed at any one time. This device Babbage was to call his Analytical Engine, and it's worth interjecting that what he was talking about was a programmable computer.

This is not a book about how computers work and I will not attempt to explain the frenetic complexities of the interior of the Analytical Engine. A model of it—put together some years later by Babbage's son—can be seen in the Science Museum in London. On the other hand it is worth looking into its guts if only to spot that it consisted of a number of distinct and partly autonomous functioning units which are very close to the functioning units of all modern computers.

In the first place, it had a set of input devices—methods of feeding numbers or instructions into its interior. Secondly, it had an arithmetical unit, or processor, which was the part of the machine that actually calculated the numbers. Babbage called this the mill. Thirdly, there was a control unit which ensured that the computer performed one task rather than another and completed all the calculations in the correct sequence. Fourthly, it had a store or memory, where numbers could be held to await their turn to be processed. Finally, there was the output mechanism itself. And there, rather over-simplified, are the five essential components of any computer, ancient or modern. For his calculation and memory devices Babbage used column after column of ten-toothed wheels, hooked together by a quite incredible collection of rods and linkages.

The prototype Difference Engine was hand-powered. One moved a lever to set the innards churning and a bell rang when that particular stage of the calculation had been achieved. One then fed in whatever else one had to, moved the lever again until the bell rang, and so on and so forth. Babbage had no illusions about the physical awkwardness of this and had planned to use steam power for his later version, the Analytical Engine. Now, if there's something partly pathetic and partly laughable about the notion of coupling the noisy, surging power of a steam engine to the numinous matter of calculating numbers, then this merely serves as another example of the fact that Babbage was really dreaming—dreaming magnificently it is true, but still dreaming—decades ahead of his time.

For the input, and to program instructions to the control unit, he leant on an invention of the Frenchman Joseph Jacquard. Jacquard had realized that when weavers of cloth were controlling their looms, they were performing a delicate, skilled, but nevertheless essentially repetitive task, and that it ought to be possible to automate the control process. For this he devised a stiff card with a series of holes punched in it. In the course of weaving, a series of rods carry the threads into the loom, and the role of the punched card was to block some of these rods and let those which slipped through the holes go on to complete the weave. At each throw of the shuttle a single card with a particular pattern of holes in it appeared in the path of the rods, thus controlling the pattern of the weave. It could also be described as a program controlling the loom, and Babbage realized that it could equally well be employed to control the sequence of calculations within his Engine.

The parallel with weaving was also spotted by Ada, Countess of Lovelace, who, commenting on Babbage's proposed machine, wrote, "The Analytical Engine weaves algebraical patterns just as the Jacquard loom weaves flowers and leaves." This intriguing woman was an exceptional mathematician and by all accounts an unusually beautiful one into the bargain. A contemporary sketch shows her to have something of the looks of Elizabeth Taylor and more than a trace of the handsome features of her father, Lord Byron. When she met up with Babbage, and realized the significance of what he was trying to do, she set out to study his designs for the Analytical Engine in depth, filling in any blank spots by pulling them out of his head in conversation. She had money and time on her side, being both wealthy and in her twenties, but even so it was a few years before she got it all together. When she did, she published everything in a long series of "Notes" entitled "Observations on Mr Babbage's Analytical Engine". They make excellent reading if you want to study his enterprise in detail, and show that she was aware of some of the philosophical problems which the construction of such a machine posed, and which have not really been resolved today. For example, on the question of whether the machine could be considered to be creative or not she wrote:

> The Analytical Engine has no pretensions whatever to origi- nate anything. It can do whatever we know how to order it to perform. It can follow analysis; but it has no power of antici- pating any analytical relations or truths. Its province is to assist us in making available what we are already acquainted with.

It was a very perceptive comment and seems to be the first ever statement of the argument which today crops up unfailingly whenever the intellectual potential of computers is discussed—*a computer can only do what you program it to*. As we shall see later, it is an attractive, though only superficially valid point, but all credit to Lady Lovelace for making it first.

The real significance of her Notes was probably in the effect they had on Babbage. Up to this point, apart from his triumph with the Astronomical Society, he had rarely bumped up against anyone who approved of what he was doing, let alone understood it. What was particularly gratifying to him was that she had taken the trouble to study his theoretical approach with the eye of a mathematician and had found no flaws in it. He knew the Analyti- cal Engine would work (in principle) and now she knew it too. All that remained was to get the wretched thing built.

But in the meantime there had been a change of government in England and the Treasury had given up financing what they now believed was a hopeless project. Time went by, the Difference Engine remained an incomplete assembly of gears and cams, the Analytical Engine a series of paper sketches, mental concepts and Lady Lovelace's Notes. The tide ebbed faster. At the age of thirty-six Ada died, and Babbage pressed on alone, achieving little. Governments came and went, none sympathetic to his ideas. Disraeli even wrote scathingly that the only possible use he could see for the Difference Engine was to calculate the vast sums of money that had been squandered on it.

But at the same time other mathematicians and engineers were scanning through Babbage's publications and Lady Lovelace's Notes with great interest. One of these was a Swedish engineer by the name of George Scheutz, who set out to build his own version of the Difference Engine. Unlike Babbage he got on with it, and so successful was he that he produced a working design suitable for manufacturing and showed the first "production model" at an Engineering Exhibition in 1855. Among the crowds who gathered round this curious, but at least visible and tangible device, was Babbage himself, now aged sixty-three and a very disheartened individual. When asked to comment on the Scheutz machine, he was gallantly congratulatory, but it is not easy, nor comfortable, to speculate on the thoughts that must have passed through his mind.

In 1871 he died at the age of eighty, and it is both safe and sad to say that he died a disappointed man, but he had grasped a concept so exciting and so revolutionary that it would some day change the world. His contemporaries seem to have dismissed him as a misguided and unreasonable genius, but a genius beyond all doubt. So certain of his brilliance was everyone that after his death a detailed examination was made of his brain, to see if it had any physical characteristics which marked it off clearly from other men. One of the leading surgeons of the time, Sir Victor Horsely, undertook the examination and, after prodding around among the millions of silent neurones, announced that it seemed to him to be no different from any other brain he had seen. No one wanted to throw it away however, and it is still preserved, in two jars of pickle, one for each hemisphere, in the Hunterian Museum of the Royal College of Surgeons, where you will be shown it if you ask nicely.

CHAPTER TWO

Computers Go To Work

BY THE TIME Charles Babbage died, the focus of industrial growth was showing the first signs of shifting from Europe to the United States, which was creaming off through immigration a steady tide of the most ambitious, bold and imaginative of Europe's citizens. The US Congress had stipulated that a census and complete update was to be taken every ten years, and this, of course, placed a nightmare burden on those who had to do the counting, checking and recording. The eleventh census was duly held in 1880, and the task of making sense of it began. Two, three, and four years passed without any concrete conclusions and when, in 1887, data was still being processed the Census Office realized that the results, when completed, would be hopelessly out of date and that the problems with the next census would be significantly worse than those of the present one. No matter which way the Census Bureau looked at it, things could not go on like this, and they were forced to consider a radically different approach. This, incidentally, probably represented the moment when a group of human beings first realized that their world was getting so complex that it was now beyond the power of the human brain, unaided, to analyse.

The solution was to hold a competition. There were a large number of entries, some pretty mad as is usual in this kind of public free-for-all, but a few were ingenious. In the end a shortlist of three was drawn up, which featured Mr William C. Hunt and his coloured cards, Mr Charles F. Pidgin and his colour-coded tokens, and Mr Herman Hollerith and his amazing tabulating machine. Tradition favoured the first two and numerous voices were raised against the idea of such data being entrusted to a machine. The contest was settled by a practical test in the city of St Louis, Missouri: Hunt's cards took 55 hours, Pidgin's tokens 44 hours and Hollerith's machine 5½ hours. All scepticism was routed and the Hollerith system was selected for the 1890 census.

Although we are talking about a time only forty years after Babbage had been wrestling to so little avail with the problem of building his Difference Engine, it will be plain that there had been a sudden advance in the field of automatic computation. A number of factors had indeed changed. Firstly, machining and manufacturing skill had accelerated on the heels of the Industrial Revolution. Secondly, the business climate was more open to the notion of machine computation, spurred by the realization that modern society would be unable to survive on pencil-and-paper computation alone. Thirdly, a new form of motive power—electricity—had turned up, and this was almost ideally suited to the driving of large mechanical calculators.

It is also important to realize that Hollerith made use of electricity in another phase of the automatic counting, ingeniously bringing it into play in the card-sorting mechanism. The Hollerith cards were, like the tried and trusted Jacquard cards, stiffish bits of paper into which holes could be punched at various pre-set points. Fine rods passed through the holes and dipped into a bowl of mercury thus completing an electrical circuit which in turn caused a clock to advance by one unit. For each of the possible positions where holes might be punched there existed an appropriate clock, and people watching the census machine at work were able to observe the battery of dials piling up the accumulated data. The reading device was exceedingly fast, and Hollerith's main problem was to invent a system which would move the punched cards across the face of the electrical scanner quickly enough. It was the first hint of the gulf opening up between electrical and mechanical processing systems, and an indication that the days of interlocking cogs and gears were numbered.

The 1890 census was completed in record time and six weeks after census day it was announced that the population of the USA stood at 62,622,250. "I am the first statistical engineer," Hollerith declared proudly and correctly, and set up the Tabulating Machine Company in Washington, DC, to handle the rapidly increasing demand for his system.

Among his first big customers were the railways—great compilers of statistics and issuers of accounts and tickets—and the Czarist government of Russia which decided to conduct a census using his machines in 1897. His company went from strength to strength, and in 1911 merged with a number of other time-recording businesses to form a conglomerate known as the Computing Tabulating and Recording Company. Hollerith died in 1929 at the age of sixty-nine, while still acting as a consultant to his immense company. By this time it had grown still more and its name was now the International Business Machine Corporation; and today, of course, it is best known as IBM.

Supposing that Babbage could have been transported a century forward in time from the 1830s, when he was dreaming up his general-purpose computer, to the 1930s—how would he have felt about the way things had developed? He would certainly have been pleased that smallish mechanical calculators, which could be looked upon as compact versions of his Difference Engine, were being marketed on a world-wide basis, and that few big businesses or government departments were without them. He would also have been gratified to see the way in which Hollerith had picked up the idea of punched cards for rapid data entry, and fascinated, no doubt, at the use of electricity in both the sorting and driving processes. But he would have been surprised and disappointed at the fact that nowhere on earth, despite a century of progress in machine design and construction, and a growing requirement for fast, general-purpose, information-processing machines, was there anything that looked at all like a working version of his Analytical Engine. And he would have a right to be surprised and disappointed. The concept and the more or less complete specification of his general-purpose computer were quite comprehensible—Lady Lovelace had worked it all through in the 1830s—and engineering skills had by now advanced to the point where it could have been built. Why then hadn't someone simply taken his design and at least had a go at building it?

There are two main reasons. The first is that by one of those curious trends of history, Babbage had become an almost completely forgotten figure in the early part of the twentieth century, and was virtually unknown to the generations of engineers who were tinkering with calculators at that time. Secondly, and more importantly, those who did cast their eyes over his drawings and caught the power of his ideas were also clever enough to realize that a purely mechanical device was simply not practical. No matter how well the components were engineered and how carefully they were assembled, the monster contrivance which would have been the inevitable end-product would have been too large, too costly, too unreliable, and—above all—too slow to be worth the investment necessary to bring it to the point of birth. In other words, the world was awaiting a shift in the nature of technology before Babbage's dream would be realized.

In the 1930s this shift was just beginning to occur, and the threads of the problem were being gathered together, quite independently, by a number of workers in various parts of the world. In the United States, large organizations such as IBM and the Bell Telephone Company were at work. In England the thrust was coming from an individual, the mathematician Alan Turing, whose paper "On Computable Numbers", published in 1936, sent a jolt of enlightenment amongst the cognoscenti. In Germany, the threads were in the hands of a young engineer named Konrad Zuse, who had made up his mind, not only to design a universal computer, but also to build one. As Zuse, unarguably, has the edge in time over all his competitors, we will look at him first.

Zuse was an engineering student at the University of Berlin in Charlottenburg, completing his doctoral thesis at a time when brown shirts and swastikas were enjoying their fleeting vogue throughout Germany. Any latent interests he may have had in the seething politics of the time were totally submerged in a personal obsession. Like so many others before him, he considered routine and repetitive calculations to be a scandalous waste of brain power, and which should as soon as possible be relegated to machines which neither cared nor complained. As a schoolboy he had been interested in automata, had made a workable change-giving machine out of the German equivalent of an Erector set and had become impressed at the potential of these kits as practical testbeds for ideas. One or two groups in the USA and Britain had attempted, with some success, to make special-purpose calculators out of these useful kits, but Zuse evidently knew nothing about their efforts. And so, untroubled by this knowledge, he sat back and thought—and had some very good thoughts indeed.

The first good thought—he claims that he was not aware of Babbage's Analytical Engine—was that one could extend the principles of a special-purpose calculator and build one capable of being programmed to perform *any* mathematical task. His second was that the way to do this was to use binary instead of decimal calculating units, and as he came to this conclusion in 1935 or at the latest 1936, he must have been the first person in the world to do so—and, what's more, to put the idea into practice. His third thought was that it would be possible to build at least a pilot working model using Erector-set parts and cheap "off the shelf" mechanical components.

In 1936, therefore, Zuse announced to his parents, with whom he shared an apartment in Berlin, that he was giving up his bread-and-butter job as a design engineer in order to stay at home and build just such a computer. His parents, Zuse recalls, were "not very delighted" at the news, but he wasted no time and annexed a table in a corner of their living room for his rudimentary model. After a while he added another table as the computer grew. Soon more tables and another corner were required, and then the centre of the room surrendered to the machine's advance. Zuse's parents retreated gracefully into the nether regions of the house and provided what financial support they could for the machine, which was now called the Z1. The Z1 was just a testbed, but it was a very successful one and it contained a number of remarkable features. There was, of course, its binary method of operation—and there was the fact that it had a memory and something vaguely equivalent to a central processor. But it also had a keyboard to input the numbers, and a system of electric bulbs to signal the results of the calculation in binary form.

The next step was to build Z2, which was even more remarkable, and incorporated two radical advances in computer design. In the first place, Zuse replaced the Erector-type mechanical switches which he had found were too clumsy and unreliable, with electro-magnetic relays—the kinds of things used in telephone switching gear. This seems to have been the first application of such relays in any computer system. Secondly, he replaced the keyboard input, which was slow and clumsy and not up to the potential of his machine, with a brilliantly imaginative system roughly the same as punched paper tape. Instead of using tape, which was not available at the time, Zuse used discarded 35mm film, into which were punched the holes which corresponded to the machine's instructions. And lo and behold, when he put all this together, it worked!

And now came a meeting of minds which might have had enormous consequences not only for the future of computing, but also for the future of mankind, if the right (or perhaps one should say the wrong) people had seen its tremendous potential. One of the most popular movies made in that period was the classic, original version of *King Kong*. It will hardly be necessary to outline the plot of *Kong* for any reader but it is enough to say that Zuse acknowledged it as one of the best films ever made. Many of his friends were of the same opinion, and had gathered themselves together—I suppose you might call it a *King Kong* fan club—to produce a stage version of the story. By any standards it was an ambitious scheme, with the climax of the show featuring King Kong lurching around the stage smashing down papier mâché skyscrapers and fending off an attack of toy biplanes. There was considerable competition for the role of Kong, and Zuse, a large man, might have had every hope that he would be the lucky one. But there was an even larger youth in the group by the name of Helmut Schreyer, to whom the prized role finally fell. And so, in a series of well-attended performances, the saga of King Kong was acted out in an amateur theatre in Berlin, and night after night Herr Schreyer, dressed in a gorilla suit, destroyed a cardboard model of the Empire State Building.

Despite their theatrical rivalry, Zuse and Schreyer became close friends, and the latter, who was looking around for a subject for his doctoral thesis in electrical engineering, showed a sharp interest in the Z1 computer. When Zuse told him he was planning to replace the mechanical memory switches with electro-magnetic relays, thus gaining vastly in speed and reliability, Schreyer in a rush of youthful optimism and insight urged him to go one better and use electronic valves or tubes. The advantage of electronic components would be a huge increase in processing speed. Telephone relays were capable of switching (and thus calculating) five or ten times a second, but tubes, if they could be made to work, might operate at hundreds, even thousands, of cycles per second. For a brief period, as they discussed Schreyer's idea, there is no doubt that both men were favoured with a glimpse of the future; but inevitably, the realities of the present pressed down on them. Tubes were rare, unreliable, extremely expensive, enormous consumers of raw electricity, and the heat they gave off when assembled in numbers would probably cause the rest of the machine to malfunction.

Zuse returned to his relays, and Schreyer went away to think about it more deeply. In 1938 the latter was awarded a doctorate for showing how electronic tubes could be employed in an ultra-high-speed digital computer; but with the coming of the war this thesis found its way onto a library shelf and apparently had no influence whatsoever on the future development of computers. Zuse worked on engineering problems associated with aircraft design, and the Henschel Company used one of his machines to help speed up the strings of calculations that are needed to solve the problem of wing flutter. A Z3 and a Z4—the latter using a few electronic components—were built, as were a series of special-purpose machines which worked solidly and successfully on aircraft and missile design.

There is another "What if?" question. Supposing some far-sighted individual had connected Schreyer's thesis with Zuse's machines and siphoned, with the implacable dedication that was such a characteristic of the German war effort, large sums of money into constructing a fully electronic computer? What effect might this have had on the course of the war? It has frequently been said that Britain's secret code-cracking computer, which we shall consider later in this chapter, ensured victory for the Allies. Might not the possession of a fully operational machine in German hands at an early stage of the war have had the reverse effect?

Fortunately the peculiarly blinkered philosophy of the German war effort prevented this happening. By 1940 Hitler was convinced that Germany had all but won the war, and directed that any scientific research in connection with warlike goals should be of a short duration only. So in 1940, when Zuse and Schreyer formally put to the authorities the very considerable potential of high-speed computers for code-cracking, they were asked if it would take longer than a year to build one. They had to admit that it would, whereupon the project was dismissed.

But the war did not end to Hitler's timetable, and most of Zuse's machines met a fiery death in Berlin in 1944. He did, however, manage to rescue his last one, the Z4, and in the closing months of the conflict traipsed south across Germany hoping to achieve the twin goals of saving his invention and avoiding capture by the Russians. Somehow or other, he reached the Alps and found a remote village; he hid the Z4 in a cellar, while his fertile brain churned away on the idea of a universal programming language for the computers of the future. All might have been well had the villagers not become suspicious about the weird contrivance he was hiding among the apple barrels. Before long the Allied authorities got curious and annexed Zuse and his computer. He was briefly interned but, as he was in no way implicated in war crimes, was released, and later went on to form a successful computer company. His friend Schreyer drifted off to South America after the war, and was also successful in business. From time to time he flies over to Germany to see Zuse and the two meet to talk about things, including computers, and—I have no doubt—*King Kong*.

At about the time Zuse was completing the Z1 on a budget which had to be scratched together on a daily basis, an attempt, on a much grander scale, was being made in the United States to construct a general-purpose computer using magnetic relays. The originator of the idea was a young associate professor of mathematics at Harvard, Howard H. Aiken. Comparing the two projects is difficult because of the chasm-like difference in scope and financial backing. But the most interesting separation point is that whereas Zuse was working more or less from scratch, designing a machine which—so far as he knew—had never even been thought of before, Aiken was consciously and deliberately setting out to construct a modern equivalent of Babbage's Analytical Engine.

In 1936, after reading Babbage's original works thoughtfully, he began to wonder whether it might be possible to combine into one unit a collection of the more effective calculating machines of the time, and in particular the highly successful 601 Multipliers manufactured by the IBM Company. It didn't take him long to realize that such a lash-up would be a complete waste of time, and that the only way to achieve a general-purpose calculator would be to start from the ground up; equally apparent was the fact that a project of this kind would need considerable technical resources and, most of all, lots and lots of money. But it was also obvious that given these useful things, an Analytical Engine, mid-twentieth-century style, could be made to work.

IBM, already a highly successful company which had made enormous sums out of selling calculators, was an obvious possibility for a touch. It was run by Thomas J. Watson, a cranky autocrat who frequently acted on hunch and who could either sink or float a project with one word. Aiken did his homework, worked out a convincing commercial case and lobbied Watson who, true to form, made an instant binary decision and handed over a million dollars. At this moment the war came and made Aiken a Navy lieutenant, but when it was obvious that his computer would be tailor-made to solve Naval problems, he was released on detachment to complete the job. There was a lot of hard work, but surprisingly few big snags, mainly because he had decided that its basic unit should be electro-magnetic relays. He never seems to have considered tubes seriously, arguing that their vast superiority in speed would be easily outweighed by their unreliability. The main design and creative work was done at Harvard, but the assembly of the system was made at IBM's headquarters at Endicott where it was first switched on briefly in 1943. It was then pulled apart for modifications and reassembled in the physics labs at Harvard.

Anyone coming up against the Harvard Mark I, as it was called, tended to gape in amazement. It was a monster, fifty-five feet long, eight feet high and containing not much less than a million individual components. Nothing like it had ever been built before, and nothing like it would ever be built again. At Watson's insistence, it had been decked out in "streamlined" stainless steel and glass, as befitting the IBM image. The effect was truly mind-blowing. To add to the sense of clinical perfection, it was staffed and run by engineers who had been drafted into the Navy along with Aiken. They were expected to behave like Navy personnel, and marched smartly back and forth across the polished floor saluting each other and, according to a Harvard scientist, who despite his scruffy appearance was once allowed in to have a peep, "appearing to operate the thing while at attention".

The Mark I received enormous amounts of publicity, particularly when the war ended and the security wraps came off. Glossy magazines carried detailed pictures of its glittering facade, which accorded so closely with the public's image of the post-war world. For all its pretensions it was an extremely slow device—the next generation of computers were well over a thousand times faster—and it was also noisy in a way that no other computer has ever been. As one stood in reverence on its polished floor, one could hear relays clicking away as the numbers churned laboriously around its innards—a sound described in someone's memorable phrase as "like listening to a roomful of old ladies knitting away with steel needles".

It did have one big effect, and that was to place the name of IBM in the forefront of computer manufacture, and mindful of this, perhaps, Watson produced the very considerable backing needed to build a Mark II model. But technology was whipping along, and experiments with fully electronic computers which had been going on in some secrecy in the USA—and in crushing secrecy in the UK—rendered the Mark II obsolete before it was completed.

The British effort in the early days of the true computers was a very considerable one, and arose because of the pressing needs of a war which had, in the early days of 1940, reached a point where the nation's survival was threatened. In military terms, Britain could forget any idea of competing with Germany as an equal and

COMPUTERS GO TO WORK

her only chance was to use her wits to bluff and outsmart the enemy until such time as the military balance could be redressed. In particular, her need was to keep one jump ahead of her opponent's moves by penetrative military intelligence. The science of code-making and code-breaking—cryptography—was evolving steadily, and before long machines were being used to create codes, which meant they could be changed from day to day. The story of how the Polish secret service captured the Germans' newest code machine, Enigma, and shipped it back to England has been told on a number of occasions, but what is less well known is that Enigma's secrets were themselves revealed with the help of the world's first working electronic computer. The site of this triumph was a country house in Hertfordshire known as Bletchley Park.

At an early stage of the war the British Government began recruiting a team of all-aces mathematicians and electronics experts; they closeted them away at Bletchley and ordered them to work out how machines could best be employed in tackling cryptanalysis. The first approach was to use electro-magnetic machines, with telephone-type relays of the kind that went into Aiken's and Zuse's devices. There was a series of them and they all had jokey British nicknames like "Heath Robinson", after the 1930s cartoonist (roughly equivalent to the American Rube Goldberg), who drew steam-driven mousetraps and other bizarre gadgets.

The remarkable thing about these machines, apart from the fact that they cracked codes, was that they were fed their information on punched paper tape, which passed through a photo-electric reader capable of scanning characters at the rate of two thousand per second. Such a stupendous rate of absorbing data was totally unheard of at the time. So fast was the tape pulled through the reader that it would rise into the air in a series of loops which would hold their position like peculiar aerial sculptures. This high rate of input merited a high rate of computing, and the team moved on from the Robinson series to the so-called Colossus series which employed tubes as their basic units. Some amazing people were roped in to work on these, including two outstanding mathematicians, I. J. Good and D. Michie, and in the background, moving from project to project as required, the seminal figure of Alan Turing.

Pictures of Colossus—the first one was installed and operating in December 1943—are hard to come by, but it looks like something that's been put together in a real hurry. All the computing was done by tubes, two thousand of them in all (an unheard-of number at the time), and to feed their guzzling appetite for information the paper tape input was pushed up somehow to five thousand characters per second. Many people think it won the war for the Allies. The Germans, confident that their Enigma Machine would produce uncrackable codes, used it in blissful complacency throughout the war, believing their telecommunication messages to be inviolate. And who can blame them? No one, with the exception of the select and silent few who were hatching it out in the rambling country house at Bletchley, could have anticipated the tremendous power of the computer once it began to work.

As soon as the first Colossus had demonstrated its worth, the construction of others proceeded at breakneck speed. Ten were built and installed before the war ended. They were, without question, the world's first electronic digital computers, but they were special-purpose machines, dedicated to the task of code-cracking and not modifiable, without very considerable difficulty, to tackle any other problem.

In the meanwhile, at the Moore School of Engineering in Pennsylvania, again under conditions of great secrecy, the Americans were working on a general-purpose electronic computer which was ultimately installed at the Aberdeen weapons-proving grounds in Maryland in 1947. It had the long-winded name of Electronic Numerical Integrator and Calculator (ENIAC), and it was the machine which ushered in the computer age.

New weapons were often ready to go into service long before their performance had been properly computed, and the Moore School project began as a top secret military effort to develop an extremely rapid machine capable of rattling off the thousands of computations necessary for compiling ballistic tables for new guns and missiles. At the Moore School the problem was put to

Dr John Mauchly and a twenty-two-year-old engineer by the name of J. Presper Eckert, who shared the conviction that the only way to tackle the problem was by harnessing the immense switching speeds of electronic tubes. Together they put forward a proposal, in August 1942, featuring a detailed design specification for such a machine, and federal funding to the extent of $400,000 was approved. They faced new and taxing problems, not the least of which was that no one had any experience of a machine of any kind, let alone a computer, employing several hundred tubes. Needless to say they had no access to the information and experience of the Bletchley team in England, and indeed were not even aware of its existence.

After a 24-hour-a-day programme stretching over thirty months, ENIAC was switched on in February, 1946. It worked on the decimal rather than the binary system, and it had almost all the characteristics of today's big computers—with one exception, which we will touch on shortly. It was massive, as were all the early computers, filling up a huge room, and it had the unheard-of number of nineteen thousand valves, or tubes as they are known in America. The electricity to supply all these would have kept a small power station busy, and the heat generated by them posed awful cooling problems. Nevertheless ENIAC worked, and it worked at very great speed. Its limitations, however, were already clear to Eckert and Mauchly. In particular it had a ludicrously tiny memory for such a giant machine. More important, while programmable in principle (unlike Colossus) it was only capable of being switched from one kind of task to another with great difficulty. To change a program, one literally had to rewire part of the machine.

While waiting for a train on the Aberdeen (Maryland) station in 1945, one of the ENIAC team, Herman Goldstine, bumped into the world-famous mathematician John Von Neumann. Both men had very high security clearances and they were able to while away the time by discussing various aspects of each other's problems. Von Neumann was working on the design of nuclear weapons, and felt handicapped by the advanced mathematics involved because of the delays in the routine checking of his calculations. When Goldstine told him about the very high speeds it was hoped to achieve with ENIAC, his ears pricked up, and from that moment on he became increasingly interested in the project. Part of the reason for this, no doubt, was that he was already considering the hydrogen bomb and hoped that computers would help in its design—as indeed they ultimately did—but a more important reason was that his exceptional brain was fired by the immense possibilities of computers. He had already identified them as being far more important to mankind than thermo-nuclear weapons. The result of that chance meeting was that in 1946 Von Neumann eagerly came in as a special consultant to the Moore team, and brought with him the vital concept of the stored program.

The development of the stored program is the major single factor which allowed computers to advance way beyond the power of ENIAC and its various contemporaries. It is also a concept of fundamental importance.

At the risk of alienating readers who have some knowledge or understanding of computers, it is essential at this point to recap a bit. A computer is a device for handling or processing information—permuting it if you like—in some way that is useful to human beings. Mostly this is to do with numbers, because so much of the information that needs processing in our increasingly complicated world is numerical. But the notion that computing is *only* to do with numbers is a misleading one, though it blinkered many of the early designers, users and manufacturers of computer systems. Numbers are themselves only concepts which have been coded for our convenience. Furthermore when they are fed into computers they are themselves coded yet again into whatever form the machine likes to work with—in the case of most computers today it is a series of binary switches of some kind. Equally, letters and words are merely coded concepts and they too can easily be re-coded so the computer can handle them.

When we get right down to it, all we have, in terms of the basic working components of the computer, is a series—possibly an immense series—of switching units, and you could say that the power of the computer is measured in terms of the number of these units, and the speed at which they can be switched. And is that all that makes a computer powerful? The answer is No. A computer can be said to be powerful not only in terms of capacity and speed, but also in terms of how many different things it can do which employ its capacity and speed. By this token Colossus was a powerful computer on two counts—speed and capacity—but an exceedingly weak one on the third, for it could only do one thing: crack codes. ENIAC was more powerful on all three counts, being slightly faster, having a much bigger capacity and also being capable, with a bit of effort, of switching from one task to another. With this third factor we are talking about the computer's "programmability".

This is not quite as straightforward as it seems, for when we speak of a computer's programmability, we might be talking either about how easy it was to change its programs—or how many and how effective were the programs that had been written for it. Anyway a general-purpose computer, as Babbage realized, is capable, in principle, of *limitless* flexibility in the way it processes information, and if there are limits they are determined by the ingenuity of the person who programs it.

Now let us return to ENIAC as it was when Von Neumann began to think about it, and see how he might have gone about trying to make it more powerful. Assuming he couldn't do anything about its speed or capacity, then the only solution would be to tackle its flexibility. The first thing would be to write some more programs—say to deal with hydrogen bomb equations. ENIAC would now be a more powerful system, and if Von Neumann wanted to he could have made it even more powerful by writing more programs, and soon he would have a whole suite of them. But then a horrible limitation of ENIAC would emerge. Although, in principle, it was now capable of doing lots of different things, its usefulness would be greatly cut down because of the difficulty of switching from one program to another. One solution might be to devise a system for feeding programs into it more rapidly—by using punched paper tape or whatever. Another solution, and it was here that the lamp of genius flickered in Von Neumann's head, would be to store the programs within the computer itself.

This resulted in two very great gains. In the first place, one could take advantage of the computer's huge processing speed and allow *it* to change programs when required; it could switch from one program to another in a fraction of a second instead of relying on the lumbering skills of its attendant human being. In the second place, and this is far and away the most important point, it meant that programs within the system could interlock and interact. Programs could call up other programs, switching back and forth as required. In principle, programs could even *modify* other programs, rewriting them to fit the needs of the moment and integrating them with yet others within the suite. From this moment on, computers were no longer fast but blinkered workhorses, woodenly proceeding down one track, but had become dynamic, flexible information-processing systems capable of performing multitudes of different tasks.

In one conceptual jump, the true power of computers moved from the finite to the potentially infinite. Once Von Neumann's concept had been worked through in the minds of the Moore School team, no one had any doubt that their next model, EDVAC, would have to be a stored program computer and indeed that every computer built from that moment on would have to be based on Von Neumann's invention. And so it turned out to be, and computers moved on an evolutionary step.

Now the pace really began to hot up. In the United States, big business began to stir the pot as IBM, Bell Telephone and Sperry-Rand started to design computers for the market-place. In Britain, which briefly led the world in computing science, powerful computers appeared at Manchester University, at Cambridge and at the National Physical Laboratory, and there was a pioneering use of computers by the giant food corporation, Lyons. But although the pace in the USA was marginally slower at first, the springs of the American economy and the huge sums of money which could be ploughed into computing soon began to pay off. Computers, often built to military requirements, appeared all over the USA, and in the early '50s IBM marketed the first small business machines.

Costs, however, were still enormous and components unreliable, and it was universally assumed that computers could never play any meaningful role in the lives of ordinary people. They seemed to be settling down into the kind of role which other highly specialized pieces of technology—submarines, cyclotrons or power stations—played in the life of the world at large. They were useful, impressive and powerful, but there could never really be many of them. And then, suddenly, from Bell Telephone Labs, came the invention of the transistor. And with it computers moved rapidly from the past and into the present.

Part Two

THE PRESENT

CHAPTER THREE

The Revolution Begins

THE MOST IMPORTANT single invention within the whole complex of inventions which we today call the computer is undoubtedly the transistor. Electfonic tubes made the first highspeed processing possible, and the stored program led the way to the possibility of computer intelligence, but the transistor outranks them all. To appreciate its significance we need to dive once again into detail.

Tubes rely for their amplifying power on a heater electrode which pumps electrons through a vacuum. This electrode is a device which has to be shaped and manufactured out of metal, and it becomes inoperative if it is reduced beyond a certain size. In any case, if it gets too small it cannot produce enough heat to activate the electrons. The transistor, in contrast, relies for its actions on particular structures of a minute size which form inside silicon crystals, and these can act as very powerful electronic amplifiers. Thus one can have a "solid state" amplifier based on a tiny fragment of silicon, and a very substantial reduction in the size of the functioning unit of a computer becomes possible—indeed the very first transistorized devices occupied less than a hundredth of the space of an old-fashioned tube. But there is another bonus. Because they do not rely on heat to drive their electrons along (transistor radios, as everyone knows, need no "warming up" period) they consume far less energy. They are also faster in operation, and much more reliable. With a bump which was heard around the world, the electronic tube hit the scrap-heap.

The coming of the transistor could not have been foreseen by any of the computer pioneers, nor could its dramatic consequences have been anticipated. The power and speed of all-transistor computers rose to a point where they were quantitatively different from anything that Babbage could have contemplated, perhaps even comprehended. Computer memories also became larger, moving from the paltry hundred or so "bits" of store in the earliest devices to thousands, hundreds of thousands, millions, tens of millions, eventually billions of words in store. Once these massive memories came into being computers began to take on a new and unexpected role. Instead of just being heavy-duty calculators—number-crunchers, to use the trade term—they suddenly became information handlers as well, offering huge and progressively cheaper repositories for the terrifying masses of facts and data which our world is endlessly generating. Their numbers doubled, doubled again and continued to double, their memory banks increased stupendously, their brontosaurus-like bulks gave way to lighter, smaller frames, their processing speeds increased astronomically, and their cost began to plummet. This may sound like technology run riot—and that is exactly what it was. Never in history had an aspect of technology made such spectacular advances.

Three major motivating forces powered this technological bandwagon, and the first, as is so often the case, was militaristic.

The problems of the military are ideal for tackling by computers. Anyone in a command position in a battle is faced with a huge inflow of information, often arriving in bursts and loaded with muddled messages which stretch the human brain beyond its capabilities. The point was nicely made at an early stage in the history of computing when the great Duke of Wellington, accompanied by his wife, visited Babbage while the latter was labouring over the design of his Analytical Engine. Asked if the principal problem of the machine lay in turning up the individual components, Babbage replied that it was more a matter of the inventor grasping the overall complexity of the system, and trying to hold in his mind the infinite variety of consequences that could arise from the interaction of its parts. The Duke, who had faced exactly the same problem when trying to control vast and disorderly assemblies of soldiers and weld them into a smoothly operating whole, knew exactly what he was talking about.

Things have got worse rather than better since Waterloo and it's not surprising that by the late '50s the military powers of the world had become highly interested in harnessing the power of computers to their own ends. The first fruits of this were largely defensive: the SAGE air defence system in the USA, for example, monitored information fed into it, manually and automatically, by tens of thousands of radio and visual observation posts across the North American continent and its oceans and by integrating this vast array kept the overall defence forces in the appropriate state of readiness. Later, computer systems were brought into play to draw up attack strategies; later yet, they found themselves, greatly reduced in size, riding along in strike aircraft, submarines and tanks. All this had its beneficial aspects. In the first place the sums of money that the United States Government can pull together when it wants to coursed through the world of computers, creating and moulding a subsidiary industry. Secondly, the stringent requirements of the military—who demanded systems that not only worked, but also worked reliably under battle conditions—tended to generate tried and tested products which could later be repackaged for the non-military market. In the third place, a huge thrust was given to miniaturization.

The second big motivating force was the Space Race. In 1957 the Russians shocked the world by successfully launching a series of artificial satellites, one containing a dog, while the Americans, who had a nonchalant belief in their own technological superiority, endured a series of fiascos in which rockets either blew up on the pad or rose grandly a couple of hundred feet into the air and fell back with a splash into the sea. The Russians had moved rapidly ahead in developing big booster rockets, and indeed they remained ahead in the Space Race until about the mid-'60s. The American response to this was partly glorious and partly megalomaniacal, and involved siphoning colossal sums of money into the goal of landing a man on the moon—if possible ahead of the Russians. The outcome of this is well known, and important inasmuch as it showed just what human beings can do if they really put their minds (and their money) to it. But it also led to an advance in computer science, predominantly because of the tremendous computer back-up which each mission required, but partly because of the real need of the Americans to miniaturize until they too had developed their own big boosters. Interestingly enough, the Soviet Union's giant rockets have probably ended up doing them a real disservice by teaching them profligacy. Such movies and TV transmissions as come from Russian spaceships show them to be cavernous things, whose interiors are kitted out more like submarines than spaceships and are choc-a-bloc with chunky equipment, including very chunky computers. The Americans, on the other hand, had to squeeze their technology, computers and all, down to size, and by doing so pushed themselves a decade ahead in miniaturization.

The third force rolling computers into action was another of Man's most basic motives—commercialism. When people who live in those parts of the world that exist under the banner of capitalism see a chance of making money out of something, they will find a way of doing it. And when they see a way of making a lot of money, they become enormously well motivated to do it. At the very beginning it wasn't clear to even the most far-sighted entrepreneur that computers were hovering on the edge of being very big business. Indeed the general consensus was that the world market for computers would be quite a meagre one. One British pioneer thought that the entire needs of the UK could be easily served by one big computer. Particularly indicative of how non-obvious was the growth potential of computers is the fact that hardly any of the many companies who were doing well manufacturing and selling desk calculators in the 1940s diversified into computers. Only IBM, lashed along by the merciless intuition of its founder, Watson, got the point.

And so, aided by spin-off from military and space research, and feeding on the growing need for their existence, computers became one of the capitalist world's major growth industries. To begin with their presence was barely felt as only large organizations and government authorities were able to afford them. Then, on the back of the transistor and with prices sliding fast, small computers designed for small businesses came into being. Companies manufacturing computers became highly profitable and ploughed their profits back into further investment, thus yielding further technological advance and further profits. As larger-capacity memories were crammed into ever-smaller spaces and steadily greater reliability was achieved, brand new applications began to arise. Machine-readable script appeared on the bottom of cheques and the banking industry was swept into the world of automatic data-processing. Airline and chain-hotel bookings switched over to computers, and after the mid-1960s no large commercial organization in its right mind would consider any other way of coping with its salaries and wages.

The result was that at about the time Neil Armstrong achieved the goal of plonking an American boot on the moon, computers had reached a point where their infiltration into large businesses and government departments was considerable. But computers themselves contain the seeds of their own growth and techno-logical advance, and the rules which govern the pace of normal scientific and industrial development do not always apply. Thus when growth occurred, it tended to accelerate, and no better example of this can be given than to look at the phenomenal way in which computers have recently shrunk in size, and gained in processing speed.

The first dimension to concentrate on is the spatial one. The components of the earliest computers were large and mechanical. Then came electro-magnetic relays, which were a little smaller, after which came tubes which, if anything, were a shade larger. The arrival of the transistor produced a quite sensational reduc-tion in size. The transistor itself is a slice of semi-conducting material (a material which is not such a good conductor as metal, but better than, say, wood), which, when it contains certain impurities in its structure, can act as an amplifier and a "solid-state" switching device. It is a curious fact that these impurities can be very small indeed, and yet the transistors still retain their amplifying power. And no sooner had the first transistors been manufactured than scientists were looking at ways of miniatur-izing them from their initial size of about one cubic centimetre to something more like a pinhead.

These levels of miniaturization were fairly quickly achieved, and while they were filtering through onto the market, the tran-sistor engineers were designing whole "logic units"—complete electronic circuits, consisting of between twenty and a hundred components and roughly equivalent, I suppose, to Babbage's demonstration Difference Engine—all connected together on a "chip" of silicon about a centimetre square. These "chips", incidentally, are now the heart of just about every electronic counting device from watches to the largest computers. We don't need to discuss their actual manufacture, which is not an easy process, but once a "master chip" has been designed and etched out, they can be mass produced.

Miniaturization did not stop when it came to etching complete circuits on a chip. With the technique known as large-scale integration, first hundreds, then thousands, and even tens of thousands of individual units could be amassed on one slice of semi-conductor. And still the process of miniaturization continued, is continuing, and so far as one can see will continue into the foreseeable future. The units of which computers are made are getting smaller and smaller, shrinking beyond the range of ordinary microscopes into the infinities of the molecular world. So rapid is the rate of progress that advance seems to be following advance on almost a monthly basis. At the time of writing the very latest memories, effectively containing a hundred thousand switching units, are being squeezed onto a chip, and may well be on the market by the time this book is published. On the horizon, or to be more exact on the laboratory bench, and scheduled for operation within a year or so, are the first million-unit chips.

Now a million is a peculiar number which gets flung around more and more as inflation makes government budgets soar into the stratosphere. It is easy, therefore, to devalue the concept of a machine made up of a million individual components, and yet which would still nestle on a fingernail. To get a rough idea of what we're talking about, suppose one expanded these units up to the size of the tubes in the original ENIAC and laid them side by side on a flat surface so that they were two inches apart—what size would this turn out to be? The answer is that it would be as big as a football field.

But let us look at it another way. When the first big computers attracted the attention of the Press in the early '50s, they were given the not totally misleading name of "electronic brains". The human brain itself is made up of minute electronic binary switching units called neurones, and there are an awful lot of them— about ten thousand million in all. But even assuming that neurones and electronic switching units are functionally equivalent, it was ridiculous, scientists used to argue, to talk of computers as "brains" and even more ridiculous to imagine them doing brain-like things. Why, if you wanted to build a computer which contained the same number of functional elements as the brain, you would end up with something the size of New York City and drawing more power than the whole of the subway system!

This daunting example was generally used to silence the brain/ computer parallelists in the all-tube days of the early '50s and it makes quaint reading when you come across it today. By the early '60s, with transistorization, the computer/brain had shrunk to the size of the Statue of Liberty, and a ten-kilowatt generator would have kept it ticking over nicely. By the early '70s, with integrated circuits, there had been a further compression: it was down to the size of a Greyhound bus, and you could run it off a mains plug. By the mid '70s it was the size of a TV set, and at the time of writing is that of a typewriter. And such is the pace of development that, allowing a one-year lag between the time I write these words and the time you read them, the incredible shrinking brain will have continued to shrink—to what size? My guess is that it will be no bigger than a human brain, perhaps even smaller. And to power it, a portable radio battery will suffice.

These careering changes, which will shortly lead to computers paralleling the brain both in size and in the number of their individual components, do not allow one to draw other parallels. Assuming one makes such a brain model and it sits there, capable of calculating at computer-like speeds, it will still be unable to perform any of the functions of a human brain. To do so it would have to be programmed appropriately, and the programming problems would be colossal. But this does not imply that it could *never* be so programmed, a topic which we will be picking up later. It is also fair to say that the computer would have an enormous edge on switching speed. The human brain would be chugging along at a hundred cycles per second, while no

TRENDS IN
MINIATURIZATION

(see p. 55)

1945   TUBES

New York

1955   TRANSISTORS

Statue of Liberty

1965   INTEGRATED CIRCUITS

Bus

1970   LARGE-SCALE INTEGRATION

Motor Car

1975   VERY LARGE-SCALE INTEGRATION

TV Set

1980   ULTRA LARGE-SCALE INTEGRATION

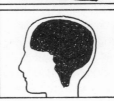

Brain

computer could be satisfied with a switching speed of less than a million cycles! Here again we have to pause and contemplate just what we are talking about.

Most people reckon a second to be rather a short period. There is not much you can do with it—blink an eye, speak one short word or read about ten characters of text. The idea that an electromechanical relay can flick back and forth twenty times in a single second sets up an image of a blurring, clattering bit of metal, and when you get to tubes operating thousands of times a second you move into a scale of time with which you have no touch-points. But what about millions of times a second? Are we not in danger of losing contact with the concept altogether? But this is just the beginning, and if you have not thought much about these things you had better steel yourself for a shock when I tell you that computers already exist whose switching potential is in the nanosecond range—that is billions of times in each tick of the clock. Once again we need to at least try to get this in perspective and can perhaps manage it by spreading time out with a broader brush. Since we so frequently hear the word "billion" employed in terms of money (I am talking about the American billion—a thousand million), let us use a context which is both monetary and temporal.

Imagine a British billionaire who decides that he is going to hand out a pound note to everyone who comes up to him—just one pound each. A long line forms and the billionaire starts handing out his pounds. He moves quickly and manages to get rid of them at the rate of one every ten seconds, but being human he can only keep it up for eight hours a day, five days a week. How long will it take him to dispose of his billion? Suppose that he has just handed over his last note, how long ago would it have been since he handed over his first one? Ten years? Twenty? Most people, when asked this question, take a jump in the dark and come up with a figure between ten and fifty years in the past. Once in a while someone will give you a date in the nineteenth century. Does that seem plausible or might it be even earlier? Does it seem conceivable, for example, that the billionaire could have started as far back as the Battle of Waterloo? Well, in fact he would have had to start before that. The Great Fire of London? No, he would have been counting away while Old St Paul's blazed. The execution of Anne Boleyn? No, he would have been counting then too. Agincourt? No. Battle of Hastings? No, further still. To cut a long story short, you would have to go back to the year 640 or thereabouts before you would see the billionaire handing over his first pound note. But that is just a taste of the cake. A billion times per second is no longer considered to be anything like the upper limit of computer processing speeds. Some recent observations indicate that on the surfaces of some of the latest semi-conductor materials, tiny magnetic elements can be seen switching, admittedly in an uncontrolled way, at rates approaching a trillion a second.

Carry the analogy to a trillionaire who wants to get rid of his money and you dive back in time beyond Christ, beyond Rome, beyond Greece, Stonehenge, Egypt and the Pyramids, before architecture, literature and language, and back to the Pliocene Age when Europe was encrusted with ice and the mammoth and woolly rhinoceros were the kings. There is no other word for it—such switching speeds are fantastic. And yet they are real: computers can operate at such speeds, and Man will find a way of making use of them.

Which brings us to the question of just what possible use could be found for these extremely fast, extremely small computers and their even faster, even smaller progeny. Surely there must be an upper limit to the speed with which people would want to calculate? Is it really going to help a company whose total tax and wage structure is handled by its own computer in one hour, to have it dealt with by the next generation of machines in one second? Alternatively, supposing that, using current memory technologies, all personnel details could be recorded on a flat magnetic disc the size of a 45rpm record, what possible advantage could there be in storing it all on something the size of a postage stamp? These may seem to be natural questions, as indeed they are, but they are not the most important ones and they miss one or two big points.

Firstly, while massive increases in processing speeds are helpful when it comes to number-crunching, they begin to have far more dramatic yield when the power of the computer is directed towards tasks of a non-numerical nature. The distinction between numerical and non-numerical needs to be made with care, but we are talking about tasks where the computer's intellectual potential, its capacity for problem-solving, for fact finding, for logical analysis rather than for purely routine calculation, come to the fore. The use of the word "intellectual" in connection with computers is also treading on dangerous ground, but once computers move from routine to analytical and integrative functions, the increases in processing speed will begin to pay off and they will be able to tackle more complex problems.

The second point concerns reductions in size. Why make computers so small that if you drop one on the floor you are in danger of walking off with it stuck to the heel of your shoe? There are three answers to this question and together they sum up one of the most important single factors about the pace of computer development over the next few years. Very small computers have enormous advantages: firstly, because they consume minute amounts of power; secondly, because they are very cheap; and thirdly, because they are extremely portable and can therefore be put to use in all kinds of different places. Indeed, we are shortly moving into the phase where computers will become one of the cheapest pieces of technology on earth—cheaper than TV sets (they already are), cheaper than portable typewriters, cheaper even than transistor radios. They will also, for exactly the same reasons, become the most common pieces of technology in the world, and the most useful.

CHAPTER FOUR

The Springs of Growth

THE SHORT HISTORY of the future which we are about to consider is based on a single, crucial assumption. This is that computer technology has not yet reached its peak, and growth in computers or computer power will continue for some time to come. But before going into the reasons for this we need to inspect more closely what we mean by the words "growth" and "power" in this context.

Computer technology can be expected to change along a number of parameters: smaller, more compact computers; faster-operating computers; computers with bigger memories; more reliable computers; and cheaper computers. But computer power could also be measured in terms of efficiency, overall numbers, usefulness and, to touch on a very controversial subject, intelligence. The first set of factors is closely tied to their design and the second is more to do with how satisfactorily they can be programmed. In deciding whether computer power had grown we would not look solely at any one of these factors but rather attempt to assess what was happening at all levels.

There are four main ways in which things could go in terms of growth.

1 Growth could stop now.
2 Growth could continue rising steadily for a period.
3 Growth could accelerate for a period.
4 Growth could accelerate indefinitely.

There are clearly variations on these themes but they are unlikely to differ significantly. All the predictions in the rest of this book are based on the assumption that one of Scenes 2, 3, or 4, or some minor variant of them, will prevail, though there could be a difference in the speed with which the developments occur and their effects become felt. If Scene 1 prevails, these predictions will not hold, and the impact of the Computer Revolution will be somewhat less dramatic.

If you believe that computer growth could stop *now*, you would have to take a radical view on a number of points: firstly that the world was unlikely to have many more computers in ten years than it does at present; secondly, that they were unlikely to get much cheaper; thirdly, that a limit had now been reached to their miniaturization; fourthly, that they were unlikely to become much more reliable; fifthly, that they were unlikely to become much more useful than they are at present (in other words, that their range of applications is already exhausted); and finally, you would also have to hold that their "intelligence", to use that uneasy word again, had peaked.

With the exception of the last point, which we will have to discuss later, the issue is quite straightforward. The fact is that there is no sign whatsoever that any of these limits has yet been reached or will be reached in the near future. On the contrary, all the signs are that the number of computers in the world is leaping upwards on a daily basis; their cost is plummeting, the pace of miniaturization is accelerating, reliability is rising, and the range of applications which can be converted to computer power, so to speak, is widening fast. These statements do not have to be taken on trust; the evidence is widely available in technical and scientific literature and has already been spelled out in numerous newspapers, magazine articles and TV programmes. But it is as well to point out that there are two major—and by no means unlikely—ways in which growth could be brought to a screeching halt. The first would arise if a third world war broke out, and the second if the Western economic empire collapsed—as has for some time been predicted by Marxist commentators. In both cases computer growth would not only stop but would probably move back quite a bit.

Having got to the point where we can agree that growth of *some* kind is likely to occur in the nearish future, we need to examine those forces which are acting to promote growth, and those to inhibit it; but to complicate matters I must first introduce a variable which I call the Joker Effect. The Joker is the card whose introduction into any game can throw the best-laid plans of all players, however intelligent, into confusion. In life this is the individual or event whose appearance can have extraordinary consequences and whose existence can never be anticipated. On the political level he is represented, say, by the bullet that assassinated President Kennedy, and at an economic level by the Arab oil boycott; at a scientific level, taking computers as an example, he is behind the invention of the transistor. In one of these cases, you will note, the consequences of the Joker's activities are bad (assuming you believe the world to be worse off because of Kennedy's death); in one, ambiguous (assuming you hold there are two sides to the oil price question); and in one, good (assuming you like the idea of really cheap computers).

The thing about the Joker is that you can never be sure which way he is going to push things. Take the case of a war between Russia and America. If nuclear weapons are employed the world will be destroyed, and certainly computer science will be set back to its origins. But suppose that a non-nuclear conflict ensues. The rival governments could now decide that the only way to achieve non-nuclear victory would be to call for a massive injection of research into developing fantastically advanced computers and then computer science might see a period of madcap advance. But enough about the Joker, whose presence and powers we have registered. Let us move on to consider the forces which might inhibit growth.

An inhibiting factor which had far more force five years ago than it has today is the possible shortage of essential raw materials. The argument is similar to that of the "Limits to Growth" thesis: you simply cannot go on having more and more of everything before coming to the point where you run out of something essential. This can apply to oil, coal, food, fresh water, even air, and in the case of computers it refers to the various metals and ceramics which are used in making their components. The argument had a plausible ring when computers were very big and used up a lot of raw material—some, like copper, being slightly scarce. Today, although large numbers of big computers are still being manufactured, the real numerical growth is coming from the small systems—currently they are desk-top size and in due course will shrink to pocket size and beyond. These contain, by their nature, such minute amounts of raw material of any kind that their development is unlikely ever to be threatened by shortages.

It is not difficult to imagine technological barriers which might cause problems for future development in computing. For example, as magnetic switching units shrink to sub-microscopic size and become more densely packed, one might find that their magnetic fields merge, and discrete (individual) switching ceases to be possible. Or one might discover that it is impossible to control the activity of the electrons in the transistors when the units go below a certain size. But these are possibilities only, and there is no evidence to suggest that they will actually occur. As it happens, one barrier has already been identified and is beginning to cause a bit of trouble; it is concerned with the speed of light. Computers are now getting so fast at calculating that the signals passing away from the central processor, which travel at roughly the speed of electricity or light, simply cannot get away quickly enough, and are overtaken by the onrush of fresh calculations. It might be referred to as an electronic log jam.

The problem loomed quite large in the old large-sized computers, for even though light will travel round the world seven times in a second, it still takes a measurable time to cross a large machine, and there is a certain amount of electronic "drag" in almost any wire or cable. This has been greatly alleviated by reducing the size of computers, but even now, with switching speeds in the billion-per-second range, a computer cannot sprawl out more than a metre in diameter before jams begin to occur. Fortunately, plenty of computers are already less than a metre across, and they are continuing to shrink in size. But the main point is that there is no sign of finite technological barriers emerging in the near future, and those barriers that do exist are either surmountable, or will only come into force when computers already have immense capabilities.

Combinatorial problems may also inhibit computer growth. This refers to the kind of difficulty that Babbage found himself up against when he began to build his first really big machine, and it is a problem that emerges whenever one tries to juggle together large numbers of things. It follows Fink's Fifth Law which says that muddle increases as the square of the number of units involved. Twins are four times, not twice as much trouble as individual children, while triplets are nine times as big a nuisance as a single child. One might well expect Fink's Law to rear its head in a very significant way in computer science, and in the early days with the big systems far more tubes would often be out at any one time than one would expect by chance. Curiously it doesn't seem to be operating with much venom in the case of microprocessors, where, if anything, reliability has increased in proportion to the number of switching units. It may be that computers will hit stupendous combinatorial problems in due course, bringing all further development to a halt; but at the moment it seems as if the reverse is true.

Decisions made by powerful forces at parliamentary or government level could, rightly or wrongly, lead to an interruption of computer growth. One such political inhibitor would be a deliberate decision by government to resist automation in major national industries in order to preserve jobs. Another would be, say, to tax computers heavily in order to interfere with what was believed to be their economically destructive progress. In non-democratic countries, particularly those which are uneasy about allowing too much information to flow about freely, political inhibitors could easily come into force to block international computer communications. They are likely to have short-term effects only, but it has to be admitted that they could impede rampant computer growth—for a period at any rate.

In democratic countries, social pressures have the edge over bureaucratic ones, and this class of inhibitors is currently recognized as being the most likely to exert pressure when the time comes. Indeed, they may already have done so. A classic example would be trade union action which resisted tooth and nail the introduction of automation where it caused loss of jobs or, less reasonably, where it hampered union power in some way. The unions are an easy target to snipe at, but their tactics are not always as block-headed or restrictive as they are made out to be, and whatever inhibiting effects they exert can only be of short duration. But social pressures, either in the form of monolithic delaying tactics by trade unions or by more spectacular "Luddite" activities by smaller groups, are a real possibility at some time in the next few years.

Another factor could be psychological inhibitors. By this I refer largely to negativistic feelings about computers which operate in the individual at an unconscious or, at best, vaguely expressed level. They are not tied to computers but reflect a basic unease with science and technology itself. This unease may have deep roots, tracing back to Man's painful awakening to the fact that he lives in a dangerous universe where survival is dependent upon physical resources, and where magical or "spiritual" back-up tends to be unreliable. It may also be of more recent origin and not unrelated to the explosion of the first nuclear weapon at Hiroshima. This attitude, whether just or unjust, expresses itself in the popularity of science fiction disaster movies, and in the glee with which the media report scientific calamities or the relish with which they pick up the exploits of the latest psychic superstar. One newspaper's headline when two Russian cosmonauts were found inexplicably dead in their space capsule after a long mission, expresses this mood neatly: "MAN TAKES ONE STEP TOO FAR!" It is clear that computing is an area where particularly deep wells of uneasiness exist.

Human inertia may be the most significant inhibiting force of all. Getting a novel technique or working strategy introduced into any large organization takes much longer than one expected it to, because of inertia in all its multifarious forms. It can vary from simple, dumb resistance and heel-dragging to laziness, inefficiency or muddle, and it has very powerful braking effects. But even the most entrenched inertia can be rendered ineffective when the innovative forces have sufficient strength. No organization, however sluggish, can hold out against a technology which decides to take it by storm. Have you noticed how pocket calculators have swept through the school system while teachers and education authorities are still arguing about whether they should be banned?

The final possible inhibitor is what is known as "the software gap". A computer is something more than a bunch of electronic components switching on and off at a frenzied rate. A vital extra constituent is the program which controls it. Programs—their collective name is "software"—are the instructions which tell the computer to do one thing rather than another, and also how to do it. The more complex the computer, the more ambitious are the tasks it can do, and the more challenging the job of writing the software. Over the years the spectacular advances in hardware have not been matched by advances in programming, and a software gap has opened up. To many computer experts this software gap is the biggest single problem, and they argue that it is rapidly becoming unbridgeable. The argument is compelling but not convincing. In the first place, it assumes that the proportion of effort devoted by the computer industry to software will remain at its present, inadequate level. Secondly, it assumes that the current techniques for writing and developing software will not improve or will only improve marginally—a most unwise assumption. Thirdly, it fails to take into account the huge army of "amateur" software writers who are beginning to appear on the scene, and who will soon outnumber the professionals to a very large degree. These are the "Home Computer" fans, people who buy a computer off the shelf to build on their kitchen table, and many of them view software development as a joyous intellectual challenge rather than a chore. Finally, and most profoundly, it ignores the fact that before too long we shall be looking for ways in which the computers themselves can be induced to tackle their own software—a development which will have, to say the least, intriguing effects.

These, then, are the forces operating individually or in concert to inhibit the growth of computers in the next decade or so. That they will have a braking effect is undeniable, but it should be marginal and is unlikely to do anything except make spectacular growth just that little bit less spectacular. The factors generating growth, rather than inhibiting it, are of great strength and enduring power.

Growing need, acting on its own, would be almost enough to ensure continued computer growth for the next two decades at least. The fact is that the industrialized world has already reached the point where it can no longer survive without using computers. This dependence upon automatic data storage and processing is at its greatest in the USA, Western Europe, and Japan, but it is also emerging as a significant factor even in the "computer-backward" giants, Russia and China. It may seem an incredible thing to say about a world which has only known the presence of computers for about twenty-five years, and one asks how we ever managed without them. There is a two-pronged answer to this. Firstly, we *didn't*—or, to be more exact, we did not manage properly. Throughout recorded history, and increasingly since the advent of industrialization, Man has lived in a state of unstable, unhappy confusion, with the majority of the population close to starvation and every country on the planet torn apart by periodic wars. Human society survived, but that is about all, and recently it has been lucky to have done that. Secondly, the world, which was complicated enough twenty-five years ago, has become unbelievably more complicated ever since. In fact, the evidence of this increased complexity is already masked by the computers we have created in order to help us out of the muddle.

Computers, in other words, have not arrived on the scene for aesthetic reasons, but because they are essential to the survival of a complex society, in a way that food, clothing, housing, education and health services are essential to a slightly simpler one. The truth is that one of the main problems—perhaps *the* main problem—of the time is that our world suffers from information overload, and we can no longer handle it unaided. Furthermore, it seems inevitable that for the next decade or so it will get even more complex. But, contrary to the popular view of the moment, computers decrease rather than increase complexity, and our future survival is inextricably tied in with a greatly increased dependence upon them. The world needs computers *now*, and it will need them more in the future; and because it needs them, it will have them.

Increased demand is another factor. A need is something one must have for survival, while a demand is merely something that one would like to have. A need is also frequently unrecognized as such, while a demand is something that preoccupies people a great deal. Demand is easily identified and manipulated for commercial purposes. Thus, as computers demonstrate their potential to generate a wide variety of consumer products, so commercial exploitation will increase and newer and better gadgets will be developed. Anyone doubting the vast power and penetration of demands should consider the motor car, which in terms of need has only a small role to play. People's need to move around the world is best met by one or other form of public transportation. But they *demand* to do their travelling in private boxes on wheels, boxes which are dangerous and expensive, but which are liked for dozens of trivial reasons. As a result the motor car industry is the world's number one commercial power. At the moment it may be hard to see what kind of demand could lead to the growth of a computer industry of an equivalent size. Would people really spend their money eagerly on a computer gadget which they didn't need? The answer is that they undoubtedly would, provided that the gadget was properly dressed up, and an excellent example is the pocket calculator.

The third major factor acting to promote growth is also tied up with capitalistic economies. As computers come down in price, decrease in size and become more useful to the average individual, their marketing range will expand rapidly. Vast new Third World markets will open up, some based on gadgets of appalling triviality—wristwatches which play computerized pop music to give just one example—but others with far-reaching social impact—pocket, personal teaching computers, let us say. The size of these new markets will ensure stupendous growth as long as they can be tapped, and the tapping may come sooner than most people would imagine.

The idea that technology itself will suggest new applications is a somewhat less obvious factor, but it is nevertheless a significant one. When a new computer, or computerized gadget, is created for a market, the essentially general-purpose nature of the device means that it spawns offspring with a different function but with a new set of equally large markets. To return to the example of the pocket calculator, which I use freely because it is a familiar one: this has already begun to generate offspring such as calculators to store telephone numbers, tell the time, act as stopwatches, bleep to remind you to do something, speak their answers to you and so on. On a larger scale, the motor car industry has already demonstrated its ability to generate subsidiary industries—car radios, instrumentation, various types of ornamentation, tool sets, bolt-on goodies, etc. The computer industry will follow the same path, but with even greater vigour. Add to this the fact that we will, in due course, be able to turn the power of the computer back onto itself, thereby effecting advances and improvements, and promoting even further overall growth. This is likely to arise first when Man recruits the computer as an aid to program or software development, but it may be a decade or so before this rather fundamental advance will be able to gather pace.

The main forces of inhibition and promotion of growth have now been paraded. How the forces balance up, and which of the three growth trends we are likely to experience is really a matter of opinion. A period of steady growth is, perhaps, the safest assumption, though even if one decides to settle on it, quite spectacular advances are going to occur within the next few years. But all the signs are that growth will be accelerating in the near future. For that reason the forecasts in the remainder of the book are based on the hypothesis of temporary acceleration. The third trend—that growth can accelerate indefinitely—seems to be the most unlikely of the three. One might even be inclined to dismiss it out of hand were it not for one factor which we have already hinted at: that there will come a point in the future when computers will be able to step in, gingerly at first, but with growing confidence, and pull themselves up by their own bootstraps. But more of that in its proper place.

Part Three

THE SHORT-TERM FUTURE:
1980-1982

CHAPTER FIVE

Of Gadgets and Gimmicks

THIS CHAPTER IS concerned with changes that are likely to take place in the immediate or short-term future, a future which comes to a close in 1982 or thereabouts. I have taken the Computer Revolution as beginning in 1975—at about the time that the first primitive microprocessors came on the market. Thus, in 1980, it is five years old and its first era has about another two years to run. It will be largely concerned with gadgetry and gimmicks— the sharp end of an immense commercial market, which will be lifting computers to the world's number one industry by the end of the period.

The second phase, the medium-term future, should run from approximately 1983 to 1990, and it is then that computers will have their most important social effects. In the third, and for all practical purposes, final phase, running from 1991 onwards, we will move out of the era of industrialization which began in the early part of the nineteenth century, and into a radically different world. The precise chronology of all this will be largely determined by the relative successes of the forces of inhibition and facilitation we discussed in the last chapter. If the inhibiting forces are dominant we might not emerge from the first phase before the late '80s, and from the second before the late '90s. If the forces of facilitation turn out to be unopposed we could be in the second phase within a year or so, and the third as early as 1985. In any case, most people alive today can expect to be staggered witnesses of the changes which the Revolution will bring.

In trying to get some idea of what form these changes will take we need to remember that there is a causal chain involved in all technological development. A need or demand of some kind leads to the development of a new piece of technology which is converted into products or applications. This in turn brings about changes, great or small, in the lives of the product's users.

In the short term the over-riding technological feature is that computers will continue to become quite dramatically smaller, while the amount of information they can hold in their spatially-diminishing memories will continue to increase. The trend is already firmly established and this forecast is based on knowledge of what the electronics industry is working on at the present time in its advanced research laboratories. At the moment, for example, ten thousand words—roughly the length of a daily newspaper—can, without any difficulty, be crammed on a silicon chip less than a centimetre square and a millimetre thick. Any item of information on the chip can be accessed and displayed on a TV screen in far less than a thousandth of a second.

But this degree of compression is no more than Stone-Age technology in comparison with what will be marketable in the early '80s, when a hundred thousand words—a longish novel rather than just a newspaper—will be storable in an equivalent chip. And even this is just the beginning: microcomputer manufacturers in America and Japan are presently working on chips which will hold a million words, something like the contents of a small encyclopaedia, while the long-term planners (those concerned with the technology we shall be using in the far-off days of the late '80s) are looking at even more stupendous compression of information. They expect to achieve this by using a new variety of storage techniques, of which the most promising seems to be "bubble memory". In this technique the individual words, coded into binary form, are stored in tiny magnetic areas which progress endlessly round and round like chains of bubbles and at a colossal speed, deep in the micro-structure of an electronic chip.

It is not just memory that is shrinking out of sight, but also the controlling and calculating elements of the computer. The central processors of the very latest systems, which would have been the size of a room ten years ago, are now so small that you can barely see them. This kind of mind-twisting size reduction can lead to some odd happenings. Recently I was showing some friends a tiny central processor which I was holding with some tweezers (my fingers were too clumsy to handle it properly). Unfortunately, even the tweezers were a bit cumbersome and the computer dropped onto the jumble which covers the surface of my desk. My friends joined enthusiastically in the search, but the chip managed to escape and hasn't been seen again.

In case this has conjured up visions of computers continuing to reduce in size almost against our will until they pass out of our universe altogether, like the Incredible Shrinking Man, it is worth saying that while the component units—central processor, program unit, memory, etc.—will undoubtedly get smaller, the overall physical size of a working computer will be unlikely to reduce to the same extent. If the things get too small humans will simply be unable to operate them. Input devices must be big enough to be operated by giant human fingers and thumbs, and output devices must be large enough to display the sizeable words and phrases which humans like to read. The overall size of the computers will not be reduced much, but more and more will be stuffed into their memories and the power of their central processors will steadily increase.

You might imagine that because you are dealing with something very tiny, the task of testing and quality control would be indescribably difficult—it is hard enough, as we all know, with big things like cars—and that this might push the price up astronomically. No doubt it would, if on-the-spot checking was attempted in the course of the chip's manufacture. Instead, the semi-conductor firms use the cavalier strategy of churning them out in huge numbers and giving them all a simple "work-or-not-work" test at the end. This leads to a ruthless reject rate which can be as high as eighty per cent—a figure which could give any other type of manufacturer a psychotic seizure—but which, because of the tiny cost of each rejected chip, is dismissed as economically irrelevant. This high reject rate is one reason why the micro-computers that actually end up being sold are so dramatically reliable; another is that, as they have no moving parts, once they start working they tend to go on indefinitely.

But cost is going to come down as well as size, and it is worth knowing just why this is so.

Firstly, and perhaps rather obviously, the smaller the computer is, the less raw material it uses up. This would be much more significant if the raw materials involved in modern microelectronics were rare, but by a quirk of fate, nature has decreed that their main constituent should be silicon, which is extremely common—you sit on great masses of it at the seaside. The second significant feature of size reduction *vis-à-vis* cheapness is that once you can design tiny computers which act as one integrated circuit on a single slice of silicon, it becomes possible to mass produce them. The initial design of the master—like the initial design of a motor car—is massively expensive. Model One of the latest Ford probably costs several million pounds to manufacture from scratch, but its offspring fall off the end of the production line at a fraction of the cost. Exactly the same applies to computers. Finally, minute computers with minute working components need only minute amounts of power to supply them, which means that they will run on small dry batteries and become portable in a way that no one could have dreamed of even a decade ago.

I keep emphasizing how dramatically things have changed; this is necessary because the scale of change is so enormous that it is far too easy to under-estimate it. A useful analogy can be made with motor cars to put things in perspective. Today's car differs from those of the immediate post-war years on a number of counts. It is cheaper, allowing for the ravages of inflation, and it is more economical and efficient. All this can be put down to advances in automobile engineering, more efficient methods of production, and a wider market. But suppose for a moment that the automobile industry had developed at the same rate as computers and over the same period: how much cheaper and more efficient would the current models be? If you have not already heard the analogy the answer is shattering. Today you would be able to buy a Rolls-Royce for $2.75, it would do three million miles to the gallon, and it would deliver enough power to drive the *Queen Elizabeth II*. And if you were interested in miniaturization, you could place half a dozen of them on a pinhead.

The outcome of these reductions in cost and size, and the huge increases in memory capacity and reliability, must be that computers will be widely used in areas which would have been inconceivable before the advent of microprocessors. As a kind of parallel bonus, certain aspects of special-purpose computing which have been available at high cost and with only marginal reliability in the past will also become cheaply available. Already some computers have the capacity to "read" typescript, printed text, and even, with a bit of difficulty, human handwriting; they can also recognize the human voice and understand spoken words and phrases. On the output side, one must also mention their ability to communicate with the user by drawing diagrams or pictures on TV screens, and also by the use of synthetic speech— the vocal equivalent of moog in which, instead of music, words and phrases are created by the computer itself. In the same category, since we are talking about the rough equivalent of the senses, we must place their feeble, but developing ability to recognize shapes. These developments, which are only the first strivings of computers to interact in a dynamic, rather than a passive, way with their environment will lead to some interesting pieces of hardware appearing on the scene. Once a computer has the power to "recognize" a shape or pattern, it could be hooked up to some kind of control system which would allow it to "do something useful" on the basis of the recognition—an example would be a simple robot with a scanning TV camera which could recognize the border between a lawn and a path, and control a motorized device to cut the grass. As a safety feature, it might be programmed to understand a few useful words like START, GO RIGHT, STOP, etc. spoken by any human voice.

Already one can sniff mass-market gimmicks in the air, and this being a capitalist society the first manifestations of the Computer Revolution will be loaded with gimmickry. Man is highly motivated to own and operate toys and gadgets. Without going into whether this is something that has been programmed into him by the consumer society or whether, as I suspect, it has its origins much further back in time, it is undeniably a major factor in determining design and marketing procedures for consumer-based industries. One can deplore the motivation and despise the triviality of the products, but on the back of this trivial gadgetry will arise truly useful products whose manufacture and widespread sale could only get under way after the initial development costs have been broken.

The real importance of the spread of the pocket calculator as a gimmick is that it has led to a huge sales outlet for chips which do routine mathematical computation—everything that Babbage ever hoped to do with his Difference Engine—and which are now manufactured by the billion at a cost of a few cents each. Riding on the coat-tails of any successful gimmick will come a second generation of devices capable of tackling a far wider range of tasks. I was one of the first customers for a calculator with a built-in 24-hour clock, a stopwatch and a bleeping "reminder" facility. I got hold of this gadget—the first calculator to be something other than just a calculator—about two years ago, and was amazed to find, barely a year later, its almost exact equivalent built into a wristwatch. Trivial? Well, maybe, but watch calculators like this are now selling by the hundred thousand.

But let us move on from this marginal product to the next phase of development where the number-only displays and the number-only keyboards of calculators are replaced by a full alphabetical array, and the calculator/computer can input and output words and phrases instead of just numbers. As it happens I have been involved in the creation of just such a device, initially designed to do simple word-to-word translation. Inside its fairly substantial memory is stored an English-French (or any other language which uses Western alphabets) dictionary, and to get a translation one simply types in a word, whereupon its opposite number appears on the display. A similar device enables one to enter words and phrases into its memory which can later be "played out" by hooking it up to an electrical typewriter—a pocket shorthand typist so to speak. Already it should be obvious that what we had originally identified as a gimmick is evolving into something with genuine practical value. But even this is just the beginning. These miniature computers—they graduate from calculators the moment they become programmable and multi-purpose—will themselves breed still more powerful offspring, whose importance we will consider later.

I have already mentioned the fiddly nature of ultra-miniaturized gadgets. Wristwatch calculators fall into this category even now.

On the other hand, the objection to picking away at their tiny buttons would be overcome if they could be used for something other than routine calculations. Watches with memories are already on the market, which can store telephone numbers and other numerical reminders. Later, when they can display letters and words as well as numbers, they will also be able to store names and addresses, reminder notes and so on. Furthermore, the main difficulty of minuscule keyboards will be overcome when speech recognition devices shrink down to the point where they can actually be built into wristwatches. Buttons as input mechanisms will then become largely redundant; calculations will be performed and telephone numbers or whatever entered into the watches' memories by spoken instructions. Indeed the majority of machines will probably become voice-controllable.

The other side of the coin—computer voice output—is also in an extremely rapid phase of development and speech synthesizers are diminishing in size and cost. One of the first applications has been a talking calculator, which not only displays the results of its deliberation in the usual array of red numerals but also speaks them aloud in the voice of a shrunken American astronaut. Ludicrous gimmick? Not really if you are blind or poorly sighted, or if you are doing chains of calculations and like to keep your eyes on what you are writing. How about a talking watch? One will shortly be on the market and may well be by the time this book is published. Another gimmick? Possibly—again unless you are blind or need to put on your glasses to read the time, or unless you are a pilot and do not want to take your eyes off your instruments, or unless you would like to be able to tell the time at night without switching on the bedside lamp.

But even if we discount this kind of development as trivial, how about instruments which speak their measurements, or containers which tell you how much they have in them? Talking altimeters, airspeed indicators and the like will be invaluable in aviation. At home there will be speaking bathroom scales, freezers which remind you to restock them, cookers which tell you how the meat is coming along, telephones that tell you how many people have rung in your absence, doorbells which inform you how many visitors you've had and when they came, thermometers which advise you what to wear before you get up. The list is endless. And despite the fact that it sounds like science fiction, most of it is technically realizable at this moment, and will be in widespread use before the end of the short-term period.

On the subject of houses, a familiar old gadget which has been around for hundreds of years is just about to get pensioned off forever—the key. Already you can obtain electronic locks which open when you punch in the appropriate combination, though they do rely on you remembering what the combination is. Human memory being as fallible as it is, the next development must be a lock which opens only when it has had the chance to scan the electronic chip built into a watch or signet ring. By the mid-1980s no one will ever need to hide a key under the doormat again.

Another place where microprocessors are just about to appear in a puff of smoke is in the motor car. For some time now it has been possible to buy a (very expensive) car with computer-controlled carburation—supremely efficient incidentally—and it will only be a matter of a year or so before these will filter down into the family car market. Speedometers which compute your average speed and fuel gauges which "tell" you in synthetic speech when gas is low will also be around shortly, and so will headlights which come on automatically when ambient light falls below a certain level. Another useful device will be a micro-processor which computes the speed of the car travelling in front and assesses whether the two vehicles are being driven at a safe distance. This kind of thing will, presumably, encourage more careful driving, once motorists have got used to the idea of being ticked off by their own cars, but vehicles which pepper one with spoken warnings and instructions—a horrific new breed of back-seat driver—may never be popular.

Less easily assailed on the grounds of triviality will be the impressive incursion of the computer into the home and office. We've already talked about domestic gadgets, but these are just a special-purpose application of computer power. A more interesting development will be the use of small computers to file all kinds of information from cooking recipes and telephone numbers to shopping lists and family correspondence, and to cope with the important but boring details of household accounts. Ten years ago the notion that the average family might some day make use of computers in this way—when a computer capable of coping with domestic requirements would cost two hundred thousand dollars and fill up half an attic—would have seemed on the edge of nonsense. Today, you can buy something to do just this kind of thing for a few hundred dollars, costing less and taking up less room than a colour TV.

Anyone doubting that personal computing is big business should pop into one of the numerous Do-It-Yourself computer stores which are springing up all over the place, and look at the weird and wonderful range of gear on offer. Better still, pick up a copy of one of the enormously successful magazines now available which are devoted entirely to this new mixture of part hobby and part industry. My favourite is the magazine *Byte* (a *byte* is a "computer word" consisting of eight "bits" or binary digits), which has a circulation in excess of a hundred thousand—a figure which many longer-established publications on politics, motoring, cooking or sport might envy. Its editorial matter is largely composed of enthusiastic articles on doors which open and close when you speak to them, computer systems which control the lighting, heating and security of your house, programs to automate income tax returns, and other similar delights. There is also a voluminous correspondence page in which the latest developments in software are heatedly debated. The advertisements are written in that unique language known as Computaspeak. NOW! IOK ROM, 5K RAM and MINIFLOPPY BACKUP ALL FOR UNDER $300 or THIRTY WORD VOCABULARY SPEECH RECOGNIZER FOR $190 are typical examples.

One of my favourite ads, an expensively produced page in full colour, shows a man sitting at the kitchen table putting the finishing touches to his own DIY computer. In the background, in soft focus, we see his smiling wife, turning momentarily from the dishes to gaze admiringly and approvingly at her husband. One ponders the significance of the scene. Is she tacitly admitting that her place is firmly in the home, particularly over the sink, while her husband attends to the manly job of building his own computer? Or are her eyes glowing because she recognizes the attractive collection of electronic doo-dads as the marvellous device all women have been seeking for millennia and which will at last free her from all household chores?

This ambiguous domestic scene may lead one, mistakenly, to dismiss personal computing as just another male "winter evening" obsession, akin to model airplane making, stamp collecting or hi-fi tinkering. It is probably true to say that the fad is being kicked off in this way—the number of women seen hanging around in microprocessor shops is still very small—but its wider applications will be appreciated in due course, as people become more tuned into what computers can actually do. This educational process will be greatly aided by developments such as the British Post Office's PRESTEL system, (or VIEWDATA as it was originally known), now in experimental service, and scheduled for full operation in the '80s. PRESTEL, as many people will already know, will connect users via a special console and TV-like screen to a huge central computer offering a wide range of information services, and a message-swapping facility. The present plan is to charge a small rental for the terminal and computer time *pro rata*. Enormously in advance of its time when it was conceived, PRESTEL has been overtaken by the gallop of microprocessor technology, and it is not obvious just what the giant Post Office computer will offer its users that they won't have by the mid '80s on their own home microprocessors. Access to huge banks of public data or library information is certainly one area, as is the personal communication facilities that it can establish between users. PRESTEL users will be able to send messages to other PRESTEL users via the computer, a kind of instant mail which must at some time make inroads into the regular postal service.

The first users of PRESTEL on any scale could well be small businesses, anxious to experiment with the possibilities of computers without committing themselves to any capital expenditure. On the other hand, the rival attractions of the new generation of off-the-shelf computers, complete with a suite of tailor-made programs for a total price of less than five hundred pounds could be overwhelming. They will be able to teach their new owners how to use them, and will also be programmed to record and store all financial transactions connected with the business, to assess taxes at each stage of the operation, check on stock control, order new stock automatically when required, record orders, issue invoices and reminder notices and even evaluate market trends.

The usefulness of the computer extends way beyond its capacity to juggle numbers. Its word-handling powers are nowadays almost as important, a shift of balance which will continue into the 1980s. The phrase now used is "word processing" and is more or less self-explanatory—you feed words, *as words*, into the computer, store them in its memory and call them up whenever you like.

To give a simple example: if you manage a business with a large number of customers most of whom have slightly different requirements, you probably use a very large card-index system. With a bit of special coding you can break the data down according to particular requirements so that a knowledgeable clerk can inspect any customer's basic needs quite quickly. It will never be an easy task, though, and the average business needs a large amount of file-space. On a computerized filing system, the space occupied by the "filing cabinets" might be no bigger than a cigarette box. To extract information you key in the word you require—let us say the name of the customer—whereupon the computer does a search through its file and pulls out all information relevant to that keyword. The keywords can relate to anything stored in the system, and it would be a simple matter if you wanted to know, say, all the customers in a particular area whose names began with A and who had ordered some particular item in the past six months. Key in the appropriate words and the data would be eagerly fed to you by the computer.

Any words stored in the system can be inspected by the computer at any time with great accuracy and speed, and it is not difficult to see how much routine filing, sorting and paperwork is eliminated and, as an aside, how much could be saved on clerical wages.

There is another use for word processors in offices: one types a letter or manuscript, corrects errors here and there, and then the complete text regenerates automatically with all amendments made and spaces and lines adjusted appropriately.

We may as well face up to the fact that in this role the word processor is beginning to eliminate the job of the copy typist and the consequences will be felt in the early '80s. Without touching on the next phase of development—word processors communicating with each other directly without going through the performance of translating their messages into letters, which then have to clump around the ponderous mail system—it is clear that the impact of computing on routine office work in the period leading up to 1982 will be substantial.

Microprocessors will be just as useful in other kinds of businesses, including the professions of medicine, dentistry and even teaching, where information storage and retrieval problems are encountered. These areas have more in common than one might think. Doctors and teachers both have to go through a long period of expensive professional training at the end of which they are expected to divide their time and skills among a large number of supplicants—hundreds of patients or pupils. It is not surprising that they are unable to give a wholly satisfactory service. The problem is that no society on earth is wealthy enough to train, let alone employ, doctors and teachers in the right kind of numbers. But computers will make significant inroads into these areas. When a patient appears in the GP's surgery, for example, his or her name will be tapped into the terminal, whereupon a complete record will immediately appear with assorted useful family details and special warnings about drugs to be avoided, etc. Fresh details will be typed in by the doctor on the spot and absorbed into the computer's limitless store.

In hospitals and clinics computers will screen patients before they see a doctor. In schools, computer teaching—initially for "drill-and-practice"—will begin to spread as costs spiral downwards. Curiously perhaps, fears that patients or pupils would resent being interviewed by a medical computer or taught by a teaching computer have proved unfounded in experiments currently in progress in both hospitals and schools.

I referred earlier to our limitless fascination with toys and games, pointing out that the microprocessor industry is already engaged in a vigorous exploitation of this obsession. Initially, as always, the first fruits will be trivial almost to the point of banality—dolls and Action Man soldiers which address their owners in computer-generated voices, toys which stop, start and progress through a limited repertoire of activities on voice command, electric train sets which buzz back and forth under computer control, and so forth. But these represent only a fragment of the potential market, and commercial interests seeking to tap the expanding "leisure" industry will recognize the limitless applications of computers for entertainment. The first big developments will spring from their incursion into micro-processor-driven games.

In 1976 I was driving across Texas listening to a local radio station when I picked up an interview with a man claiming that he would shortly be marketing a computer-controlled chess player. The interviewer sounded incredulous, mainly because he couldn't conceive of a computer actually playing chess. I, too, was incredulous, not because I couldn't accept the idea but because I couldn't see how one could get a good chess-playing program onto a cheap computer so soon. I had been playing against cumbersome chess programs for some years and while they had generally beaten me—I am a poor and careless player—I used to shudder at the logistical difficulties of getting the huge programs into action and at the ponderous nature of their play. But not much more than a year after I had listened sceptically to the broadcast, a micro-based chess game, complete with board and luminous display to announce the computer's moves, was on the market. Not much later I was playing one myself—and getting beaten. They are still a bit expensive, but they are getting cheaper all the time. Furthermore their chess-playing strength is rising and there are versions which already give club players a thrashing. Being beaten by a computer is an odd sensation, but it's one that will before too long be experienced by even the world's leading chess players.

Other two-person board games, checkers, Chinese checkers, and even more complex games such as Go will soon come with built-in computer opponents. But the most spectacular growth will occur in the realm of games employing the domestic TV set, where a tremendous market is already opening up.

TV games have been around for over five years, but because their importance lies more than skin-deep I want to say a bit about their principles of operation. The essence of any TV game, from the simple to the most complex, lies in the fact that computers can push out information to the external world in a variety of different ways. In the very earliest computers, numbers appeared in a window, sequences of lights flashed, or patterns of holes were punched in cards or tapes. A later development allowed them to control electric typewriters or teletype terminals. The trouble with these mechanical methods is that they are hideously slow in terms of what the computer could do, and the next logical development was to arrange for it to generate photoluminescent spots on cathode-ray tubes, a technique which is employed in a slightly different way in the re-creation of the picture on our TV sets. In the case of TV, of course, no "intelligence" or processing power is employed at either end, and the set is merely a display unit which slavishly captures and reproduces the signals generated at the TV transmitter. In the case of the units used for computer output, in contrast, the end product is sequences of luminous characters which are actually under the control of the computer.

Now, if the computer can control a cathode-ray tube so that it can create patterns in the form of letters and words, it can obviously also create other patterns—geometric shapes for example. Using the simplest programs and the cheapest forms of display, the shapes or patterns are generally square or angular luminous areas—like the squares which form the "bats" and "balls" of the first TV games of table tennis. These games were limited only by the processing power of the chip and later, as the chips grew "smarter"—to use the latest expression for increased processing power—they were able to keep automatic score, add sound effects, and more recently to handle more complex dynamics—extra playing pieces, different angles and speeds, etc. At the time of writing, quite elaborate battle games can be played—warfare seems particularly suitable for TV simulation— with the microprocessor using its intelligence to control the movements of one set of pieces—tanks, bombers, UFOs and so on—while the human player responds by operating a simple control lever or wheel to change the position of his own units and fire off missiles appropriately. Direct hits are recorded by flashes of light and satisfying bangs and the computer notes and announces the winner at the end. Other variations feature gun battles between cowboys, with covered wagons and cacti acting as bullet deflectors, or motor races in which one steers the car down a twisty track by using a miniature steering wheel. This genera-tion of games is already common in amusement arcades and pubs, and by 1980 they will be widely available for attachment to home TVs.

Hot on their heels will come even more elaborate and exciting versions, some of which are already being testbedded on large computers. They are on the edge of the incredible and have a compulsion which is genuinely alarming. Once one has been exposed to them one's sole goal in life seems to be to continue playing them. My favourite at the moment—it is available on most scientific and business oriented computers, and will filter through to the public within the next year or so—involves an attempt to land a space capsule on the moon.

A realistic picture of the lunar landscape comes up on the screen, with mountains, valleys and volcanic areas clearly depicted. In the top left-hand corner a cartoon space capsule appears, retro-rockets blazing, and begins a slanting descent to the lunar surface. The object is to effect a soft-landing. The direction of thrust of the rockets and their power are controlled by touching a "light pen" to a set of controls displayed on the screen. The light pen is a device which signals information to the computer by emitting a pulse of electrons whenever the screen is touched. To increase or decrease power you slide the light pen up and down a luminous scale. To change direction you point the light pen at one of a set of arrows and this makes the capsule rotate in the required direction. There is a limited amount of fuel, displayed conveniently on a gauge and, of course, a limited amount of time as the capsule relentlessly slips down towards the surface. First efforts are inevitably met with abject failure, the capsule crashing with humiliating biffs and showers of dust, but slowly one begins to master the complex skills involved.

When the rocket gets below a thousand metres in height, the

initial large-scale picture vanishes and you are treated to a vivid close-up of the appropriate area of the lunar surface, complete with pock-marked craters, boulders and the wrecks of previous crashes (the computer remembers them all!). This close-up gives you the detail necessary to effect a proper soft-landing. Slowly you improve (people, scientists included, are prepared to spend an awful lot of time learning how to land a rocket), and finally the grand moment comes when you make your first soft-landing. At this point the computer delivers a congratulatory message and a tiny astronaut steps out of the capsule and plants a little flag.

But that is not all. With increased skill and familiarity you begin to notice novel features on the moon's surface. For example, on one stretch of plain, near a cluster of boulders and by a tricky volcano, a MacDonald's hamburger stand is to be found. True *aficionados* learn not only how to find this particular portion of the lunar landscape whenever they want to, but also how to land their capsule right by the stand, achieving the satisfaction of seeing their astronaut get out, walk up to it, order two cheeseburgers and a Big Mac "to go", and march back to the rocket which takes off in a cloud of dust.

I have gone into the details of this fantastic—there really is no other word—computer simulation to give an idea of what the present generation of such games can do, and a hint of what might be expected from subsequent generations. It is not necessary to talk in detail about other existing games such as computer Monopoly, in which one drives a car through a cartoon town featuring the familiar streets and utilities of the Monopoly board, or the superbly hair-raising space battles featuring the spaceships and personalities of *Star Wars*, but they are mentioned because they are the shape of games to come.

Large industries will grow along with them, but their real significance lies in the fact that their intellect-grabbing capabilities—they are very real—will one day be harnessed in the service of the colossally powerful teaching computers which will appear on the scene in the mid-to-late 1980s.

CHAPTER SIX

Political, Economic and Social Consequences

IN THE PREVIOUS chapter we concentrated on technological changes which, because the forecasting periods are so close, are relatively easy to identify. As there is always a lag, and one of very variable duration, between the onrush of a technology and the changes which follow in its wake, it is dangerous to pronounce confidently on the political, economic and social consequences that will occur within such a short period of time. The best one can hope to do is to highlight a sample of areas in which, it seems, change, even upheaval, is inevitable and allow these to emphasize the significance of the Computer Revolution. I have chosen six of the areas most ripe for change, with the caveat that these are not necessarily the most sensitive, unsettling or threatening.

Firstly, we will witness the growth of a vast new industry. In the 1970s, the computer industries of the Western world began a period of extremely rapid growth and this, spurred by the advent of the microprocessor, will ensure that in the early 1980s they will become the world's number one industry with the amazing firm of IBM spearheading the drive. IBM's economic strength is phenomenal. Their orders in hand at the moment of writing, for example, exceed the total amount of their deliveries from the years 1950 to 1979! While I have been writing this book, I have watched them hoisting themselves up the *Fortune Magazine*'s list of the world's great companies, leap-frogging over such giants as Gulf Oil in the process. They now stand at number seven and, if the present trends continue, must soon displace General Motors from the number one spot.

The unseating of this seemingly omnipotent giant from the throne of capitalistic power will have symbolic as well as economic significance, as it will indicate the end of the great motoring era which began at Henry Ford's Dearborn factory in the '20s and whose twilight was signalled by the Yom Kippur oil crisis. There are, it is true, certain elements of doubt about IBM which are worth discussing because they serve as another reminder of the rapid rate of change which the industrial world is facing. From the beginning IBM's marketing policy has been strongly oriented towards providing maintenance and software support services. IBM machines, always noted for reliability and power, have been sold at highly competitive prices but with the requirement that customers commit themselves to a long-term maintenance contract. This policy, which few can resist because of the inherent attraction of IBM machines, leads to bonds of deceptive strength being formed with the company. The strategy has worked very well for IBM in the past and has allowed them to run rings around the opposition, some of whom, like the radio giant RCA, have pulled out of the computer business altogether in despair. Only Honeywell, Sperry-Univac and a few others— with about 20% of the market between them compared to IBM's 70% headlock—have offered any semblance of a fight.

But now the picture is changing. Having built their strength on a policy of long-term maintenance contracts, IBM appear to be totally committed to the manufacture and distribution of big systems—"mainframes" to use the trade term—and to have missed out on both minicomputers and microprocessors. If this is so then the rocketing rise of IBM may come to a halt in the near future. There are other scribblings on the wall. As computer technology in all its phases from hardware to software has become less expensive, there have been some forays into the field by small companies flying under the twentieth-century equivalent of the skull and crossbones. The most famous of these is the Amdahl concern, run by a former IBM designer who set up on his own and is now busy manufacturing IBM-type systems at a much lower price.

Equally significant is the fact that the most successful company in the minicomputer field (the generation of computers before the micros), Digital Equipment Corporation, who were never in the big mainframe business and have left IBM standing in this market area, have as yet been unable to make any penetration into the growing "personal computer" market. All this may seem like computer industry gossip but a highly important point lies buried among the anecdotes: the pace of technology is now so dramatic that those companies deeply involved and highly successful in one phase of development cannot always adapt quickly enough to maintain the lead in later phases. There are historical precedents— the ocean liner companies, none of whom were able to involve themselves in commercial air travel, and the automobile industry, which has been unable to maintain a finger in the aircraft manufacturing pie. The difference is that it is no longer a matter of making a bridge from one industry to another, but simply of crossing from one phase of a single industry to the next.

But however these internecine struggles turn out, one thing is certain: *the* industry of the coming decade is going to be computers and computer-based electronics. The imminence of this shift in the importance of computers is now apparent to many big industries, including the oil and automobile manufacturers who are diversifying as rapidly as they can. General Motors, for instance, has invested in semi-conductors, and Exxon (Esso in the UK) recently swallowed up in one swift gulp the promising microprocessor firm of Zilog. Evidence of this rocketing growth can also be seen if one scans the "trade" papers like *Computer Weekly*, in which issue after issue breaks its own record for display and "situations vacant" advertisements. When the rest of the commercial world finally gets the message the effects on the stock market will no doubt be something to behold.

Secondly, bureaucracies will rely increasingly on computer modelling. A few years ago a group of scientists, economists and geo-politicians sent a quiver through the Western world by publishing a brief document entitled "Limits to Growth". The group, who called themselves the Club of Rome, were reporting on the results of the first large-scale exercise in computer modelling, and their findings made newspaper headlines for months. Their message was quite simple: growth, in the terms that Western capitalism has accepted for the past hundred years, cannot go on indefinitely without (a) running out of raw materials; (b) overpopulating the world; (c) running out of food, and/or (d) poisoning the biosphere with industrial pollution. The significant thing about the message was that it had sprung from the bowels of a computer. The members of the Club had fed a jumble of data about various aspects of present industrial society into a mainframe and asked it to predict the consequences if things persisted on their present—or on any one of a number of alternative—courses. For unmitigated capitalists the computer's pronouncement was a grim one—growth must shortly stop or Western civilization would collapse.

The Club of Rome arguments are exceedingly interesting. They can of course be disputed, and indeed swiftly were, as rival groups fed their own sets of information into their own machines and came up with (somewhat) different answers. It all depended, everyone pointed out, on what kind of information you put into the computer in the first place. True—but the really important feature of the Club of Rome exercise was that, while there might be argument about which set of data was the "right" set, once it had been fed in, the consequences predicted by the computer, unpalatable though they might be, were unarguable. Once the premises had been accepted, no economist, no politician, no individual whatever his expertise or standing could dispute the computer's conclusions.

This has deeper significance than one first realizes, for it seems to me to represent the first occasion when the world as a whole recognized, and responded to, the judgement of a computer. Like it or not, even the most ardent anti-computerist would admit that the computer, lacking emotions, hunches and prejudices, would consider and generate only the stark facts of the matter. Of course, all it was doing was using its talent for sorting through data and boiling it down, but at a speed which would have been beyond the capabilities of an army of statisticians. The Club of Rome exercise had more than its fair share of impact—some people trace the influential but eccentrically misguided "small is beautiful" movement to the aftermath of the "Limits to Growth" debate. But by the end of the short-term period such exercises will be a major feature of all bureaucratic planning, whether stemming from business empires or governments. It is a significant trend, for it signals the imminent emancipation of Man from, on the one hand, the rule of the committee and, on the other, the inspired hunch of the autocrat.

Another significant feature of the short-term future will be the rise of Japan. At a conference in London towards the end of 1977 I was treated to lunch by the vice-president of one of Japan's largest computer companies. In excellent English he gave me a blow-by-blow account of his country's industrial strategy for the 1980s. Japan, he pointed out, has a population of about a hundred million (about twice that of the UK) and few natural resources. It has risen to be the world's most efficient and successful post-war economy on the basis of starting completely afresh with brand-new factories and no clogging industrial heritage, a shrewd and nationally determined assessment of what world markets were likely to be in the '50s and '60s, and a deep-seated and universally accepted understanding that without a huge export-based industry it would be unable to feed its population. Britain, he told me, had come out of the war with antiquated factories, a heavy industrial commitment to the past, a misplaced assessment of world markets, or more probably no assessment at all, and a fallacious belief that we would somehow muddle through however rough the economic waters. And without rubbing in how wrong we had been and how right they had been, he went on to say that Japan was now facing up to the next phase of the future.

The oil crisis and the various shifts in the balance of political and economic power throughout the world meant that Japan would be unable to maintain, let alone increase, its standard of living in the years to come if it relied on such archaic means of making money as selling motor cars, cameras, tape recorders and the like. The solution was simple and blazingly unambiguous. His country had to make itself the number one computer power of the 1980s, designing, making and selling the stupendous range of computers and computer-based products which the world of a decade hence would crave. To achieve this end the Japanese Government, in consortium with industrial investors, was injecting about seventy billion dollars into the computer industry in the decade 1975–1985. By the end of 1979 thirty billion of that will already have been invested, and the Japanese thrust—whose rewards one must remember do not mature immediately—will be half way home. Almost half that stupendous budget, incidentally, would be spent on computer training and teaching—about three billion dollars a year. Since that rather unsettling lunch, I have had few doubts that the most striking feature of the short-term future will be the emergence of Japan as the world's dominant computer power. No doubt that was the impression my host wanted to leave me with, and if so, he certainly achieved his goal.

The first economic consequences of the Computer Revolution will be felt in the short-term future. The snap reaction of the press to the recent flow of information about the wonders of semi-conductor technology has been that it will lead to sudden mass unemployment, and as a result we have been treated to a flood of Shock-Horror news headlines. This reaction has a thread of realism in it, for widespread computerization must have considerable effects on patterns of employment. But the picture will be far less gloomy than that painted, for two reasons. Firstly, employment patterns will change rapidly but not as precipitously as they did, for example, at the onset of the depression in America in the '20s, or in Germany following the collapse of the Mark. Secondly, the Shock-Horror emphasis is based largely on an anachronistic usage of the word "unemployment", which still conjures up an image of men in cloth caps lining up on a rainy street for free bowls of soup. The new "unemployment", if we can use the dread word at all in this context, will be of quite a different order, and much closer to a kind of affluent redundancy; we will discuss this in more detail in a later chapter.

Nevertheless economic consequences will arise. It is unwise to single out any particular industrial unit, or area of employment, but one turns automatically towards the newspaper and motor car industries, which in the UK in particular have been vehemently resistant to automation and will shortly become quite horribly uncompetitive if this resistance persists. The motor car industry is in double trouble because its product has passed its peak of demand, while the newspaper industry is not only heavily over-manned but is, at the same time, committed to antiquated production and distribution methods. These, of course, are not the only strands of industry which will be affected. Increasing computerization and industrial automation, while biting most fiercely in the middle term, will begin to noticeably affect patterns of employment well within the short term. Indeed, they have *already* had effects, but these have been masked by political manoeuvres and by such tactics as government subsidies on over-manned sections of the economy. This has been possible because of its relatively minor scale, but the days when such tactics can continue to be successful are numbered. Initially the shock will be partly cushioned by large-scale redundancies and hefty redundancy payments, by enforced early retirement and by absorbing as many young people as possible into pre-job education or training schemes. But even these tactics can only succeed for three to five years at the most, after which time there will be a sudden, and possibly rude, awakening to the realization that patterns of working life are about to change in a most radical and irrevocable way.

The first practical evidence of this shift will be reflected in a cut in the working week to an average of thirty hours, a retirement option (with strong inducements) at fifty-five or even fifty, and annual vacations of at least six working weeks. In tandem with these changes must come the first major questionings of the "work ethic". Leaving aside for the moment a discussion of the use to which people will put their increased non-working life, the notion that it is morally reprehensible not to be working hard all the time—"the devil finds work for idle hands to do"—is deeply ingrained in our culture. Other strongly entrenched ideas—the notion of the inequality of women for example—have, it is true, been uprooted in the past, but not without a toughish struggle. More important, the timescale over which these changes have occurred has been extensive enough to let people and society adjust. No such luxurious timescales will prevail as the work ethic dissolves before our eyes.

The short-term future will also see a growing public awareness of computers, with clear-cut attitudes beginning to emerge out of the amorphous pool of confusion or indifference that presently exists. From newspapers, magazines and TV programmes about computers it is easy to get the impression that there already is a public awareness in this area, and that it is characterized by strong feelings of distrust and animosity. This is a misleading view as anyone who takes the trouble to talk to a reasonable range of "ordinary" people will find out. Most people have very little conceptual understanding of computers, what they are or what they can and might do, and have only the most hazily-formed attitudes to them. Their most likely image features ranks of flashing lights and reels of magnetic tape, gleaned from TV programmes of the *Six Million Dollar Man* variety, or of "intelligent" computers such as HAL in *2001* or K9, the talking dog in *Dr Who*.

The poverty of most people's ideas about computers is strikingly demonstrated by the fact that any discussion of them, nine times out of ten, revolves around a computer recently installed to a chorus of raspberries, or one of a range of anecdotes about monstrous gas or electricity bills.

Within the short-term future such ignorance will end, mainly because the average person will increasingly be face to face with computers in the course of everyday life. This may be the computer at work into which information has to be fed, or the personal microprocessor which an electronically-minded neighbour is assembling at home, or the synthetic voice on the phone that gives information about train timetables or weather forecasts, or, possibly, the tiny teaching computer which the children are using to help them with their exams. This new social awareness will, needless to say, bring big changes in its wake, the first manifestation of which will be a rush of interest in learning about computers. People will feel the need to be informed and they will go wherever they can to get this information. For those who *are* informed, employment opportunities will be prodigal, while those who remain ignorant, resistant or unwilling to learn will find the world an alarmingly alien place. This in turn could lead to sharp polarizations of attitudes, with some segments of society, for a variety of motives, forming an anti-computer bloc, and other sections—again from a mixture of motives—forming pro-computer groups. But the era of indifference and ignorance will be over.

The growing lure of games and gadgetry is a difficult notion to put over, but it is characteristic of the peculiar problems we will shortly have to contend with. It is tied up with the enormous potential for titillation and engrossment which the next generation of computer-driven games will provide. Even today's games, such as the cartoon moon-lander, can be compelling to an extraordinary degree, and I have been both surprised and irritated at how much I am drawn to them. The need to achieve mastery over the task set by the game is clearly a prime motivator but its power as a credible, continuously exciting simulation of some aspect of one's fantasy life is also a big factor. And if games like the moon-lander are merely the first computer "life simulations", what fabulous adventures, what overwhelming involvement can we expect from later versions? We won't have to wait long to find out, for before the end of this era computer games will have reached such heights of realism that for many people they will be a major hobby. This could be viewed as a good or bad development. At first thought it might be seen as replacing the largely passive entertainment of TV watching, which would be a most welcome trend, but this may be missing an important point. The trouble is that one knows very little about the long-term psychological effects of this kind of preoccupation.

A parallel area of uncertainty will serve to emphasize the point. At the time of writing the educational world is in the grips of a debate about the use of pocket calculators by schoolchildren. The question is whether the regular use of these devices will stultify a child's capacity to do mental or even pencil-and-paper arithmetic. The snap answer is that it must—the act of calculation involves practice and training, and if you do not get it you can never expect to develop the necessary skills. To this one can glibly respond by asking whether it really matters if these skills are not developed. Calculators are cheap and universal and do the job more quickly, so why bother to fumble around with the sums in one's head?

At this point a subsidiary and much deeper question is exposed. Supposing the knack of doing "sums" in one's head dies out—

will that necessarily hamper mathematical capabilities? Might not the reverse be true? It is possible that natural and "intuitive" mathematical powers are at present being inhibited, perhaps severely, by the formal discipline of learning trivial computational rules. Alas for psychology, for education, for teachers and for pupils, one has to say that one simply doesn't know. We are already embarked on a course which might have quite sweeping effects, either beneficial or destructive, on the development of human mathematical abilities, and not only have we no answers to some of the critical questions that need to be asked, but we have not even begun to formulate the *questions* properly. In the meantime the spread of personal calculators—and other computer gadgets—goes on, and as the present generation of schoolchildren mature into young adults by the end of the era, its first effects will show themselves.

With these glimpses of the short-term future we move on, with a forgivable mixture of trepidation, excitement and uncertainty, to look at the medium term, the years between 1983 and 1990.

Part Four

THE MIDDLE-TERM FUTURE: 1983-1990

CHAPTER SEVEN

Into the Exponential

BY THE EARLY years of the 1980s the Computer Revolution will be in full swing, and even those individuals most detached from the march of technology will be aware of its progress. But the deeper consequences will not have had time to mature and will only begin to surface, like a series of magically generated mushrooms, in the following decade. They will be greeted with shock and surprise, for by this time the rate of change in technology and its by-products will have passed from the historically linear phase and will have entered the exponential section of the growth curve.

Many people are familiar in general terms with the concept of exponential growth, but few people—mathematicians and computer experts included—have an intuitive as opposed to an academic grasp of its nature. In linear growth the increments of change remain constant, and as a result the future is easily predicted. In exponential growth the increments of change increase steadily, the simplest example being growth to the exponent 2, which is better known as a doubling effect. If plotted on a graph this gives a curve which starts off relatively flat but soon begins to accelerate upwards at an amazing rate. To give an example: take a sheet of paper of average thickness and fold it over on itself fifty times. Forget for a moment the physical difficulty involved and ask yourself how thick the paper will be when you have completed the operation. Remember that you are doubling the paper's thickness fifty times, so you should talk of its *height* and expect something pretty spectacular.

Most people who have not already heard the answer to this or a similar teaser talk about something a few inches thick. Others, realizing that a novel concept is involved, talk of a few feet, while bolder souls offer up Nelson's Column or even the Empire State

Building. Once in a blue moon someone will produce Mount
Everest in triumphal certainty that they have stretched their
imagination far enough. But few realize that the stupendous
block of paper will have pushed far above Everest, right out of the
atmosphere, past the moon, beyond the orbit of the planet Mars
and into the asteroid belt. Human beings just do not have a
conceptual experience of the exponential. In our brief life-span
we normally experience only linear change, and although the
universe is full of exponential change, it is either irrelevant to us,
or so overwhelming when it occurs that there is nothing we can
do about it. Most explosions, from hand grenades up through
hydrogen bombs to supernovae, have a brief exponential component. Our inability to face up to such problems as impending
global food shortages, atmospheric pollution and—most widely
cited—population growth, are excellent examples of this weakness.

The point is important, for computer technology is embarking
on a period of exponential growth, and social and economic
changes will probably occur in its wake, for a brief period at any
rate, at the same conceptually unmanageable pace. The first
person to spell this out was Alvin Toffler whose book *Future
Shock,* published in 1970, warned that the world was moving into
an era of change which would stretch existing institutions to their
limits, and strain psychological concepts beyond breaking point.
Future Shock was criticized for being sensationalist, but it is clear
when one re-reads it ten years later that Toffler himself underestimated the rate at which things were going to move. His book
showed an astute awareness of impending technological developments, but it contains not one single reference to the most sensational instrument of change of all—the microprocessor—for the
very good reason that when he wrote it the microprocessor did not
exist. No clearer testimony could be offered to prove how fast
things are now coming upon us.

In attempting to plot the course of events over the four years
assigned to the short-term future, it was convenient to concentrate first on likely technological developments, then on politico-
economic changes and finally on social and psychological issues.
The pace is already so great, however, that making specific

technological predictions about what will be available either in the research laboratories or on the production line *after* the year 1982 is extremely hard. One thing, however, is certain: human society is going to make a radical change in the way it handles and stores information. This may not seem particularly earth-shaking, but it could turn out to be one of the most momentous developments that Man has known.

CHAPTER EIGHT

The Death of the Printed Word

BIOLOGISTS HAVE ATTEMPTED to define the crucial differences between Man as a species and other animals, notably the higher primates. The task is not as easy as it might seem, for many of the talents that appear to be critical—upright posture, tool using and making, a high degree of social organization—even the use of language, if one accepts the latest studies of chimpanzees who use American Sign Language—turn out not to be exclusively human. But in one respect Man does stand qualitatively apart from all other animals: his use of a written language.

The invention of writing was the most revolutionary of all human inventions, for in one great blow it severed the chains which tied an individual and his limited culture to a finite region of space, and to a restricted slice of time. Through the act of writing, one human being could express ideas or facts which were communicated to another individual. These facts could then remain as a permanent record after the originator had forgotten them or had passed away into dust. The significance of permanent data storage is the principal and perhaps the *sole* reason why Man is so absolutely the dominant creature of the planet. All non-human animals carry their knowledge and experience with them when they die. Man can preserve the richest fruits of his brain power, and stockpile them indefinitely for his descendants to feed on. The gigantic advances in human societies which have taken place over the last ten thousand years have been due to this capacity to record and preserve information; the principal system employed has been making marks in the form of inky squiggles on paper or, in earlier times, chopping chunks out of stone tablets.

This has served us more than well, but it is also obvious that the system has limitations. As the world's pool of "facts" has swollen—science alone, it is estimated, generates about six million new facts every year—so the problem of storing them has escalated. Books and documents are manageable in small numbers, but there comes a point when the amount of space needed is so great that it becomes uneconomic, both in financial and volumetric terms. In many businesses and in places such as hospitals, the cost of housing the written records on which the organization depends has risen to the point where it is greater than the cost of accommodating the people—clerks and administrators—who use the records. Data extraction, too, becomes progressively more difficult. In the early days of "book technology" a simple filing system of the A to Z variety was adequate, and a well-trained clerk could find his way around by referring to a parallel filing system in his own brain.

The problem, like so many others which we are facing today, has been neatly anticipated in science fiction. One story tells how, despite the use of microfilm and other information-compression devices, ninety per cent of the world's surface has to be given over to data storage and the inhabitants have to squeeze into a tiny area of living space. Huge artificial satellites are then employed and in due course the moon, too, becomes a filing cabinet. Hundreds of years pass; the information increases remorselessly and so does the storage problem, until all the other planets in the solar system have their surfaces (and interiors) crammed with "libraries" and file warehouses. The story concludes with an expedition across interstellar space in a search, not for adventure or the glory of colonization, but for fresh worlds on which to dump Earth's files and records. On the outbound voyage, however, they bump into an alien spacefleet coming from the opposite direction, so to speak, and on an identical mission. Like much science fiction, the story stretches the problem area to its limits, but nevertheless it makes an effective point. There is an endemic weakness in any technique of information storage which relies on the written or printed representation of concepts, and that is the size of the individual data units. Letters and words cannot be too small as humans would be unable to create, copy or read them.

So long as this remains the *only* valid method of recording data, the cost of paper, printing, distribution and storage will be a continuing problem. But one of the most startling features of the Computer Revolution (which, incidentally, is often referred to as the "data processing revolution") is that print and paper technology will appear as primitive as the pre-Caxtonian hand-copying of manuscripts seems to us. In sum, the 1980s will see the book as we know it, and as our ancestors created and cherished it, begin a slow but steady slide into oblivion.

The book has been such a long-loved and useful companion to mankind that one should not speak lightly of its decline and ultimate disappearance. Nevertheless there are a number of reasons why this is imminent. Books and computers have one important thing in common—they are both devices for storing information—and on at least three parameters the computer is so vastly superior to the book as to defy comparison.

The first parameter involves the size of the basic data unit, which, in the book, is the printed word or number, whose lateral dimension is in the order of two to five millimetres. In a computer the data unit is mind-blowingly different—an electronic switch whose dimensions have to be expressed in hundredths, even thousandths of a millimetre. Even existing microprocessor techniques can compress literary information at least ten thousandfold, and in due course the entire contents of a book will be located on a single silicon chip. But this is just the beginning. By the late 1980s, if data compression techniques continue on their present curve, it will be possible to store very large books, perhaps even sets of books, on a microchip and a whole library in a space about the size of one of today's paperbacks.

The next parameter of difference concerns cost. In the days before printing, a book was a one-off job; a scribe copied from a specially prepared source and the costs had to be related to the amount of time he took doing the transcription. While type-setting was a relatively skilled and laborious business, the automatic generation of facsimiles through printing brought the cost of books down and made the knowledge contained in them available to a wider audience. The consequences of this wave of information washing across the world included the first serious challenging of the establishment religions, the questioning of medieval social values, the great intellectual uprising of the

Renaissance, and the industrial and scientific revolutions of the eighteenth and nineteenth centuries.

Now the essential point about books is that in comparison with handwritten manuscripts they are *cheap,* and this cheapness led to their proliferation. But chips are going to be even cheaper, and on a scale which will make the economic gulf between handwritten and printed manuscripts seem tiny. The initial cost of compressing the book into chip form will, of course, be no less than the present cost of setting it up in typescript, but from that moment on everything is on the side of the computer. A book which sells by the million can, it is true, be kept to an extremely tempting price — you can buy the paperback of the latest Harold Robbins for about three dollars — but the majority of that sum is locked up in the unshrinkable costs of raw materials, distribution and retailers' profits. By the late 1980s its computerized equivalent could be available at something like twenty cents, as raw material and distribution costs reduce sensationally with miniaturization.

Furthermore, the notion of a chain of retailers — bookshops in particular — must shortly by called into question. When computer books can be mailed by the dozen in small envelopes, or even, at a later date, transmitted instantaneously by cable or microwave, it seems inevitable that publisher-to-customer sales will dominate the publishing industry. Profits on individual books will be down, but the cost of each work will be so low that many people will be able to buy every work published, instead of selecting a limited number to suit their pockets. The book-purchasing habit could well spread to a far wider population, a trend which the substantial advances in education and cultural learning brought about by computer-based teaching of the next decades will emphasize.

Initially the third parameter of difference seems to weigh against the new technology. Old-style books not only store the information but also display it for anyone who has learnt to read. You pick up the storage device, open its covers and there, arrayed along its pages, are the rivers of information coded into words. It is marvellously convenient and aesthetically gratifying as well. The chip or computer book however, is merely a slice of silicon holding information in machine code, which is essentially a series of binary statements—strings of zeros and ones. These cannot be read by the naked eye, and even if you scanned them with a high-power microscope you would only see the minute transistors holding their electronic signals. And so a translation device is needed to read an electronic book—something to scan the array of transistors, interpret their codes and convert them into whatever language the human uses.

The read-out terminals of the late '80s will be about the size of the average book today, and, of course, you will only need one of them. The screens on which the text is displayed will vary in size depending upon what one wants—page-size for the hand-held book, wrist-size for quick reference and portability, a ceiling projection for reading in bed in absolute comfort (at last!). The speed of text generation will be variable with automatic "page turning" as a standard feature. Different colour displays could also be offered, and a variety of different typefaces, while for children, those with poor vision or for anyone learning to read, the print could be projected in large characters. These developments are not just science fiction dreaming. Computer-generated "books" of this kind using TV sets as their displays instead of printed pages are already being built and tested, and the first commercial versions may be on sale early in the 1980s. Later years will see a reduction in their price, an increase in their general convenience and an enormous spread of their use.

The objection can be raised that electronic books, although marvellously cheap and convenient, have none of the aesthetically satisfying qualities of traditional printed books—the feel of a fine binding, the sensuous touch of paper pages and so on. The aesthetic needs of the book lover are most likely to be served by making the chip-readers themselves pleasant to look at and to touch—binding them in leather with gold clasps and with the display screens elegantly framed and mounted, for example. The chips themselves, each containing a book or set of books, will of course be easily interchangeable.

So far we have been talking about the book as an entertainer or informer, and to this extent the "books" of the 1980s and beyond are not really different in principle from today's. But in one respect they *do* differ, and it is here that the electronic book revolution will have its greatest impact.

The book as we know it is an essentially *passive* device, merely transferring information from one mind, that of the author, to another mind, that of the reader. But the book of the 1980s will no longer be passive, for it will be a sifter and interpreter as well as a purveyor of information. Dictionaries, to give the most simple example, will offer packages of relevant information on command. You type into the chip-reader a word or a phrase describing the problem area and the computer will respond, probably with one or two questions probing the nature of your interest, and finally generating a balanced summary with appropriate background information. Many encyclopaedias and "study courses" attempt to provide such guides at the moment but they are static, severely limited frameworks which rely on the user's motivation and basic research skills. The "smart" encyclopaedias of the late '80s will *do their own research,* acting literally as study partners to anyone who needs to access any of the complex patterns of information contained within them.

This extension of what we were describing in a previous chapter as "word-processing power" will be the first application of intelligence in what we would once have called a book, and it will rely on fairly substantial advances in computer software. Before any dictionary can become intelligent enough to "know something about its contents"—which is what one will be asking it to do—it must know in what parts of its store the various words are located, and it must also have some means of linking concepts together. Suppose that one wanted it to generate a package of useful information on, say, air pollution: it will need to "know" that information on industrial waste, on oil resources, on smokeless fuels, on the difficulties of legislating for "clean air", on the potential of solar energy, etc., is all relevant, whereas stray information about other kinds of pollution must be ignored.

Scanning and classification is quite easily performed by human beings, but is simply too much for computers with their present, rather feeble, intelligence. Nor is it a trivial problem to equip computers with the kind of programs which would allow them to perform these operations, and without which the kind of "intelligent encyclopaedia" we have been talking about will be impossible. But, significantly perhaps, this is the kind of problem area which appeals most to those computer scientists who are currently engaged in the field of machine or artificial intelligence. It is also the area into which increased effort is likely to be pumped in the near future, for, once real progress has been made, the gains are likely to be immense. In teaching and education, the dynamic book could have a breathtakingly powerful role, and there is an obvious spin-off to industry and commerce. Once again in a capitalist world, the forces of the market-place prevail, and the promise of this commercial spin-off will be enough to ensure that the intricate programs allowing this kind of "intelligent" data inspection and retrieval will ultimately be developed. In some areas the effects will be wholly beneficial, in others marginal, and in yet others, highly controversial. Among the most notable developments will be that we shall see the computer beginning to poach on the preserves of a group of human beings who, at present, seem to be securely protected from its advances.

CHAPTER NINE

The Decline of the Professions

THE EROSION OF the power of the established professions will be
a striking feature of the second phase of the Computer Revolution. It will be as marked, and perhaps even more so, as the
intrusion into the work of the skilled and semi-skilled, although
the notion of precipitous unemployment among factory workers
and clerks tends to be the centre of debate.

The vulnerability of the professions is tied up with their special
strength—the fact that they act as exclusive repositories and
disseminators of specialist knowledge. This is true whether one
is talking about the symptoms of illness and the keys to its
treatment, which are presently in the hands of the doctors and
physicians, or the weird permutations of tax laws and entitlements on which accountants thrive, or the fantastic tangle of
information which makes the practice and implementation of the
law so formidably restrictive to the lay person. It is important not
to undervalue the professions or the complex information
packages they handle on our behalf. They are the end-product of a
process of labour specialization which began when men first
undertook the hunting and women and children the berry-
gathering in the most primitive human societies, and they have
come into being because the social evolution of mankind has
made life increasingly complex. In this respect they have served
us well.

The professions, as you might expect, guard their secrets
closely, insisting on careful scrutiny and rigorous training of
individuals who wish to enter their ranks. But this state of
privilege can only persist as long as the special data and the rules
for its administration remain inaccessible to the general public.
Once the barriers which stand between the average person and
this knowledge dissolve, the significance of the profession

dwindles and the power and status of its members shrink. Characteristically, the services which the profession originally offered then become available at a very low cost.

There are some clear-cut examples from the past. At one time the arts of reading and writing were classed among the great mysteries of life for the majority of people (and still are for many, many millions), and individuals trained in these arts could command good fees for their services. Another group once esteemed to the point of exaltation, the clerics, were assumed to have unique moral and spiritual expertise with a hot line to God into the bargain, and they enjoyed exceptional living standards on the basis of this occult knowledge. It may seem that there is a pretty big difference between reading, writing, sermonizing, etc., and interpreting a legal document or making a medical diagnosis. But the difference is largely illusory, and arises because, although most of us have managed to penetrate the secrets of the former areas of knowledge, few have made much headway with the latter. In the final analysis, the raw material of a modern profession is nothing more than information, and the professional expertise lies simply in knowing the rules for handling or processing it. No clearer example can be given than the case of medical interviewing which computer experts have been looking at now for almost a decade.

To the layman, the questions which a doctor puts to the patient at their first meeting are suffused with wisdom and insight, and give the impression that the doctor is proceeding towards his goal with uncanny understanding. On the basis of the information gathered he makes his "diagnosis"—a decision as to which of the many possible illnesses the patient is suffering from—and then out of a seemingly bottomless jar of remedies, he selects the one most likely to effect a cure. More often than not the patient recovers and the magnificently complex practice of medicine has once again justified itself. All this may be impressive to the outsider, but on closer inspection it is revealed as something altogether less marvellous. The initial questions (the "history taking" in medical parlance) are extremely easy to formalize, and the preliminary diagnosis—for example, a possible gastric ulcer—and the decision about further investigation and treat-

ment—a recommendation to X-ray, a special diet and so on—
follow more or less automatically in the majority of cases.

Computer programs have already been written which take satisfactory histories in a large variety of common complaints, make
simple recommendations for follow-up studies and even offer
tentative diagnoses. And they do it all with such panache that the
majority of patients interviewed by the computer prefer it to the
doctor. There is also clear evidence that many patients are more
truthful when they talk to the computer and are more willing to
reveal their secrets to it than to a human being. In some experiments in a Glasgow hospital patients suspected of being
alcoholics were interviewed by a specially tailored computer
program; they admitted to drinking fifty per cent more alcohol to
the computer than they did to the clinic's highly trained consul-
tants. In other experiments, patients visiting psychosexual
clinics showed real eagerness to chat about sexual hangups to a
computer, in striking contrast to their reluctance to talk to the
most sympathetic resident psychiatrists. These examples, to be
fair, are merely indicative of some aspects of medicine, but they
are enough to suggest that the barriers of mystique which
surround the profession are beginning to crack. Certainly an
increasing number of computer experts and doctors believe that
by the 1980s, large areas of medical practice will yield up their
secrets to the computer.

The first signs of this will be the appearance of computers in
hospitals, and a good deal of the "front end" of medicine—
routine interviewing, screening and advice-giving—will be
performed by microprocessors. There will also be a steady
transfer of the bulk of patients' records away from the inefficient
and costly system of files and folders—the bane of hospital
administration—onto central computers. Not only will this allow
instant access of relevant data but it will also be substantially
cheaper. Contrary to popular mythology, by the way, computer-
based records can easily be protected from prying eyes by simple
systems of codes and computer-generated checks, and would be
inaccessible to the average nosey-parker. And those peculiarly
optimistic blackmailers who are supposed to be forever itching to
make use of the information about the ingrowing toe-nail you

suffered from in 1964 would much prefer the present, easily scrutinized, forged and copied paper records.

Anyone horrified at this picture of a medical practice apparently devoid of human content need not be worried. Spreading computerization will give the patients *more* contact with the living human doctor, who will become less of an interrogator and glorified records clerk, and will be able to spend far more time with the patient discussing the things that really matter. Indeed the computer is likely to emancipate the doctor, allowing him to exercise the native talents and numerous skills for which the long period of medical training has prepared him. Equally, anyone fearing that computer interviewing and rudimentary computer diagnosis must eventually lead to computer "decision-making", and in particular decision-making of the "cut off that leg" variety, can be reassured: surrendering routine and time-consuming medical matters to a computer is not the same as handing over matters of life and death. It will be a long time, one suspects, before these powers are taken out of the hands of our fellow human beings. Nor is the practice of surgery in its present form likely to slip easily into the world of cybernetics for numerous reasons, among them the sheer difficulty of transferring subtle psychomotor skills from human to computer. Even so, the medical profession is by no means inviolate from automation, and the '80s will see great changes occurring in its practice, efficiency, cost and in its public and self-image.

The law, which seems even more mysterious and impenetrable, will also find itself being subjected to the quizzical gaze of computer programmers and systems-analysts. And when it does, its impenetrability may turn out to be equally illusory. Legal matters, it is true, have a different kind of depth and subtlety of muddle and are embedded in obscurantist statement and Latin phraseology. Precedent is all-important—what happened in this case in 1964, to that judgement in 1888, to that appeal in 1932. But this is precisely the kind of information which can easily be lodged in a computer's brain, and which can be called up at the press of the right button by anyone following the simplest book of rules.

It is difficult to see how the 1980s will get far under way before the economic advantages of codifying the law in computer terms are recognized. Presumably the main thrust towards computerized legal administration will come from big companies who would like to simplify or eliminate this traditionally expensive facet of their internal bureaucracy. On the other hand, there will be those who find the intricacies of company law and its opportunities for putting up smoke-screens too profitable to surrender and will resist the advent of computerization accordingly.

There are curious parallels between medicine and law, indeed between all the professions. Just as there will be specialists within medicine who remain, at least temporarily, impervious to the threat of computers—the surgeons who are craftsmen skilled in the use of the scalpel rather than repositories of medical knowledge—so there will be their equivalents in the other professions. In the case of the law the favoured experts will undoubtedly be the lawyers who, as all but the most starry-eyed admirers of the judicial system will admit, are really operating as a special-purpose arm of the theatrical profession, skilled in the use of oratory, rather than as great disseminators of knowledge and wisdom.

Another profession of social prominence—though it has never achieved the status or economic standing of medicine and the law—is teaching. Once again there are striking parallels. It is a characteristic of most professions that they require long and expensive training periods. After these have been completed the trained individual then has to "time-share" his abilities among too many supplicants for him to be as effective as he could be. Universal, personal medical care and personal, dedicated tuition are clearly marvellous goals for the world to aim at, but they are economically unattainable even in the richest societies. That they *are* desirable, and presumably worthwhile, is attested by the fact that once one has scrambled to the top of the capitalist ladder and become a millionaire (or, in other societies, climbed high enough up the political pecking-order), just about the first services one makes available to self and family are personalized medicine and teaching. But these services are likely to be available to us all in the very near future, and the changes will be even more striking and effective in the case of teaching than in medicine.

Bringing the computer into education is an ambition that has turned out to be extremely difficult to fulfil for three major reasons. The first is that no one, not even the most experienced and eminent teacher, the most knowledgeable educator or the most perceptive psychologist, has the faintest idea what the best methods of teaching are. We do not even know how human learning takes place, or what ensures that one thing is learned rather than another. Motivation is known to play some part and intelligence is assumed to be important. Reward and punishment are also involved, though not in as clear-cut a way as most people like to believe. Social interaction is supposed to facilitate learning, as are attitudes to teachers, other pupils, schools, etc. Yet we have to admit that thousands of years of academic effort all add up to very little understanding of what the teacher is doing when he teaches and how the pupil is learning what he is being taught. And only when we do understand can there be a science of teaching or education.

Secondly, although people know very little about the educational process *per se*, they are convinced that they *do* know something, perhaps a lot, about it and that it is essentially a simple process. It was this myth that led to the disastrous experiments with teaching machines, programmed text books and the like which galloped across the bewildered world of education in the late 1950s and early '60s.

Teaching machines (which were not, of course, computers) were never enormously common, and the period for which they were around was a pretty short one. Here and there in the basement of a school where the head has not been ruthless enough to get rid of the junk of decades past, you will stumble across a nest of them, gathering dust among out-of-date text books and assortments of non-metric measurers. Generally they were boxes roughly the same size as a TV set, electrically-switchable projectors which could handle a sequence of slides, featuring pictures or text of some kind. In more "advanced" designs, the carousels were replaced by film-strips which could be displayed frame by frame or with brief bursts of movie action. In some cases a sound-track was added. The pupil sat in front of all this, responding to questions on the screen by pushing one of a small range of buttons. When the button was pushed, the machine, after a lot of grumbling and swishing, would produce an appropriate response, followed by another question.

In designing the machines due attention was paid to the findings of the Harvard psychologist, B. F. Skinner—almost exclusively based on the behaviour of rats in puzzle boxes—on the importance of rewarding correct responses and punishing, or at least not rewarding, incorrect ones. So whenever you made a right decision, the machine laboriously displayed a slide with some enouraging phrase, such as "Well done! You were quite correct." If you were wrong the slide said something like, "No, that isn't right. You have not taken such and such into account. Now push the return button and have another go." When you pushed the return button you were faced with the previous decision point again, but this time the "correct" decision was easy to identify and you could march on to the next phase of the program. At the end of the "lesson" the very superior marques of the machine would have totted up your score.

The above is a fair description of teaching machines and their goals, and it is not difficult to see why they were unsuccessful. For one thing, the "dynamic" component of the programs was largely illusory. True, at each step in the process the pupil had a choice, sometimes of three or more possibilities, but these were barely enough to eliminate the "lucky guess" element which enabled the effectively untaught pupil to advance beyond his level of understanding. In addition, whenever the incorrect button was pushed one tended to come up against the same "Bad luck" messages over and over again, a feature of the machines which all who ever used them came to know and hate. The trouble was that the devices—no matter how noble their aims—were, in the end, just somebody's old slide show, put together in a time remote from the pupil's, and whose basic lack of intelligence was only too swiftly exposed. To make matters worse they were almost always unreliable, being of such notoriously touchy components as tape recorders and slide projectors, and by the same token not cheap. Programmed text books, which guided the pupil on a branching excursion through their pages, were much cheaper and suffered no mechanical faults, but their pretensions to dynamism were an order of magnitude worse and their attempts at personal conversation even feebler. Once you had discovered that page 46 harboured the message, "No that is not quite right. Go back to page 36 and read the text once more," you never felt the same about the book again.

It is easy, as always with hindsight, to identify the weaknesses of the approach. But it is also easy to see why it was superficially so attractive and why many education-based companies, including publishers and audio-visual-aid manufacturers, lost large sums of money in this new enthusiasm. But the whole saga was based on two fundamental misjudgements: that we knew something about the principles of good teaching, and that these principles were essentially simple and so could be embodied in a simple machine.

There is a third reason why CAI (Computer-Aided Instruction), or CAL (Computer-Assisted Learning) as it is sometimes abbreviated, has been slow to advance, and it is of great importance in determining the pace of evolution of computers as a whole. It is that, to date, there has been little evidence that large sums of money are to be made out of teaching, whether by human or automatic means. The capitalist world is only interested in things which make profits, and only takes risks with things which look as though they are going to make very big profits indeed. And within this frame of reference, teaching and its associated products are pushed aside as being non-starters, and would on present terms remain so. But the terms are beginning to change.

The change evidently reflects a growing realization on the part of governments that national wealth depends to a high degree on the educational standards of their peoples. If one had to pin it down to a date one would probably choose 1975, which was the first year when combined world expenditure on education exceeded defence and military budgets, a statistic which most people find very surprising. This could be interpreted as indicating that the world is at last moving towards peace, but it is probably more realistic to accept the by no means objectionable alternative that it is attempting to move away from ignorance.

More and more money is now being pumped into the educational system, and it is reasonable to assume this will continue. It is difficult to understand why an education-based industry comparable to the enormous weapons industry does not already exist. The fact is while stupendous sums of money are injected each year into teaching in its various forms, hardly any of these find their way into consumer-based products. Billions of dollars are spent on the construction and maintenance of schools and universities, billions again on training teachers and paying their somewhat niggardly salaries. These easily take the lion's share of the total financial allocation, and books, paper, educational aids, etc., have to squabble over the scraps. Educational research—which should be the most important facet of education—fares even worse.

Until the last year or so, the only part of the education industry which could be regarded as being consumer-based—to the extent that it churned out non-permanent items by the million—was text-book publishing and the like, with pencils, erasers and other knick-knacks following along behind. The qualification "until the last year or so" serves to remind us once again of pocket calculators which are now owned by a high percentage of school-children in Europe and America. They are the first wave of a new range of products that will, in the course of the 1980s, transform the educational system and at the same time create a new industry to capitalize on this development. Pocket calculators, as we said earlier, are very important straws in the wind, and the speed with which they have swept through the Western school system—while educationalists are still standing around uneasily musing whether they are a good thing or not—is an indication of the shape of things to come. Their intrusion into the schoolroom is only one facet of their intrusion into the world as a whole, and their huge sales are related more to their appeal as gimmicks than to their general usefulness. But the second wave of highly advanced super-miniaturized technology will be directly geared to the educational process, and will be even more attractive to prospective buyers. It will also, after a few false starts caused by over-enthusiasm and a rush for quick profits, lead to major changes and advances in the teaching process itself.

This will be based on the development of portable, personal teaching computers, devices no bigger than the average pocket calculator of the late '70s, and selling at about the same price. The prototype of these devices (with the provisional code name of MINNIE, and developed at the National Physical Laboratory in England) is worth describing because it gives a good idea of the form they will take. At first glance MINNIE looks just like a calculator and weighs about the same. Closer inspection reveals that it has more keys than the standard four-function device, and these not only cover the numbers 1 to 10 but also a full set of the letters of the alphabet. There are keys for "space", "delete" and other functions. Hit the keys and the appropriate number *or letter* appears in the display. But there is more to it than that. When you switch the device on, a sequence of glowing letters appears to introduce the machine to the user: "HELLO, MY NAME IS MINNIE. I CAN ACT AS A FRENCH-ENGLISH DICTIONARY, OR I CAN TEST YOU ON YOUR KNOWLEDGE OF FRENCH. WHICH WOULD YOU LIKE, THE DICTIONARY, OR THE TEST?" If you want the dictionary you type in the letter D, whereupon you are invited to choose French-English or English-French; and then MINNIE obliges with the appropriate translation of whatever word you type in. MINNIE tests your vocabulary by putting up a sequence of words for you to translate; it tells you if you are right or wrong, and gives the correct translation after three unsuccessful goes. At the end of the exercise (one can choose the length of the test) it spells out the score.

In its earliest form MINNIE had a relatively small vocabulary—a few hundred words only, and operated off a microprocessor chip with a memory of about two kilobytes. Even so, users found it really helped them to brush up their French—or any other language for which it was programmed. But these tiny memories are completely unrepresentative of what such teaching aids will come equipped with as we move into the '80s. Chips containing over a hundred kilobytes of information—the equivalent of thousands of English words—are already being manufactured, and even bigger memories are on the drawing board. By the mid-'80s complete book dictionaries will easily be packed into MINNIE-type devices, and by the end of the decade the chips of these tiny computers could contain not just one, but several common languages.

The language application is probably the one for which such devices are most easily programmed, and pocket computer translators and vocabulary teachers will soon be found in the briefcases of travelling businessmen; and as production soars and prices plummet, in the pockets of school teachers and schoolchildren as well. The basic components of pocket teaching computers are no different from those of calculators—a larger keyboard and a more elaborate display are the only minor changes—and once a commercial impetus is given to their development, the production lines will roll them off, by the million and then by the billion, and each unit will shortly be as cheap as (possibly cheaper than) today's calculators. It is worth emphasizing this point, because the low cost of the gadgets will ensure that they, like their predecessors the calculators, will sweep through the educational system of the Western world. Teachers and educators may as well face up to this fact and should decide now how to meet the challenge when it comes, for one thing is certain: any tactic that involves banning or prohibiting their manufacture and sale is doomed to failure. Commercial pressures of unstoppable strength are already building up and, like it or not, the pocket teaching computer will soon be upon us.

It is tempting at this point to look back at the dashed enthusiasm of the 1960s for teaching machines, and ask why the weaknesses of these devices are not equally inherent in their successors. Surely one teaching machine is, at heart, just the same as any other and the advantage of size reduction would scarcely be enough to matter? The question is fair, but behind it lies a basic failure to comprehend the huge power of computers. This power has reached the point where even those who are closely involved do not have any real grasp of its immensity. I myself get only brief flickering glimpses of it. Recently, for example, I decided to write a program for a microprocessor using machine code. Machine code is the language that the computer actually speaks, and it is really just a sequence of zeros and ones. Higher level languages, such as FORTRAN and BASIC, use English words and phrases and are much quicker and easier to work with but the little microprocessor I was using did not understand either of them, so I was faced with communicating with it in the only language it could understand—strings and strings of zeros and ones.

The task was to program it to play a moon-landing simulation and after some hours of appalling brain fag I finally succeeded. The program had seemed, as I slogged away at it, to be quite gigantic and intuitively I felt dangerously close to overloading the tiny computer's memory. So strong was this feeling that when I found that to make the program run in a more interesting way I would need to add an extra loop involving fifty or so steps—another few hundred ones and zeros—I did some anxious calculations to see how much of its memory was left to use. When I realized my lengthy, tortuous program had used a barely detectable fragment of just *one* of the system's twenty or thirty mighty memory units, the shock was hair-raising. It was as if I had walked to the crest of a minor ridge expecting to see a gentle slope falling away in front of me, only to find that I was standing on the rim of the Grand Canyon. The programming task had given me a particularly graphic yardstick against which to measure the system's true capacity, and it made me wonder what the effect would have been had I "grasped" the true size of a really beefy system instead of a cheap microprocessor. Personally I suspect that an insight on this scale would be beyond the capacity of the human mind, in the way that the awful wastes of time and space defy comprehension. The point is that even those closely involved in computing rarely get a sniff of the true power of their charges and it is scarcely surprising that those who only see them from a distance misunderstand and underestimate their potential. Unfortunately, before one can understand the vast difference between a teaching machine and a computer, one has to have at least a glimmering of it.

Teachers working in schools where anything smaller than an elephant has to be chained to the floor to prevent it vanishing into the mist will no doubt smile wryly at the thought of portability as an advantage. But remember that the computers of the '80s will be cheap and common rather than rare and expensive, and there is really no substitute for a gadget that travels with you. One of the winners of a "Brain of Britain" contest attributed his great knowledge to the fact that he had a set of encyclopaedias in every room in his house so that whenever he wanted information he could get it immediately. We all know the feeling. Things accessible *now* and on the spot are a hundred times more useful than those which are at a distance—even a short distance—in time and space.

Then small things, on the whole, are cheaper than big ones because they use up less raw material and can be produced in very large numbers. The old teaching machines were electromechanical gadgets, combining the subtle swiftness of electricity with the unhappy slowness of machinery. Electro-mechanical devices are relatively simple to design, but extremely difficult to mass produce and, once they reach a certain price level, increase in production runs will not do much to reduce the cost per unit to the public. Teaching *computers* on the other hand are basically all-electronic, with no moving parts—other than electrons—and are easy to mass produce. They cost little more than the raw materials of which they are made, and they have the great advantage of being extremely reliable.

The computer has a flexibility of function which is unique. MINNIE-type systems can be used as dictionaries, as drill-and-practice aids in mathematics as well as in language, as personal diaries or information systems, as game-partners and even, as things move on a bit, as conversationalists. But their value is not so much in *what* they teach as *how they will go about it*. The flexibility of a modern computer, small or large, is, to all intents and purposes, infinite and the range of tasks it can perform is limited only by the range of programs which can be written for it.

Teaching computers will be genuinely "smart". By this I mean that they will adjust their responses in a wide variety of ways, constantly giving the impression that they are "interested" in teaching by the way in which they structure their communication to meet the needs of the moment. For example, instead of pushing a limited range of buttons of the multiple-choice variety, your responses will be typed into the system in a more or less open-ended way; the computer will respond not by throwing up an obviously pre-prepared message on a screen but by generating a sequence of words and phrases which come up at conversational pace. A typical interaction could go something like this:

Computer: HELLO, HAVE I MET YOU BEFORE? WHAT'S YOUR NAME?

User: PETE.

Computer: PETE. WOULD THAT BE PETE SMITH?

User: YES, THAT'S RIGHT.

Computer: OH HELLO AGAIN PETE. WE WERE WORKING TO-GETHER LAST THURSDAY ON FRENCH TRANSLATION. I SEE WE GOT UP TO LEVEL SEVEN AND YOU WERE GETTING EVERY-THING RIGHT. WOULD YOU LIKE TO RUN OVER A SHORT TEST ON THAT LEVEL AGAIN OR SHALL WE MOVE ON?

User: LET'S MOVE ON.

Computer: OK PETE. WHAT DOES THIS WORD MEAN: JARDIN?

User: GARDEN.

Computer: FINE. NOW WHAT ABOUT ITS GENDER.

User: FEMININE?

Computer: THAT WOULD MAKE IT "LA JARDIN". DOES THAT SOUND RIGHT TO YOU?

User: MASCULINE THEN.

Computer: I THINK THAT WAS JUST A GUESS BUT YOU'RE RIGHT. JARDIN IS A TYPICAL MASCULINE NOUN. THERE'S NO "E" ON THE END OF IT, AND "IN" IS A TYPICAL MASCULINE ENDING. HOW ABOUT THE WORD "VIN"? WHAT DOES IT MEAN AND WHAT IS ITS GENDER?

User: WINE AND IT'S MASCULINE.

Computer: RIGHT. NOW THINK ABOUT THIS. SUPPOSE YOU WANTED TO SAY "PASS ME SOME WINE" IN FRENCH. WHAT WOULD YOU SAY?

User: PASSER-MOI LE VIN.

Computer: DO YOU MEAN PASSER? ARE YOU SURE ABOUT THE SPELLING?

User: PASSEZ?

Computer: YES THAT'S BETTER PETE. NOW SOMETHING ELSE WAS WRONG. YOU WOULDN'T SAY "LE VIN" BUT "DU VIN". DO YOU KNOW WHY?

User: NO.

Computer: WELL, IN THE CASE OF . . .

The above transcript gives a good idea of the kind of dialogue which people could be having with personal teaching computers by the mid-to-late 1980s. It is evident that the interaction is much closer in spirit to the way humans exchange information than is the approach of the old-fashioned teaching machines. The computer is capable of identifying and "understanding"—to use the word rather loosely—a range of common words and phrases, which prompt appropriate responses from it. In fact its *true* understanding is rather limited, but this is not a limitation which is easily identified by the human user. Even if the human goes through the program a second or third time, and gives precisely the same responses, it is possible to program the computer to randomize its own phraseology so that one rarely finds it saying the same thing twice. This apparently open-ended conversational ability gives the human the impression that he is communicating with something with a good deal of intelligence, and this impression persists even when one knows the computer's limitations, and the nature of its "imitation intelligence" is explained. The reason for this is that, in the long run, we are not concerned about *how it is* something works, so much as *what it actually does*. If a machine appears to be conducting a sensible conversation with us, to be interested in us, to be understanding our problems and to be motivated to correct them, then this is more than enough for us to enter into communication with it.

Of course, it is possible to throw the computer program out of joint by typing in nonsense or misleading it in some way. If it asks you what the English equivalent of the word "vin" is, and instead of saying "wine" you produce some ridiculous response such as "tennis match", it will not recognize the response as being sillier than if you had said "fine" or something linguistically closer. This inability to respond to the absurd may, in the earlier teaching computers, prove a slight handicap, but this could be overcome with more subtle programming. As most teachers and pupils know, even the most intelligent and well-meaning humans can have their teaching strategy torn to tatters if pupils refuse to play the game by the rules; but for people with any degree of motivation to learn, the computers will be infinitely more acceptable than teaching machines.

One of the strongest arms of the new industry which will spring up around computer-aided learning will be devoted to developing and evaluating the huge suites of programs which will extend the range of areas which computers can handle and give them their real teaching power. Herein lies the final key to understanding not only the future of teaching computers but also much of the future impact of computers on society. The realization that miniaturized, super-cheap, highly reliable computer technology will open up markets of staggering size, at first in Westernized societies and later in the Third World, must lead to a ruthless commercial investigation of the most profitable marketing areas. And one of the biggest untapped markets in the world is the application of computers to education.

Sceptics may here marshal their forces and point out that it is one thing to develop a technology capable of providing interactive personal tuition, but it is another, and far more difficult thing to determine the best methods for doing so, and to ascertain just how effective these methods will be when put into practice. The argument is valid—so much so that it is clear that no large-scale sales of teaching computers can possibly come about until these issues are at least partly resolved. But they may be resolved with a rapidity which takes the teaching world by surprise. For by the early 1980s, in order to catch this gigantically profitable market by the throat, commercial organizations will have begun to pump colossal sums of money into investigating the nature of the teaching process and developing powerful and effective teaching programs as a result. By the mid-to-late 1980s their research will probably begin to make headway and for the first time Man may develop a true Science of Education, and with it a real understanding of the nature of learning.

It is true that sequences of text appearing on calculator-size displays can only fulfil the most simple teaching function, but computers are advancing on a variety of fronts. Portable computers can already be plugged into TV sets, allowing full-colour displays and even the generation and manipulation of graphic material—sophisticated versions of the games that we were talking about in previous chapters—and can be linked up to other computers to allow "group" work. Voice output in the form of limited synthetic speech is already available at low cost, and in many of the language-teachers the computer will not only display the text but also speak it. Computers which recognize the human voice and could correct spoken words and phrases, drawing attention to pronunciation and accent problems, are unlikely to be commercially viable before the tail-end of the middle term, but they will come. Really powerful interactive computers capable of having extensive conversations with their users, whether in a didactic role or merely to satisfy the requirements of intellectual chat, will not be available until the 1990s or later; they will depend on developments in artificial intelligence, which we will discuss later.

One conundrum after another will be posed by developments of this kind, of which the response of the teaching profession to the part-threat, part-challenge of the computer is only one. We may as well pose some of the others. Who for example is going to determine the standards by which teaching computers operate? Given large amounts of time, some kind of co-operative mechanism could be set up between government, education authorities and the commercial organizations involved, so ideas and teaching strategies can be passed through the conservative buffers of committees and other "safety first" organizations. The end-product of all this would be a slow, dull, but educationally "safe" computer-taught curriculum. But limitless amounts of time are *not* going to be available. The first companies to bring pocket teaching computers on the market are going to make a commercial killing, and while precautionary mutterings may come from governments and the teaching profession itself, the Gold Rush atmosphere of the moment is likely to carry everything before it.

This is not necessarily a matter for panic. Teaching, as it is presently carried out, has changed very little in millennia, the only significant difference being the greater number of human brains that are subjected to the process; the various educational experiments of recent years are merely froth on the surface of an uncharted ocean. No one involved with providing a standard, equitable education for the vast throngs passing through the state schooling system will pretend that what is offered at the moment is much more than a desperate gesture. Anyone disputing this should take a look at the cultural and scholastic levels of the majority of seventeen-year-olds popping out of the end of the urban school system.

Another conundrum concerns the differential rate at which, at least in the early stages, the teaching computers will penetrate their market. The experience of pocket calculators already gives some leads. Their ownership, it is true, is widespread among children, but in many cases it has a status value only, and after the devices have been fiddled with ostentatiously in class or on the playground, they are forgotten until, batteries bulging, they find their way into the wastepaper basket. But there *is* a kind of bright child, usually coming from an educationally and culturally up-market home, who takes to the calculator like a duck to water, exploring its myriad permutations for sheer pleasure and, in doing so, acquires an intuitive grasp of fundamental mathematical concepts. Maths teachers are already familiar with this small but interesting breed who stand out so markedly from the rest of the class. This kind of elitism is even more marked in schools where computers are available for on-line use and experiment. Here groups of skilled programmers emerge, contemptuously dismissive of those who have not accepted the challenge of the computer's mystique. Sharper divisions will appear as the first teaching computers come on the market, and some children seize on them with voracious eagerness while others ignore them altogether.

This will no longer be a matter of a calculator or a programming elite, but rather an elite who will feast on the huge range of intellectual and fact-giving possibilities that the computer can provide. If this trend becomes at all strong, we could find ourselves with a generation of children sharply divided between those who have amplified their own brain power with that of the computer and those who remain wedded to the haphazard ignorance of the past. The problem might seem insoluble: there are always those who seize the gifts which society offers and those who, either from ignorance or lack of motivation, reject them. Fortunately, again for basic commercial reasons, concerted efforts will be made to ensure that, after the first wave of gimmick penetration, teaching computers sell to *every* child. To achieve this, the computers and the programs they offer will be carefully prepared to make sure that the user, at whatever intellectual or cultural level, will be highly motivated to use them. To the beginners, the backward or the poorly motivated, they will be lucid, non-patronizing, and endlessly patient, adapting themselves to the ebb and flow of the pupils' interests and progress. To the brighter, more advanced child they will be challenging and demanding, but still endlessly patient.

Does it seem too much to hope that such devices could exist? In fact they are already being developed in research laboratories in Europe, the USA and Japan, and the first trial models will be marketed in the early '80s. Does it seem incredible that a tiny package no bigger than a calculator could pick up the reins of the teaching profession? Step back and look at how little a young adult often has to show for ten years of traditional schooling, and the computer as a teacher will suddenly seem altogether more credible. The truth is that the world is about to move on from the era where knowledge comes locked up in devices known as books, knowledge which can only be released once the keys to their use have been acquired. In the era it is about to enter, the books will come down from their shelves, unlock and release their contents, and cajole, even beseech, their owners to make use of them.

CHAPTER TEN

Of Money and Crime

THE USE OF money dates back to the time when human societies first grew large and efficient enough to allow some division of labour. One man tilled the soil and produced vegetables, another hunted wild animals and produced meat. Later, "service trades" such as tool-making and blacksmithing appeared, at which point the simple swapping of produce was no longer feasible. Trade began to take place in something both portable and universally acceptable—in the first instance, useful metals. Metal as a token of exchange is still with us, though it is no longer the dominant form of currency. Paper banknotes, brought into play as a means of coping with the growth and increasing complexity of the world's economies in the early twentieth century, are now a far more important component of the economic picture, with cheques following close behind them.

But money, whether in the form of coins, notes or cheques, is only a statement of the fact that the holder has delivered into society an equivalent amount of goods or services. It has filled this role in a most satisfactory way for millennia, but it is still only a *record* of an individual's or an organization's wealth within the terms of their society, and could swiftly be replaced by any other form of record which proved simpler, cheaper or more portable. Well, something very dramatic is about to happen to money, and to the financial mechanisms and institutions that go with it. The changes are already in motion, and have been for a decade or so, though their effects to date have been constrained and their full implications have not been widely grasped.

It is no coincidence that the world's big counting houses were among the first to spot the economic benefits of computerization. The starting signal was the banks' move to machine-readable recognition of cheques, which made it convenient for monetary information to be fed rapidly into computers. This set the stage for their wider use, and a further step towards the replacement of *physical* money by electronic money came with the appearance of credit cards. These handy devices—they should really be called *debit* cards of course—are the first nails in the coffin of traditional financial methods. At present, they are simply plastic promissory notes which declare an individual's credit-worthiness and act as a vehicle for recording any financial transaction the owner makes with them. Today this is done by the clerk at the purchasing point who uses a special machine to stamp up a sales voucher which is later mailed to a central computer. In the next phase (probably in the middle-term future), the card will be fed into a computer terminal which will scan it to ensure that it has not been stolen and that its owner is credit-worthy. If it is happy on these two points it will instantaneously debit the owner's account at a central computer.

Direct computer scanning of cards and automatic transfer of funds pose substantial problems, but no one should assume that the banks would not find this method of exchanging records immensely preferable, in terms of accuracy, simplicity and economic efficiency, to the present cumbersome system. Credit cards, as we have said, represent the first step down the road to the elimination of cash and cheques—and anyone who has followed the argument about the immense superiority of computers for recording, processing, transferring and retrieving information will appreciate that this trend is inexorable. But it is not only banks who will gain from the coming of electronic money.

The disadvantages of coin and paper money are already becoming obvious in other quarters. For some years, filling stations in the less salubrious parts of the United States have been refusing cash after six o'clock in the evening in an attempt to discourage hold-ups. Even a small bunch of dollar bills is, in our disjointed and greedy society, sufficient incentive for murder, whereas a collection of credit card receipts is not. Cash is, by its very nature, universally transferable and extremely difficult to trace. The credit media of the future will present another face, and it is clear that as they replace existing monetary units, a shift in the nature of money-based crime must take place.

At the slam-bang end of the scale, wage-snatches and bank robberies must gradually become less attractive propositions as the proportion of transferable cash dwindles. More and more firms will pay their employees by direct transfer into their bank accounts, and more and more people will turn to cheques and then to credit cards for the majority of their purchases. Many professional people in the Western world already do the bulk of their purchasing in this way, but it is still a minority practice. As thieves turn their attention away from traditional targets and concentrate instead on those businesses which, for one reason or another, still rely on the turnover of large amounts of banknotes, so even these conservative strongholds will be forced to consider the virtues of credit cards. There is already evidence that the criminal community is beginning to appreciate the wind of change. In some American cities the attention of muggers has shifted away from affluent-looking pedestrians whose wallets are likely to be lined with treacherous credit cards to the less obviously affluent who, paradoxically, are more likely to be carrying cash.

Credit cards, it is true, are eminently stealable, and if used with resolution and cunning can net the thief very large sums. But they *are* more risky than cash, and becoming increasingly so. The new generation of cards come with personal colour photographs on the back, which makes their illicit use far more difficult. But by the middle or end of the '80s, when most cards are fed directly into a scanning computer terminal at the point of purchase and each card receives an automatic screening check, their theft will become even more pointless.

For a brief period there will be an unpleasant spin-off from this, for anyone whose credit card is stolen will almost certainly be murdered at the same time to prevent him from reporting its loss. But this horrible attempt on the part of criminals to fight back against the incursion of electronic money will fade when the use of a card will require some "unforgeable" back-up identification. This could be a secret code number which is punched into the terminal when the card is presented, or, in more advanced systems, the card will be equipped with a built-in computer chip which identifies its owner through his fingerprint pattern or some equally unique sign.

Obviously crime is going to be squeezed in a variety of ways, and the shift away from cash is just one of these. For a period, the emphasis of the determined criminal will have to be channelled into crooked businesses, or into theft of property, or blackmail and kidnapping. But even these will soon lose their lustre. Most crooked businesses rely on substantial tax evasion, or on the unrecorded transfer of funds in the form of large numbers of untraceable bills. The electronic transfer of money, however, tends to make business transactions readily accessible to government authorities, and it is likely that income and other tax will be deducted automatically as any transaction takes place. The savings to the revenue-collecting authorities will be enormous, as will the convenience to the individual and to all but the most shady of business organizations. The replacement of paper cash by its electronic counterpart will be a gradual process though, and organized crime will continue to function for a time on the basis of the remaining pools of cash. Interestingly enough, the criminal fraternity may well be the last group to value and employ these essentially worthless bits of paper.

The plight of the casual criminal will be even more acute. With stolen credit cards useless and cash increasingly hard to find, he will be forced into theft of property—watches and jewellery, household items, motor cars, etc.—so we can expect more armed assaults on homes, stores and warehouses. Once again this will be a transient phase, for all stolen objects have to be disposed of, and offered for sale in exchange for cash—and when cash is no longer widely used, the acquisition of large numbers of watches and jewels will become pointless. The only items which would continue to have a limited general value and which might become a kind of criminal world currency are illegal objects which are nevertheless greatly desired—drugs of various kinds, stolen works of art, and so on—and these could circulate in a barter ring like the shells of the Trobriand Islanders.

The drop in petty crime and theft will certainly mean less work for the police, but the time when money is neither totally *in*, nor totally *out*, will be an uncertain and socially restless period. Sophisticated home security systems, most with some degree of computer control, will come into fashion; there will be routine videotaping of all callers, and complex microprocessor-controlled sensors scanning property, feeding computer-enhanced images to police or security organizations. Such security systems could be difficult to defeat by even the most ardent and experienced professional criminal. Unlike their electro-mechanical predecessors—electronic eyes which ring alarm bells and so on—the micro burglar alarms will operate on a variety of principles, acting as autonomous units in unpredictable parts of the house, so that knocking out one unit will have no effect on the others. The introduction of such systems in a limited number of homes or offices will cause criminals to concentrate their attention on the less protected segments of society, and as these too gradually "computerize" their home defences, the residue of the population will be subjected to increasingly desperate assaults. To counter this the police will equip themselves with a great variety of computerized devices—pocket computers which contain complete and regularly updated criminal records, for example, and sophisticated methods of identifying suspects.

The work-load of the police will be much eased by a reduction in motoring offences of all kinds. The continued decline of the motor industry and the increasing world shortage of gasoline must cut back non-essential private motoring. In the late 1980s people will be amazed at the amount of aimless driving their predecessors did a decade earlier. Furthermore, every car will come with built-in safety features. At the time of writing, the world's biggest automobile companies are conducting, in partial secrecy, tests with "collision-proof" vehicles, which have batteries of microprocessors capable of detecting "danger" in the form of other vehicles travelling too close or approaching on a peculiar course. The sensors, which are chip-size computers equipped with pattern recognition programs, will be extremely cheap, particularly when mass produced on the scale that the automobile market allows.

By the late 1980s these sensors could be standard, or even compulsory, equipment in all cars, together with other safety monitors such as microprocessors which monitor tyre wear, brake power, steering alignment and so on. They may even have the capacity to disconnect the car's electrical system if they "think" that any of its mechanical systems are in a dangerous state. A car which refuses to start when its driver has ingested too much alcohol has often been joked about, but it could well be the only type on the road in the late 1980s. By then most cars will be virtually theft-proof though, as we have suggested, the rewards for car theft will be falling off markedly. Another factor ensuring a reduction in road-based crime will be a substantial change in the working pattern of the majority of people in Western societies, thanks to the new communications possibilities which computers provide, which will reduce the need for human beings to move around from place to place.

Although the forces of law and order will be less concerned with the classic patterns of crime, they will find themselves preoccupied in coping with greatly increased civil disturbances. These are likely to arise because of the convulsive changes which society will undergo in this period and as the old institutions which preserved social cohesion lose their binding strength. The first tremors of change have already shaken contemporary society. A major factor is undoubtedly the collapse of the traditional values of the past—orthodox religion, nineteenth-century democracy, nationalistic idealism, the supposed inviolacy of the law, the immutability of social class—combined with the lack of any replacement suited to the world of the present. As the pace of change quickens and produces greater distortions in the fabric of society, the inevitability of conflict between the elements has to be accepted.

One development will be the growing use of the computer by antisocial elements as a weapon of crime, as a weapon against the police themselves, or in a destructive assault on society. The possibilities of computer crime—when clever crooks with programming knowledge induce computers to transfer sums of money from one bank account into another for example—have been widely debated recently, and there have been some spectacular hauls. The solution is to create more secure computer systems, and while nothing in this world is *absolutely* inviolate, computers can, in the long run, be made far more secure than any bank vault. The penetration of computer records and files could also be used for such second-stage crimes as blackmail, but again it has to be said that it is much easier to break into steel filing cabinets, open cupboards, or lift a briefcase from a locked car or office, than it is to break through the numerous security checks which most modern computers provide.

The basic attraction of computer-penetrative crime is that it is possible to do it from a distance by accessing the computer over the public telephone network or private data line, thus introducing a new kind of leisured remoteness to the task and a bewildering absence of the criminal from the scene of the crime at the moment he is committing it. But access to computers is going to be less dependent upon public data lines as small local computers carry more of the relevant information. Of course it might be argued that with the new microcomputers all the criminal has to do is to steal the whole device and crack it in the leisure of his own home, but the same argument applies to a filing cabinet. The latter, however, will yield to a jimmy and a bit of brute force, while the former only to a skilled and highly intelligent operator.

One very real possibility is that, in the early days of the period at any rate, criminals who realize the increasing dependence of police forces on data handling and processing machines will make every kind of effort to disrupt police computer networks. It is certain that they will have some spectacular successes. With a bit of ingenuity, particularly before completely secure systems have been built up, a criminal could arrange to feed the police network with misleading information, deflecting attention from planned criminal exercises or "fouling up" counter-measures. Attempts to "erase" police records, or introduce erroneous information will be even more common.

Another source of trouble will be the activities of antisocial groups not directly concerned with crime itself: terrorist groups, minor political parties with extremist views and, later, activist anti-computer groups. This last group pose a serious threat as many of their members will themselves be dissident computer experts equipped with the maximum amount of destructive knowledge. The political groups will have more power, mainly because of their larger numbers but also because there is a chance that the dramatic advances in computers of the 1980s will be unwelcome to some of the world's biggest political blocs. There is not much doubt that any slack in police work resulting from the shift away from crimes of theft will be more than taken up in coping with a new plague of antisocial forces, perhaps aiming at the destruction of the "computerized society".

The principal issues raised by these social upheavals will be those of personal freedom and the rights of the individual *vis-à-vis* the bureaucratic power of government and state. The problem is one that always faces a society when it finds itself threatened. When pushed beyond a certain point even the most tolerant of societies, even the most committed to liberal ideals and civil liberties, will pick up all the weapons it has at its disposal and defend itself vigorously. Potent new weapons will shortly be available. Computers and electronic devices could be employed in a number of ways, the most effective and potentially dangerous being the provision of low-cost "personal chips". These will not only identify each individual accurately, but also, if required, locate him anywhere and at any time through a multitude of special sensors—again relatively inexpensive to install in large numbers. The individual location feature will, of course, be far more difficult to push through than the personal identifier, though any government sufficiently unscrupulous or desperate could do so with few problems. If in doubt, consider the restrictions of personal liberty which people are prepared to accept in the case of war or political unrest. To give one example out of many: ten years ago air travellers would have been horrified to think that it would soon be customary for them to submit to a thorough body search, the X-raying and photographing of their baggage, and constant electronic surveillance before boarding an airplane. Yet this all came to pass with barely a demurring voice.

Protests and campaigns on the part of organizations which defend civil liberties and resist the encroachment of bureaucracy are likely to be extensive and powerful. But the "Law and Order" lobby, gaining strength from the general confusion and malaise which must dominate the '80s, could have the edge of the argument, and they will be aided by two "hidden" factors.

The first is the sheer, unarguable convenience of having a tiny, completely personalized chip which offers a multitude of functions. By the late 1980s it will be increasingly difficult—impossible, if events move as quickly as some people think they will—to avail oneself of many public (and private) services without an electronic identifier which can transfer funds into or out of one's credit account. The universal power of the chip over-rides the objection raised by many people to the notion of a totally cashless society. How on earth, it is often asked, could one pay for *really* small sums using a credit card? The answer, of course, is that the credit card is just one link in the chain of personalized credit identifiers, and each advance will become smaller, more powerful and more foolproof. Ultimately it will probably be located in the amazing devices which will be worn where wristwatches are worn today, and which will incorporate a wide range of functions of which telling the time will be only one. They will be able to identify their owners on the basis of some combination of factors, easily monitored by their elaborate sensors—say, blood pressure, pulse or electrical skin resistance—and would be inoperative when worn by any other individual; they could even send out warning signals identifying their precise location if stolen. But theft, as we have already said, will be pretty pointless by this time, and the theft of the personal identifier will be the most pointless crime of all.

The second factor which will favour the spread of personalized identifiers and even, perhaps, personal locators, is that such devices are already in widespread use. Anyone who does a reasonable amount of international business travel is struck by the awful precision with which his movements around the world, his acquisitions and activities, are known to the vast central computers of his credit cards. Every purchase made, every hotel room booked, every meal eaten, every bar bill charged—all these are translated into electronic signals and engulfed by the new breed of global computers. Anyone who has anything to do with credit cards—and most people accept their very real convenience—is already participating in the evolution of the universal personal identifier, and it would be a rash individual who felt that this evolution was not still in its early stages.

While so many of the facets of the contemporary world which we take so complacently for granted are being scattered to the winds, another great transformation will be occurring. Again it is connected with processing information in electronic rather than physical terms, but it concerns the way in which the world of the 1980s will *disseminate* information, and not simply process it.

CHAPTER ELEVEN

Of Work and Robots

THE BASIC UNITS in which we store information will shortly become so minute that whole books or even libraries will be available on a single chip, and the average individual will be able both to afford and store huge amounts of "reading material" and other factual data in his home. But cost and storability are but two of the advantages of electronic data handling. A third dimension of improvement concerns the speed and ease with which electronically coded information can be passed from place to place. The laborious process of moving a letter from one part of the world to another shows the limitations of traditional methods of coding and transmitting information.

First the letter has to be written, on many sheets of paper if it bears anything but the briefest of messages; then it has to be sealed into an envelope of some kind and taken to a collection point such as a mail box; to remove it from here a human being has to physically transport himself from a central point, probably in a motor car, and after visiting lots of other points returns to the place of origin. Here another human examines the letter, along with thousands of others, sorts it into a particular box, after which it is removed to another sorting place and is finally despatched, by at least two forms of transportation, to its destined city or country. Here the whole process is reversed; all the while involving human beings shunting themselves around in the characteristically slow way they go about their business, and the letter is finally dropped into someone's mail box where it is opened and ultimately read. That this monster chain of events can hold together well enough to allow a letter to leave a house in Europe and arrive, only three days later, in a house in the USA is a magnificent example of the way in which human beings can learn to co-operate efficiently for the common good. It is also a riveting example of an approach to information transmission which is as archaic as the postal system set up by the early Egyptians in the time of the Ptolemies.

The 1980s will see the first widespread use—it is already in limited operation—of its replacement: electronic mail. The procedure is madly simple. The letter is typed into a word-processor—a typewriter with a microprocessor built into it—which holds it in store along with any other material that is fed in, until its owner indicates where it is to go. The word-processor itself is connected to other word-processors, either by a direct private line or via some kind of microwave transmission. All the sender has to do is to give his own system the appropriate address, and within seconds the letter is in the target microprocessor ready to be displayed on a TV set or printed out on a typewriter. Electronic mail has obvious advantages, but there are also drawbacks. One is that the mail can only be passed from one suitably equipped point on the network to another—from someone with a word-processor to someone else with one. By the middle of the 1980s, though, most major businesses will be using word-processors and where they lead, others must follow. It can be predicted that, before the end of the '80s, a business without word-processing, communicating typewriters will be about as competitive as one which tries to operate without a telephone today.

Another problem is that most existing electronic lines, telephone wires or microwave channels have a limited carrying capacity and become overloaded if there is really heavy traffic. There are a number of ways this can be solved, and the world's leading communication and data processing organizations are working on them now. As a result, many people believe there will be limitless electronic mail by the end of the '80s, or the early '90s at the latest.

One approach is to provide more channels by making use of the huge potential of communication satellites. A main drawback of the satellites at the moment is the relatively high cost of construction and of launching them into space. Capitalist economics again plays a big part here, for as the need for satellites grows, so ways will be found to manufacture them more cheaply. Already the electronic components and microprocessors which are important constituents of all satellites are in mass production, and NASA has made no secret of the fact that they expect the Space Shuttle— due to begin weekly round trips in 1980—to carry large numbers of communications satellites and to put them into space at an amazingly low cost. Some of these satellites are already earmarked for person-to-person paging—nothing less than the two-way wrist radio (or TV) that Dick Tracy pioneered.

In discussing the ease and rapidity with which we will be able to send information around the world, there is a tendency to look upon everything in terms of its effects on the postal service. But the greatest impact of electronic mail and its by-products will be on the business community as a whole, and in particular on its mobility. Each morning in the average city great numbers of people climb into automobiles or public transport and begin a wearisome journey to their place of work. The chances are that they spend the productive part of their day talking to other human beings, or receiving pieces of paper with marks on them; reading and interpreting these; generating fresh marks on new pieces of paper, and passing these on to some other human being. All this is part of the woof and warp of modern commercial life (even if it is not as essential an activity as most participants care to believe), but it will begin to change in the 1980s. As the impact of communicating word-processors is felt, the world of industry and commerce will notice a decreased need for its paper-handlers. The first to go will be those who look after the files of information which present society creates; next will be those who handle communications and routine accounts; next those who take short-hand and do routine typing (word-processors make no errors). They will be followed by the people who supervise paper-handlers and who make decisions about what they should do, and, by the early years of the medium-term future, the numbers of these people needing to make the trip from suburb to city office will fall off markedly.

Once again it is tempting to step back and ask whether it is worth introducing such stupendous changes into such enormously complex systems? The answer is that it most certainly will be. Once computers infiltrate a society, their virtues override any intrinsic objections to their use, and their continued infiltration and ultimate domination is from that point inevitable. They achieve their subtle take-over by demonstrating first their usefulness and, when that has been established, their indispensability. The laws of survival in the modern world apply and those companies that employ computers to their maximum effectiveness will achieve monumental economic advantages. Those that reject or ignore them will sooner or later find themselves in ruins.

The medium-term future, therefore, will see the first real shift towards a decentralization of commercial and business life. The importance of the city office, with its *mêlée* of agitated human beings passing each other redundant messages through the archaic medium of paper and printed word, will be rapidly eroded. More and more often, office and home will be combined, the public transport system will give way to giant data communications networks, the business motor car will be traded in for the latest video conference system. For the first time since Man began to behave as a social animal and gather his kind together into ever larger working and communicating units, a significant contrary trend will emerge. The cities will empty and expensive office blocks will gather dust. For centuries Man has been accustomed to the notion that he must travel to find his work; from the 1980s into the 1990s the work—such as there is to do—will travel to meet Man.

We shall not have to wait until the 1990s, however, to observe the effects of computerization on non-clerical jobs. These still provide the greatest number of opportunities for paid employment in Western society, and cover a continuum from those requiring an extensive period of training and practice—certain machine tool operations for example—to those of the "digging holes in the road" variety, in which muscular power and physical endurance are at a premium. The computer will make its biggest and swiftest incursions into the skilled and semi-skilled segments of employment, leaving the muscle-based trades relatively untouched for the time being. There are a number of reasons for this, of which by far the most important concerns the evolving science and technology of robots.

The robot, as everyone who has opened a science fiction comic or watched an SF movie will appreciate, is heavily and misleadingly typecast, its unvarying image being that of a largish man formed out of streamlined metal. It has legs with rollers or wheels, arms with clumsy pincers and a face complete with eyes. There is also a mouth from which tinny speech issues, and a nose which appears to be purely decorative. In the combat versions the arms have built-in guns and the eyes emit death-rays. This image, which is essentially that of a man made out of Erector parts, is a constant and enduring one and illustrates the simple-minded view people have about robots and what role they are to play in our future. In fact, one would be hard put to think of a greater waste of effort than constructing man-shaped general-purpose robots which wander about the place engaging in stilted conversation.

An American firm recently built, and at least pretended to put on the market, a mobile, talking, general-purpose robot supposedly capable of understanding spoken commands. This ludicrous object was hawked around the world until the press and TV, who had shown themselves to be more than usually gullible, finally realized that the whole thing was a spoof. The "robot" which was, as usual, vaguely man-shaped, was in fact a tin box on wheels controlled remotely and in secret by a cunning fellow using the kind of radio controls that steer model airplanes around the sky. It could no more understand speech or act independently than could the individual nuts, bolts and aluminium sheets of which it was constructed. The real mystery is what the manufacturers hoped to gain by the exercise, unless they were eccentric millionaires engaged in a major hoax. Anyone with even a smattering of knowledge of robotics or computer science could tell simply from a description of the thing, that it just could not be what it claimed to be. No possible application of present technology—or even of the technology of the 1980s—could create such a device and offer it for sale at the quoted price of twenty thousand dollars. Candidly even twenty million dollars wouldn't buy one.

The motives of its creators remain a puzzle, but the whole farce illustrates the canyon-like gap that separates people who know something about computers or robots from the rest of the world, no matter how intelligent or well-educated they may be. This message was rammed home to me when an American journalist of international repute told me that he had been convinced of the authenticity of this "robot" because he had been present at a cocktail party at which it drifted around serving drinks and engaging in casual conversation. Nothing I could say, no argument that I could offer, no plaintive assurance that the science of robotics simply could not have advanced so dramatically, could dissuade him from his belief. Decades of science fiction books and films had prepared him to accept the notion of Instant Mechanical Men without raising an eyebrow.

But if a robot is not a metal or plastic human being, programmed to do everything from washing up dishes to putting out the cat at night, what exactly is it? The word came into popular use with Karel Capec's famous play of the early 1920s, *RUR* (Rossum's Universal Robots). The robots in question (they were androids actually, as they were biological systems, human in form, which had been synthesized by Rossum in his laboratory) acted as zombie-like serfs who eventually took over the world. Later they became "human" when they discovered that they could "love" one another. The play, which has heavy Shavian overtones, now has historic rather than aesthetic merit, and its author, an *émigré* Czech with more than a touch of Kafka about him, chose the word "robot" because of its common usage in Teutonic languages for slave labour. The play deserves to be read if only because it raises a number of fundamental issues about robotics and machine intelligence and, in particular, the question of whether there are moral issues at stake in the construction (or destruction) of human-like, thinking or even "feeling" machines. These issues were also raised with considerable foresight in Mary Shelley's *Frankenstein*.

Computer scientists and engineers understand present-day robots to be devices capable of performing automatically some task normally performed by human beings. They are rarely assumed to be capable of tackling more than one task and are never "general-purpose" in the way Rossum's androids and

Frankenstein's monster were. Some scientists even object to the use of the word "robot" at all, arguing (as the most recent edition of *Encyclopaedia Britannica* does) that the dividing line between a robot and a machine capable of repeated performance of a task such as putting caps on bottles is too vague to justify the use of a separate term. But the line is not, in fact, as blurred as all that. There are essentially three categories of machine: simple machines, programmable machines and robots.

Simple machines, to all intents and purposes, are nothing more than powerful mechanical muscles; they are either controlled by a human being, or have been designed and constructed to perform an endless series of repetitive acts. Hydraulic excavators, steam engines and motor cars all fall into this category.

Programmable machines are more sophisticated. They are devices which can be programmed to do any of a number of different tasks or, in the more ambitious cases, a sequence of tasks. The program is set into the device by the human who controls it. They have only become widely used in recent years, though some of the very earliest versions were invented at around the same time as the first simple machines. Jacquard's loom was a programmable machine—and it was also one of the first true machines.

The robot is different, and in an important way. It, too, is capable of performing a variety of tasks, or a sequence of tasks, but the choice of tasks at any particular moment is determined not only by a pre-set program, but also by some information *fed into it from the outside world which is relevant to the task it is performing*. The information it absorbs is fed into it through sensing devices attached to its own structure, and not by command signals from a human. A simple machine, or even a programmed one, is capable of performing quite a complex task, but it will go on doing it indefinitely in really blockheaded fashion until something intervenes to stop it; a robot, on the other hand, will take account of change in its environment and adjust its behaviour accordingly.

To develop the point further, one can consider a possible test for robots which I call the "Carmichael's Hat Test". In the classic British movie about industrial relations and automation, *I'm All*

Right Jack, there is a scene in which Ian Carmichael is visiting an automated sweet factory. Pre-cut slabs of a repellent kind of toffee pass along a conveyor belt and into a tunnel where they are coated with chocolate and capped with a cherry. Nauseated at the sight, Carmichael reels and inadvertently places his bowler hat on the belt, whereupon it proceeds through the tunnel and emerges coated with chocolate and decorated with an array of cherries.

Now it might seem this was the giveaway mark of a simple machine as the device was not capable of detecting that it was faced with a bowler hat rather than a chunk of toffee. On the other hand, the graceful way in which it coated the entire surface of the hat and the aesthetic arrangement of the cherries on the top indicate that the system was more intelligent than one had suspected. Why did it not merely cover that portion of the hat which approximated in size to the "target" toffee bars? How was the device able to ensure an even coating over the subtly curved surface? How did it know where to position the cherries—and for that matter how did it decide to give it more than one cherry? The inescapable conclusion is that the machine was equipped with a size-monitor, a shape-detector and had some kind of aesthetic appreciation as well, and this makes it by present-day standards a rather smart robot.

Robots *make decisions*. The decision may be simple or complex, but it is made by the *machine* and it is made on the basis of some apprehension of the external world. Present-day technology could not create a robot which could solve the problem of the proper coating of Carmichael's Hat. At the moment, industrial robots are capable of only rudimentary shape discrimination and are confined to locating positions where particular operations have to be performed—as the celebrated factory robots like UNIMATE do when they perform accurate spot-welding on motor cars and machine parts.

At present, robots are used for jobs which are either unpleasant or dangerous for human beings—repairing equipment which operates underwater or in great heat, or where there may be dangerous gases. There are a few experimental exceptions to this, but the main thrust of robot research in the '70s has been directed towards tackling the problem of running machinery in hostile environments. Here the robot is doing something which would otherwise be impossible and so the high cost is acceptable. As long as a large, "old style" computer is needed to control each robot, costs are always going to be high and robots are not going to be applied to the kind of operations done by skilled and semi-skilled human beings.

But the picture changes when the computer costs a few dollars rather than a few thousand, and when it is small enough to be easily integrated with the basic equipment. Such developments are being made now in Japan, in Eastern Europe, in some parts of the USA and in a few places in the UK, and this is the first indication that the robot is about to become both convenient and sensationally cost-effective. In the late 1980s, a vast array of tasks which could previously only be performed by highly-trained human beings, including the majority of those involving the control of factory machinery, will suddenly fall to the robot. Any country or industry which fails to keep pace with these developments will soon be in trouble, for a robot-based industry will produce goods at highly competitive prices.

If anyone doubts the truth of this, they should look at the two most successful post-war economies, Germany and Japan, both of which were forced, thanks to the attentions of the British and American bombers, to start their industrial lives afresh in the late '40s. Using factories and manufacturing equipment tailored to the mid-twentieth century they forged ahead of countries like Britain and, to a lesser extent, the United States, who were committed to ageing and relatively inefficient technologies. But those imbalances which have led to the strength of the German Mark and the Japenese Yen have arisen on the basis of quite small advances in automation, and because a greater proportion of the design, manufacture and distribution of German and Japanese products is done by the machine, and less by the human being. Even there the machine's share of the burden has largely been concerned with the replacement or amplification of muscle power, and as long as it has been thus limited, automation has only penetrated a fraction of industrial life. The coming of in-expensive robots will allow much deeper penetration of labour-intensive industries.

Jobs which have, up to the present, been largely unaffected by the advance of automation are those in which the role of the human is to control and guide a machine. They represent a special partnership: the machine does the work which is beyond the human's strength, capability or endurance, while the man looks after those components of the task which are beyond the machine's processing powers. The man may operate a machine tool to cut out a complex pattern from a metal plate of varying thickness, control a powerful drill to excavate a tunnel, or inspect a series of finished manufactured objects to check that they meet required standards. In all these cases, the machine does something, the result is inspected by the human, a decision is made, the machine is either reset or repositioned, and the next phase of the task is implemented.

Despite the complexity of these operations and the sophistication of the man–machine partnerships involved, the human inspection and decision-making are often relatively trivial operations and not, in principle, difficult to transfer to a machine. Take precision-welding: the system has to be equipped with (a) a sensing device capable of scanning the area to be cut or welded, (b) a set of programs to recognize the required patterns or shapes which the machine is to produce, (c) a decision logic which matches the sensory input against the recognition programs and judges whether an acceptable match is being made, and (d) a means by which the decision logic can "reach back" down to the welding or cutting surface to correct or guide it. Experimental computers capable of this have been in existence for decades. They have remained strictly experimental because they have been cumbersome, unreliable giants, trailing wires all over the place, taking up the space of half a dozen men and gobbling up enough money to hire a hundred.

But the microprocessor will change all this. No longer will cybernetic systems be large, unreliable and expensive. They will be smaller than human brains, far more reliable—and untiringly so—and far, far cheaper to maintain and operate. As the 1980s unfold, the man–machine partnership which began in the nineteenth century and reached its peak of efficiency in the 1950s will be elbowed aside by the first true industrial robots.

By the end of the next decade industrial robots will be in widespread use, and another phase of the emancipation of Man from the need to work for his living will have been achieved.

It is interesting, and mildly ironic, that the impact of the Computer Revolution will be greatest in those areas where high levels of skill and training are normally required and which, at one time, were assumed to be the *least* likely to succumb to automation. Conversely, those jobs which are currently assigned a low rating on the economic and social scale—jobs like packing and unpacking, cleaning and simple maintenance, truck driving and door-to-door delivery, even such despised tasks as clearing away dishes in a canteen—are likely to be relatively immune. This will be so until the whole pattern of industrial life and social interaction has been turned inside out by the computer, and the concept of jobs as essential ingredients of human life has vanished into the past.

To most people the notion of a society in which a steadily increasing share of work is handed over to computers and computer-controlled machinery is both difficult and disturbing. Perhaps the whole issue can be placed in a less threatening framework if we accept that all the changes which will take place in the remaining decades of this century are the continuation of an unvarying trend towards increasing world affluence which advances in parallel with a decreasing requirement to work. In primitive societies the poverty was such that all members of a group—male, female, old and young—had to work for the whole of their waking life simply to find food and ensure survival. With advances in technology and science, Man gradually achieved a greater mastery over his environment, and his work-load was reduced and the wealth of his society increased. With a few notable exceptions this trend has continued at a gentle pace, achieving a powerful surge of acceleration at the time of the Industrial Revolution.

The scale of change over the last century alone has been enormous and needs to be spelt out. Consider the case of a coal miner of the third quarter of the nineteenth century, working twelve to fourteen hours a day, six days a week, in abominable conditions—and earning barely enough to keep his family in malnourished discomfort. Would he be able to comprehend, let alone believe, the life led by his counterpart of the late 1970s? Today's miner still works hard, and in unenviable conditions underground, but he enjoys a standard of living which even the affluent middle class of Victorian times might envy: a warm, dry house, ample food, clothing and other essentials, education up to and including university level for his children, his own car, sophisticated electronic devices in his home, holidays in a Mediterranean hotel and so on. This is not intended as a patronizing homily on how lucky today's miners should consider themselves to be, but merely to emphasize the gulf in affluence between the life style of two equivalent groups separated by a mere century of technological advance.

It is easy to accept these changes. But they are remarkable, and we should be surprised every time we think of them—almost as surprised as the miner of 1879 would be if he were suddenly time-warped into the present day. But perhaps the most surprising thing of all is that we should have any doubts about the continued development of this trend. The history of the economic life of Man graphically illustrates that by increased productivity he has been able to pay himself more and more for doing less and less. Sixteen-hour working days have given way, in a century or so, to seven-hour days. In the next decade or two, the seven-hour day will become a five- and perhaps even a four-hour day. And as we hand over the job of providing wealth to the computers we have created to help us, it will be further reduced and eventually the nil-hour day will arrive. The trend may have its ups and downs but its direction is inevitable, and the 1980s are the decade when mankind as a whole will at least realize this fact.

But one of the main problems faced by the inhabitants of the medium-term future will not be understanding the truth, but learning how to cope with it. It should be clear from a discussion of these sensitive points that the Computer Revolution faces us with a choice between a world transformed either into a paradise or into a disaster area. The transformation could take place within the mid-term, but the most likely period would seem to be at some time in the 1990s. It may be hard, looking at the uneasy catalogue of problem areas that the 1980s will throw in our faces, to see how we can hope to pass through even that period unscathed. The world is already complicated to the point of desperation, and the complication is almost entirely of our own doing. In order to support a growing, increasingly more affluent civilization, we have applied science and technology mercilessly to assist us. The result has been an even more complex world, demanding even deeper excursions into advanced technology which in turn complicate the world yet further.

Is there any way out of this technological trap? Possibly, but only by taking a momentous step whose consequences are frighteningly hard to assess. The step is this: realizing that the problems of the world are moving out of our grasp we may shortly decide to look to our new companion, the computer, for a helping hand. When the limited powers of the human brain are stretched to the limit, our only option will be to turn to the theoretically limitless powers of the machines for assistance. And the machines, slowly at first but ever so surely, will gather themselves together and oblige.

Part Five

INTERLUDE:
ON INTELLIGENT MACHINES

CHAPTER TWELVE

The Nature of Intelligence

THROUGHOUT THIS BOOK I have, with suitable qualifications and apologies, used the word "intelligence" in connection with computers, computer programs and, occasionally, machines, without defining the word. Definitions, even those in the best dictionaries such as *The Shorter Oxford*, have an ambiguous quality. The complete *Oxford English Dictionary* (quite unmanageable in its thirteen-volume glory, but likely to be very manageable indeed when compressed into the electronic microstructure of a chip) offers "the faculty of understanding; intellect" as its prime entry. But what do we mean by "understanding"? Or "intellect"? Turn to page 3493 where "to understand" is defined as being "to apprehend the meaning or import of", "to judge with knowledge" or "to comprehend and reason". A bit circular? Back, therefore, to page 1455 and "intellect" which is described as "the faculty . . . of the mind or soul by which one knows and reasons (excluding sensation and sometimes imagination); power of thought; understanding. Rarely" (it adds) "used in reference to the lower animals."

With all respect to *The Oxford English Dictionary*, these definitions do not help much; there seems to be an element of contradiction, or at any rate confusion, within them. Even worse confusion exists in the average person's mind, a fact which can easily be established by asking anybody to explain the word. Occasionally people will suggest that it must somehow be associated with consciousness, with learning, with thinking, or even with "intuition", whatever that means. If you press for further definitions—of consciousness, learning, thinking, etc.—you can be sure that the word "intelligence" will creep back in, and the circularity of the exercise is revealed.

Tacitly it has always been assumed that intelligence is something possessed by all humans, and which might or might not be an attribute of the higher animals. The latter point was the kind of thing that philosophers lighted upon, rather in the way that they speculated about whether certain classes of animals, by their nearness to God, might be said to have souls. In any case the outcome of the argument, whatever form it took, would have had no practical consequences. Only with the feeble stirrings of the science of psychology in the mid-nineteenth century was the word really subjected to any kind of inspection, and it wasn't until the First World War that this inspection became at all rigorous.

The stimulus was the US Army's need to classify its huge emergency intake of soldiers along some kind of ability continuum, and to get some measure of each man's native "mental powers". To achieve this, military psychologists designed a battery of written and multiple-choice tests which were really measures of educational and cultural background. Today's tests, working on the assumption that all humans do have some kind of innate mental ability, strive to avoid cultural factors and aim at assessing something which might be best described as "mental agility" and which is revealed by the quick perception of relationships or incongruities. How useful or how valid such tests are— the idea that one defines intelligence as that faculty which is measured by intelligence tests is a standing joke amongst psychologists—is not the issue here; I have only introduced the point in order to ask whether, when we speak of intelligence, we are indeed speaking of the kind of thing that is being measured by such tests. Forget the validity of the IQ tests themselves for a moment, and ask whether the ability to perceive relationships between objects and patterns, to solve problems of varying complexity and to see fresh ways out of mental puzzles, can reasonably be called intellectual activities. I think all will agree that these are at least some of the pertinent factors, though there may well be others. So far so good.

Now if these abilities are taken out of the pencil-and-paper test environment, it can quickly be seen that they are very much part of the day-to-day life of all human beings and also, inescapably, of many animals. The non-human primates—chimpanzees and the like—are certainly capable of perceiving the relationship between different objects and of finding their way out of a maze, and so are domestic animals such as dogs and cats. So unless one is prepared to take an irrationally hard line and declare that intelligence is something which is an attribute of the human brain or mind *alone* and, by definition, cannot be present in any other thing (a point of view which would be awfully hard to defend) then intelligence, to some degree, is present in at least some animals.

Two questions now arise. Firstly, assuming that we agree that the primates, dogs, cats and even rats have intelligence, where on the phylogenetic scale do we draw the line? Do hedgehogs have intelligence, for example? Why not? But what about bees? Or earwigs? And secondly, what about machines? For some time computers have been capable of perceiving relationships between different categories of objects in the external world (though admittedly in a rather laborious manner) and are also able to solve certain types of problems. So again, unless one was prepared to take a stand and define intelligence as something that could only be present in biological systems, and not things made out of electronic components, one is forced to accept the notion of *machine* intelligence. At this point in the argument, most humans ask the question which every computer scientist has come to dread: "But a machine's intelligence, if you *must* use the word, is purely automatic. Surely it can only do what you have previously programmed it to do?" The answer to this is unexpectedly simple: the same is true of animals and humans.

The higher animals, as we said, have the capacity to solve problems and perceive relationships, and from this we inferred that they were equipped with some degree of intelligence. Now, "solving problems" and "perceiving relationships" are merely phrases used by humans to describe various patterns of behaviour, and they can be summed up in the phrase *adjusting to changes in the environment.* And here we come to the most basic and fundamental definition of intelligence that one can find. Intelligence is the ability of a system to adjust appropriately to a changing world, and the more capable of adjusting—the more versatile its adjusting power—the more intelligent it is.

This is a good, general-purpose working definition. Like most general-purpose definitions, however, it lacks true explanatory power, making sense at the level where we see animals escaping from mazes and so on, but not, except with a great measure of latitude, where we find humans solving crossword puzzles or writing books about computers. To see how such a definition can be expanded to cope with the subtler facets of intelligence, we first need to identify the principal factors that make a creature versatile or flexible in the way in which it adjusts to its environment. By my reckoning there are six major factors in all.

Sensation (Data Capture): The word "sensation" has quite a tight meaning in psychology and physiology, and implies the receipt of environmental information by some organism. This includes the function of the eye when it "catches" photons impinging on the retina; the ear when its internal structures vibrate in harmony with pressure waves; the olfactory mechanisms in the nasal passages where special cells detect the presence of free-floating chemicals, and so on. Sensation, by this definition, is a property shared by humans and all animals. Even the lowliest creatures such as amoebae, which consist of just one more or less homogeneous cell, are responsive to changes in their environment, moving away from certain stimuli and towards others. But is it just a matter of receiving information or stimuli?

Imagine a toy soldier which is standing up in the middle of the floor. It is hit by a toy cannon shell and falls over. Can it be said to have demonstrated the faculty of sensation? Clearly it *is* responding to environmental change or stimuli, but is doing so in a totally passive way. It has only two things it can do, remain standing or fall over; it will remain standing forever if it is not touched, and will fall over if anything strikes it with a great enough force. This will be true whether it is something that is "bad" for it, like a cannon shell, or "good" for it, like, say, a paint spray which would preserve it from corrosion. Obviously the soldier is not "sensing" the environment in anything but the most far-fetched usage of the word and this is really because *it does not differentiate between stimuli.* The enslavement of the amoeba, however, is less total. Its range of responses is very limited—"go towards" this, and "come away" from that—but it does have *some* room for manoeuvre because of built-in mechanisms that detect which of the appropriate stimuli, "nice" or "nasty", are present in its environment. Here the living thing is qualitatively different from the non-living thing: it can adjust to changes in its environment. Now let us replace our amoeba with something that is not a biological entity, such as a mechanical tortoise.

The mechanical tortoise was an interesting toy invented by the eccentric British neurophysiologist, Grey Walter. It consisted of a metal box on wheels, vaguely tortoise-shaped, and was equipped with a bank of light-detecting photocells on its front end which, if you were in a good humour that day, you might call a head. The tortoise was so constructed that if light shone on the photocells, its motor would go into reverse and would continue to reverse— pulling it away from the light—until the luminance had fallen to the point where the cells were no longer activated. Here the tortoise would rest, endlessly, until more light came its way, when once again it would back off. Later versions of the tortoise led far richer lives. When their batteries were low a switch inside would make them move towards the darkest corners of the room where Grey Walter had placed battery chargers, to which the things would connect themselves. When "replete" they would ramble off to some neutral corner of the room and so on *ad infinitum*. The tortoises were quite easy to construct and Grey Walter, and anyone who visited his lab in Bristol, used to have enormous fun with them, but their existence posed the question— as he intended it should—as to whether they were *sensing* beings. By any definition current in the life sciences they certainly were, because—crude though they were—they came equipped with devices which could discriminate between light and non-light. So, for that matter, can radar scanners, radio telescopes and the like, but they are, on the whole, purely receivers, hooked up to screens and displaying information immediately it is received, whereas the tortoises (and the amoeba) have one other critical function. Unlike the radar scanners, not only do they detect the presence or absence of a particular stimulus, but they also *respond* to it in some appropriate way.

But how do they "know" which stimuli to avoid and which to

seek out? This brings us to the second building block of intelligence.

Data Storage: This concerns the way in which many living systems make use of information received by their sense organs and by doing so increase their power to adjust to the world. Both the amoeba and the mechanical tortoise differ from a toy soldier in the way they respond to the environment. Now, superior though the amoeba/tortoise systems may be to toy soldiers they are still enormously limited. Although they can discriminate between different conditions in the environment and make appropriate responses or non-responses, *this is absolutely all they can do.* When born, or created, they can do all they are ever going to be able to do in the way of sensory discrimination and behavioural response. Any significant change in the environment—the disappearance of white light and its replacement by red light or by, say, sound—would completely overwhelm their decision-making processes. No matter how long they are in these new conditions, they will remain totally impotent and ineffective until the original light/dark dichotomy returns. But the majority of living things have the capacity to change their behaviour as a consequence of their life experiences. Looked at in the most simple sense, this is what we mean by learning. Could it also occur in machines?

The tortoise, which "knows" that its batteries will be charged in the dark corners of a room and which only goes there when its batteries are low, is an intelligent system of the simplest kind. It can make "decisions", and has a choice of three courses of action: it can run away from bright lights, which it does whenever they appear, or it can head for dark corners, which it does when its batteries are down, or it can roam around in the gloaming which it does at all other times. The internal mechanisms of the system can be looked on as a simple set of programs or command mechanisms, each of which is triggered into action by one of three sets of stimuli: bright light, low battery indicator, or the absence of both bright light and low battery stimuli. But let us suppose that the battery chargers are suddenly brightly lit instead of being in total darkness. The tortoise that has been wired up to run away from lights will run away from the battery chargers, come to a stop and "die" because its instincts are now directing it towards anti-survival rather than survival.

The tortoise could be rewired so that light now means "go to" rather than "go from", and all will be well until the environment is switched round again. Or it could be upgraded and given some more powerful rules. These could be as follows: "Go away from light unless batteries are low and chargers are not found in dark corners. If batteries are low and chargers are not found in dark corners, go *to* light and see if chargers are there." A further set of instructions of the "If/then" variety could easily be built in to allow the tortoise to survive in a quite unstable world. Far more sophisticated instructions would have to be developed, however, to allow it to cope with much more than the most rudimentary lighting changes. Nevertheless, what we have been describing would be a quantum jump on the mainly instinctive tortoise. Indeed, by suitable programming, its life could be made infinitely richer provided that (a) it was equipped with a powerful range of sensors designed to capture a broad spectrum of information from its environment; (b) it had enough room to store all the information it received from its constantly changing environment; and (c) it had, within it, a computer powerful enough to integrate the huge amounts of new information being fed in, and to relate these to the multitude of new or rewritten programs with which it was already equipped. Points (a) and (b) are essentially the first two factors of intelligence—data capture and data storage. Point (c) is something new, and we call this "programmability". But to say an entity is programmable does not help much. What kind of programmability are we talking about? Do we mean that it has lots and lots of programs, or that its programs are particularly powerful ones, or particularly quick to operate? The more one thinks about it, the more one realizes that "programmability" is not one factor but several, and that each is a major parameter of intelligence in its own right. The first is concerned with the system's speed of operation, or how quickly its program can be executed, and it is the third factor in intelligence.

Processing Speed: This is the rate at which the individual components of the entity's system can switch from one state to another. The more rapidly information can be processed, the more rapidly it can adjust to changes in its environment and the more versatile it is in coping with problems. A mechanical tortoise, made out of Meccano or Erector-set parts, which could only change direction after a great heaving around of levers and pulleys, will be much slower to adjust than an all-electronic tortoise. Computers, as we have said, are already incomparably ahead of any biological rivals in processing speed. Most animal nervous systems have a switching speed of about 2ohz, while even the most sluggish of today's computers switches about a million times quicker!

Software Modification Speed: This is a more elusive concept, and must not be confused with processing speed. What we are talking about here is the speed or ease with which the entity can *change* its software, or create new programs where necessary. To take the tortoise again: at first all its programs tell it to go away from lights and into dark corners when its battery is low. In a later version we equipped it with more complex sets of instructions which told it to go *towards* light whenever it found no chargers in their usual place. Now imagine yet another program which tells the creature to wander round all over the place whenever chargers do not turn up in the expected place, and which, when chargers have finally been located at Point X, erases all out-of-date programs which say they are at Points Y or Z. This would be an adaptive program and, contrary to popular belief, it is *not* difficult to write and prepare such programs for even quite simple computers. No one is pretending that the learning programs which control the human brain—or those that control the rat, the fish, or even the earwig— are anywhere near as simple in execution. In really complex brains there may be millions, perhaps billions, of interlocking programs, and they are constantly restructuring in order to take account of the changes in the average organism's environment. The key to understanding this factor is to realize that we are not talking about the system's capacity to modify its own software but rather about the *speed and ease with which it can do so.* This factor assumes increasing importance the more complex the creature, for the more programs there are, the more important it is that they can be changed or rewritten quickly.

A subsidiary factor here is the entity's ability to undertake its own software modification, as all biological systems do, rather than have them done by an outside source, as is currently the case with most computers. Automatic self-programming is a great bonus, but it is *not* a prerequisite for high intelligence. A computer could be extremely intelligent by our model, and still have the bulk of its software modification done by humans. In practice, though, most highly intelligent systems would have to be self-programmable to a significant degree.

Software Efficiency: The word "software" is a generic term for the sets of programs which control *any* complex information system, and is as applicable to the programs that control the brain as to those that control an electronic and lifeless computer.

The concept of software efficiency needs further explanation. There is more than one way to write a program. For example, one could write the instructions "Go to this, if such and such, and then do that," in a casual, discursive way, adding in clauses here and there, clarifying vague instructions by further explanation, and still end up with an overall command that achieves its goal. But it may only achieve its goal in a highly roundabout way, using up a lot of what is known as "central processor power". Computer programs of this kind tend to be the sort of thing that beginners write, but they are never popular with other programmers since they are essentially wasteful and time-consuming. Conversely, one can write the programs in a most efficient way, particularly if one is a skilled programmer and plans the procedure well in advance. When completed, these "efficient" programs run very quickly, are error-free and waste little of the computer's brain power.

Software efficiency is probably rather constant in all biological systems as it has been developed and tested over a long period of time—many millions of years at a conservative estimate—and may not be a major factor in determining *differences* in intelligence between animals. It is sure to be a major factor when we come to making intellectual comparisons with computers whose programs, at the moment, are wildly inefficient and will remain so for some time to come. The reason for this is that they are written by humans and the only penalty for inefficient writing is a cumbersome, slow computer system which breaks down and produces million-pound electricity bills. Biological computers, on the other hand, have their programs developed by a ruthless process of trial and error in the hostile environment of our planet, where the penalties for inefficiency are merciless death.

Software Range: The speed and efficiency with which the programs control an animal's central nervous system are crucial factors in intelligence, and so is the *range* or programmes with which the brain is equipped. In the mechanical tortoise the programs were few in number and limited to detecting the difference between light and dark, and all the creature could do was roll forwards or backwards, and plug itself into a wall socket. As we move up the phylogenetic scale, from the lower to the higher animals, we find that the range of tasks which a creature can perform increases steadily. Admittedly, higher animals are not capable of doing *every* single thing that their lower relations can—bees can fly, whereas monkeys cannot—but the range of tasks a monkey can perform is far wider than that of, say, a parrot, a trout or a donkey. Some creatures can do certain things with supreme skill—take a spider's web-making capacity for example—but almost always you find that this is just about the only complex act of which the creature is capable, its party-trick if you like. When a spider is removed to an environment where its web-making abilities are irrelevant it is swiftly reduced to the intellectual level of the mechanical tortoise.

The preceding discussion indicates that what we casually term "intelligence" is an amalgam of a number of different faculties, all of which are innate—built into the organism and present at the time of birth. In the course of life these abilities are exercised as the result of the creature's interactions with the world around it, and it gradually becomes more and more able to cope in a frequently hostile, always changing environment. This means, incidentally, that one should discriminate between a being's *innate* intellectual endowment which it shares with all other members of its species, and its achievement or performance level, which will vary from individual to individual and which depends on its experience and opportunities throughout life. A human being brought up in a minutely restricted environment—like Kasper Hauser who was raised from birth by a lunatic and was kept in a darkened cellar until he had reached the age of twenty-one—will appear incapable and ostensibly unintelligent in comparison with one who has lived in a more open, stimulating environment. The logic of this argument seems to be heading towards the controversial view that all members of the human species are, in terms of their intellectual endowment, more or less identical at birth, and that the vast differences which appear to exist in human intellectual performance are all to do with their experiences in life—the opportunities which the world has offered to their software. Tempting though it may be to follow this point through, it is not really relevant and we had better move on: but first, because they are so important, let us summarize the key factors again:

Data Capture Ability: An entity is intelligent to the extent that it can extract information from the universe around it. All other things being equal, the better its data capture (sensory) abilities, the more intelligent it is.

Data Storage Capability: An entity is intelligent to the extent that it can store information once captured, which can be referred to on future occasions to improve its ability to adjust. The greater its data storage capacity, etc . . .

Processing Speed: An entity's intelligence is partly a function of the speed with which its brain/computer can process information. This refers to the switching speeds of its basic units which in the case of most animals are neurones, and in computers, are micro-transistors.

Software Flexibility: An entity is intelligent to the extent that its software is rapidly and easily modifiable. This may be one of the most important of the factors.

Software efficiency: The way in which the system's software has been written will affect the entity's capacity to adjust to novel happenings in its environment. The more efficient the software (the quicker it runs, the less prone to errors or breakdowns, the less "program space" it occupies) the more intelligent the entity.

Software range: The bigger and wider the range of programs with which a system is equipped and with which its central processor can cope, the more intelligent is the creature.

And these six factors, taken in isolation and together, are what constitutes intelligence in animal, man or machine.

We now have a working definition of intelligence and it might be interesting to devise some kind of scale to measure it and then to rank various creatures against it. The traditional human IQ tests yield a score which runs between 0 and an upper limit of about 200, with the "average" human score running out at 100. It is based, as we said earlier, on a series of tests of mental agility rather than of general knowledge and, obviously, it is Man-oriented. The brightest chimpanzee on earth would be lucky to score 10 or 20. And where would one place a dog? An IQ of a half of one per cent perhaps? How about the hedgehog then, or an earwig? The questions are obviously absurd within the context of human IQ tests, and indicate that a wider range is required if we are to encompass the scope of animal, to say nothing of machine, intelligence. Constructing such a wide scale is an important exercise, because it will help to put in perspective the vast gulf that separates existing human intelligences from existing computer ones.

Let us take as our starting point the "average" IQ of *homo sapiens*, which on traditional scales is 100, and call it instead 1,000,000. The least intelligent human being might have an IQ of about 70 on the traditional scale, and the brightest about 170. On our new scale the range would be 999,970 to 1,000,070. Right down at zero we have our toy soldier, block of wood, rock, or whatever. On this macro-scale, the amoeba and the mechanical tortoise might have IQs of 10 or 50 at the maximum, whereas an earwig would be loftily placed at about 5,000! Most fish would

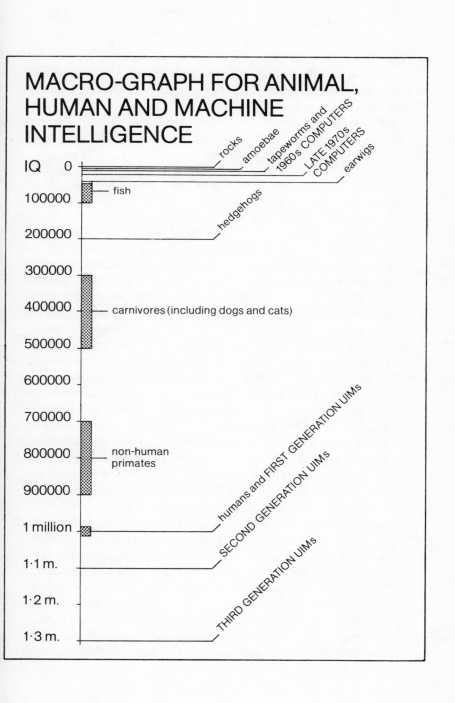

MACRO-GRAPH FOR ANIMAL, HUMAN AND MACHINE INTELLIGENCE

IQ 0 — rocks
— amoebae
— tapeworms and 1960s COMPUTERS
— LATE 1970s COMPUTERS
— earwigs

100000 — fish

200000 — hedgehogs

300000

400000 — carnivores (including dogs and cats)

500000

600000

700000

800000 — non-human primates

900000 — humans and FIRST GENERATION UIMs

1 million — SECOND GENERATION UIMs

1·1 m.

1·2 m. — THIRD GENERATION UIMs

1·3 m.

come out at between 50,000 and 100,000; hedgehogs, rats and the like could hit the scale at 200,000; dogs and cats at 300,000 perhaps, and the non-human primates would vary between 700,000 and 900,000.

Zoologists may disagree with the rankings and the numerical values should not be taken too seriously. The important thing to realize is that if one is to make comparisons between the various animals on the phylogenetic chart, a scale of this spread is essential. And now the question is, where does one place computers?

Warren McCulloch, a profusely whiskered, egoistic and undeniably brilliant protagonist of artificial intelligence who died in 1970, a year or so before computers really began to take off, once remarked that the very best computer of the time had about the intelligence of a tapeworm. It was an interesting remark, characteristic of McCulloch, for tapeworms and computers have some interesting points in common. In the first place both are relatively immobile—the tapeworm just sits there attached to the wall of the intestine, while the computer just sits there on the floor of its air-conditioned room. Both tapeworm and computer are fed and serviced by things which are not tapeworms or computers, and can therefore be classified as parasitic. In fact, if we take our six "Intelligence Factors" we can make an interesting comparison. Data Capture Ability: poor in both the tapeworm and the standard computer, as neither have much in the way of sense organs. Data Storage Capability: here the computer comes out way on top having a storage capacity massively in excess of the tapeworm's, most of whose "memory" will be devoted to "reminding" itself how to shed its egg-laden segments, how to re-attach itself to the intestinal wall, how to "repair itself" and so on. Processing Speed: again the computer beats the tapeworm by a huge margin. Software Flexibility: low in both entities but the tapeworm has a minute edge in the sense that it is largely self-programmable. Software Efficiency: the tapeworm wins here, for those programs with which it is equipped are extremely efficient, having been rigorously tested over millions of years. Finally, Software Range: the computer definitely comes out on top, though the number and range of programs needed to run a tapeworm's digestive and reproductive systems should not be underestimated. A glance at the score-sheet shows three to the computer, two to the tapeworm and one even, which makes McCulloch's parallel not a bad one.

Where exactly would we place the tapeworm and the McCulloch-era computer (assuming we agree they are roughly comparable) on the macro-scale? My guess, which is as good as anyone's, is that they would be located somewhere around 1000—in other words much higher then the amoeba/tortoise, but way below an earwig and, of course, remotely distant from anything of the rat or hedgehog variety. This might be the cue for that substantial segment of society which is *not* keen at the notion of machine intelligence to take comfort. The gulf between the tapeworm and Man is so wide as to inspire jocularity. This complacency would appear to be even more justified when one has to admit that, although computers have advanced quite dramatically in the ten or fifteen years since McCulloch introduced his analogy, they still make only a piteous showing on the graph. The reasons for this are quite simple: the kinds of advances that computers have made are confined to aspects of their existence which make them attractive and useful to humans—reduced size, lower power requirements, and sensationally lower cost—but which really have nothing to do with their intellectual capabilities.

On the purely intellectual front, little advance has been made in widening or improving their sensory capabilities. They can scan specially printed documents very rapidly, but tend to be totally put out by even the most minute changes in type style, quality, etc., and are pretty hopeless when it comes to sustained recognition of three-dimensional objects. A really good "seeing" or "perceiving" computer of the late 1970s, with loads of memory and very elaborate software, can recognize simple three-dimensional shapes such as blocks and pyramids, and could tell the difference between a cup, a saucer, a spoon, and a teapot, if they are set against a plain background with carefully controlled lighting. Change the lighting so that the shadows shift their positions, or introduce an ambiguous item such as a coffee-pot or gravy dish, and even the world's most powerful computer will be reduced to imbecilic level. But before laughing and jeering too much, one ought to accept that this shows not so much how dumb

computers are, but how fantastically magnificent human beings—
or any animals capable of that kind of perceptual discrimination—
really are.

Speed of adaptation of programs and program efficiency have
not developed much, but real advances have been made in software range. Modern computers can be applied to a far wider range
of tasks than they could in McCulloch's day, a decade and a half
ago, and in some very limited areas—such as chess playing—the
power of specific programs has advanced quite substantially.
Memory capacity has expanded, of course, but even the computers of the '60s had almost infinite memory banks, the main
problem being the time they took to access the information. Only
on the parameter of processing speed have things changed really
dramatically and it is this, rather than any other changes, that has
effected a significant and most praiseworthy increase in computer
IQ. Even so I would be very hesitant about locating the very
brightest of today's systems at much higher than 3000 on the
scale—substantially above a tapeworm but still, you will notice,
below the earwig.

On the other hand one must not forget that while Man has
reached the one million level on the scale only with the greatest
difficulty and after *several hundred million years*, the computer
has passed the tapeworm and is coming up on the earwig fast after
not much more than twenty-five years of comparable evolution!
Another five years at the present rate of progress, and the earwig
will have been left behind and the hedgehog will be looking over
his shoulder. You might think, "Too bad for the hedgehog, but
there is still no measurable threat to Man," but that overlooks the
possibility that the rate of progress might increase substantially—
a factor which we will be considering in a little while. More
importantly, it also overlooks a subtle aspect of the whole matter
of intelligence, particularly as it relates to our macro-chart. Biological systems (which, until the advent of the computers, were
the only intelligent things around on this planet) are multi-
purpose devices. Their principal purpose, as Richard Dawkins
points out in his magnificent book *The Selfish Gene*, is not to give
a whole lot of animals of varying degrees of complexity a good
time for a few months or years of life, but rather to act as vehicles

which ensure the survival and continued evolution of the gene—the package of coded information which all living things carry buried in every cell in their body. This horrendous concept—the total prostitution of all animal life, including Man and all his airs and graces, to the blind purposiveness of these minute virus-like substances—is so desperately at odds with almost every other view that Man has of himself, that Dawkins' book has received a bleak reception in many quarters. Nevertheless his argument is virtually irrefutable.

Unfortunately it is also extremely simplistic, as the author himself admits. It fails to acknowledge the significance and richness of the numerous *sub*-goals which are integral to and entirely supportive of the "main purpose", if one can call it that. The first major sub-goal, for example, which manifests itself as a prime goal for the individual beings that carry the genes round inside them, is that of *survival,* and a whole range of sub-sub-goals, each served by complex sets of programs, are to be found nested under that heading. These include mating and care of the young, eating and drinking, running away from some animals and chasing others. And within each of these sub-sub-goals there are yet more nests of sub-sub-sub-goals and so on.

Now the crucial point here is that as biological systems advance up our macro-graph they tend to acquire more and more of these sub-goals, each of which is supplied with and driven by its own set of programs. Thus the higher up the IQ scale, the more complex and more elaborate is the creature's software package—a rule of life which is absolutely fundamental and inescapable. Any creature "striving" for the survival of its genetic package throughout time and "choosing" intelligence as one of the weapons in its armour must pay this penalty. There are creatures who have not "chosen" intelligence as their prime weapon. Tapeworms which rely on internal parasitism, and limpets which rely on keeping out of mischief in a suit of armour on rocks have had a good long run for their money. Their life may be horribly dull, but you can bet that their genes are more than satisfied! Plants (which have only limited intelligence by our six-point plan) are other examples.

But whereas advanced biological intelligences have to carry

round huge software packages simply in order to survive, computers are not bound by the same constraints. Their relative position on the macro-graph and their rather sluggish rate of progress give a highly misleading indication of their true status and potential. For example they do not, and I am sure never will, have to devote any software to supporting a complex reproductive system; humans kindly attend to all these matters for them. Nor does any software have to be given over to maintenance and repair functions, or to providing immunological defences against bacterial or viral assaults. Once again humans wait there in the wings to build and restore. Nor do they need elaborate suites of programs to enable them to hoist their bodies all over the place in search of food or to escape danger. Nor yet—it is a formidable list of bonuses whose significance becomes more and more apparent as one thinks about it—do they need a huge range of interlocking programs to allow them to enjoy good food and drink, nor the host of other sensory thrills which most biological beings experience, from basking in the sun to making love.

In other words, if you are only interested in *intelligence,* and not in psychomotor co-ordination or in the major task of keeping a complex body alive and active, then the chance of the computer evolving rapidly up the graph is far greater than you would intuitively realize. Add to this a stunning fact which most people, including computer scientists, have tended to discount. In certain limited, but important, areas of intellectual achievement— taking intelligence according to our six-factor schema— computers have long ago by-passed hedgehogs, rats, monkeys, chimpanzees, and even Man. In processing speed they are already so far in advance of biological systems as to defy comparison. More specifically, computers are far superior to Man in handling numerical information and computation of various kinds. These achievements may sound like "purely automatic computation", but they are nevertheless an integral part of human intellectual performance. Nor should they be dismissed because they are "just to do with numbers"; the main reason that advances have been confined to these areas is because they were precisely the areas where Man needed most help and where he first decided to put the computers to work.

But there are other areas of development which are closer to our intellectual tender spots. It used to be said that no computer could ever be programmed to play a half-way decent game of chess. If the experts who made that kind of statement ten or twenty years ago are not eating their words by now they should be, for by the end of 1978 computers existed which would crush 99.5 per cent of the world's chess players. Some have almost reached International Master level—and if this does not make you feel the computer's hot breath on your neck, then nothing will. As a last resort the sceptic may fall back on cataloguing Man's supposedly unique abilities—his power of reason, his creativity, his capacity to show aesthetic judgement and above all, perhaps, his power to *think*. Surely these are unique, and no possible acceleration of computer intelligence will make up for them? To answer this question I want to introduce—or re-introduce rather, since he cropped up in an earlier chapter—the man who was the first person to face up to this problem and think it through to its conclusion. His name was Alan Turing.

CHAPTER THIRTEEN

Can a Machine Think?

IN THE EARLY years of the Second World War when the British began, in ultra-secret, to put together their effort to crack German codes, they set out to recruit a team of the brightest minds available in mathematics and the then rather novel field of electronic engineering. Recruiting the electronic whizzes was easy, as many of them were to be found engrossed in the fascinating problem of radio location of aircraft—or radar as it later came to be called. Finding mathematicians with the right kind of obsessive brilliance to make a contribution in the strange field of cryptography was another matter. In the end they adopted the ingenious strategy of searching through lists of young mathematicians who were also top-flight chess players. As a result of a nation-wide trawl an amazing collection of characters were billeted together in the country-house surroundings of Bletchley Park, and three of the most remarkable were Irving John Good, Donald Michie, and Alan Turing.

The first two were precocious intellects who, true to their early promise, have since gone on to make a considerable mark on the world of science. After the war, Michie, a multi-disciplinary character from the beginning, founded a Department of Machine Intelligence and Perception at Edinburgh University where his ambitious and imaginative goals included robot design and construction. Unfortunately, the scheme was a decade ahead of its time and failed to attract the financial support it needed. Had it been forthcoming, Britain might have pushed into the lead in this controversial aspect of computer research.

Jack Good, after a period of top secret work for the British Navy and a Fellowship at Oxford, zoomed off to the USA and is now a Distinguished Professor of Statistics at the Virginia Polytechnic Institute. His impeccable scientific credentials—he has a list of about a *thousand* published scientific papers, reports and notes in his curriculum vitae—do not prevent his enjoying an idiosyncratic approach to life. His keen interest in palindromes (phrases like ABLE WAS I ERE I SAW ELBA) led him on one occasion to write to Her Majesty the Queen suggesting that she appoint him a peer of the realm. His reason for making his request was that when people saw him approaching they would certainly remark, "Good Lord here comes Lord Good", which he felt would have sufficient aesthetic merit to justify the peerage. The Queen may, or may not, have been amused . . . Professor Good is also, incidentally, the originator of the concept of the Ultra-Intelligent Machine, a particularly exciting notion which we shall discuss later.

The third member of this unique trio was Turing himself. Older than Michie and Good by a decade or so, he had already stamped his presence on the face of science, notably by one immortal paper published in 1936 entitled "On Computable numbers, with an Application to the Entscheidungsproblem". Toe-curling though that may sound to the layman, the paper is read with rapturous joy by mathematicians and it is generally agreed to be one of the most important single papers in the foundations of computer science. It is frightfully tough going but it can be summarized without too much difficulty. What Turing was doing was to latch on to the thought that had occurred to his predecessor, Babbage, as he surveyed his giant Analytical Engine: once you have constructed a machine which can calculate *one* set of mathematical operations, then it ought to be possible to construct one to calculate *any other set*. Furthermore, it ought to be possible, in principle, to build a single machine which, through the appropriate manipulation of its interior (we would call it programming today), would be capable of coping with any or all of these calculations—a universal computer in other words. Babbage had a hunch that this would be possible—or, to be more exact, could see no reason why it should not be so—but could not take things much further. Turing set out to show that a universal computer *could* be constructed, through a rigorous mathematical argument which made mathematicians all over the world pause and prick up their ears. From that moment it was inevitable that one day there would be a science of computing, though few of those who read the paper realized just how quickly it would come about.

If contemporary accounts of what the workers at Bletchley were talking about in their few moments of spare time can be relied on, many of them were a bit over-optimistic if anything. Both Good and Michie believed that the use of electronic computers such as Colossus would result in major advances in mathematics in the immediate post-war era and Turing was of the same opinion. All three (and one or two of their colleagues) were also confident that it would not be long before machines were exhibiting intelligence, including problem-solving abilities, and that their role as simple number-crunchers was only one phase in their evolution. Although the exact substance of their conversations, carried long into the night when they were waiting for the test results of the first creaky Colossus prototypes, has softened with the passage of time, it is known the topic of machine intelligence loomed very large. They discussed, with a *frisson* of excitement and unease, the peculiar ramifications of the subject they were pioneering and about which the rest of the world knew (and still knows) so little. Could there ever be a machine which was able to solve problems that no human could solve? Could a computer ever beat a human at chess? Lastly, could a machine *think*?

Of all the questions that can be asked about computers none has such an eerie ring. Allow a machine intelligence perhaps, the ability to control other machines, repair itself, help us solve problems, compute numbers a millionfold quicker than any human; allow it to fly airplanes, drive cars, superintend our medical records and even, possibly, give advice to politicians. Somehow you can see how a machine might come to do all these things. But that it could be made to perform that apparently exclusively human operation known as *thinking* is something else, and something which is offensive, alien and threatening. Only in the most *outré* forms of science fiction, stretching back to Mary Shelley's masterpiece *Frankenstein*, is the topic touched on, and always with a sense of great uncertainty about the enigmatic nature of the problem area.

Good, Michie and their companions were content to work the ideas through in their spare moments. But Turing—older, a touch more serious and less cavalier—set out to consider things in depth. In particular he addressed himself to the critical question: Can, or could, a machine think? The way he set out to do this three decades ago and long before any other scientists had considered it so cogently, is of lasting interest. The main thesis was published in the philosophical journal *Mind* in 1952. Logically unassailable, when read impartially it serves to break down any barriers of uncertainty which surround this and parallel questions. Despite its classic status the work is seldom read outside the fields of computer science and philosophy, but now that events in the computer science and in the field of artificial intelligence are beginning to move with the rapidity and momentum which the Bletchley scientists knew they ultimately would, the time has come for Turing's paper to achieve a wider public.

Soon after the war ended and the Colossus project folded, Turing joined the National Physical Laboratory in Teddington and began to work with a gifted team on the design of what was to become the world's most powerful computer, ACE. Later he moved to Manchester, where, spurred by the pioneers Kilburn, Hartree, Williams and Newman, a vigorous effort was being applied to develop another powerful electronic machine. It was a heady, hard-driving time, comparable to the state of events now prevailing in microprocessors, when anyone with special knowledge rushes along under immense pressure, ever conscious of the feeling that whoever is second in the race may as well not have entered it at all. As a result Turing found less time than he would have hoped to follow up his private hobbies, particularly his ideas on computer game-playing—checkers, chess and the ancient game of Go—which he saw was an important sub-set of machine intelligence.

Games like chess are unarguably intellectual pursuits, and yet, unlike certain other intellectual exercises, such as writing poetry or discussing the inconsistent football of the hometown team, they have easily describable rules of operation. The task, therefore, would seem to be simply a matter of writing a computer program which "knew" these rules and which could follow them when faced with moves offered by a human player. Turing made very little headway as it happens, and the first chess-playing programs which were scratched together in the late '40s and early '50s were quite awful—so much so that there was a strong feeling that this kind of project was not worth pursuing, since the game of chess as played by an "expert" involves some special intellectual skill which could never be specified in machine terms.

Turing found this ready dismissal of the computer's potential to be both interesting and suggestive. If people were unwilling to accept the idea of a machine which could play games, how would they feel about one which exhibited "intelligence", or one which could "think"? In the course of discussions with friends Turing found that a good part of the problem was that people were universally unsure of their definitions. What exactly did one mean when one used the word "thought"? What processes were actually in action when "thinking" took place? If a machine was created which *could* think, how would one set about testing it? The last question, Turing surmised, was the key one, and with a wonderful surge of imagination spotted a way to answer it, proposing what has in computer circles come to be known as "The Turing Test for Thinking Machines". In the next chapter, we will examine the test, see how workable it is, and also try to assess how close computers have come, and will come, to passing it.

When Turing asked people whether they believed that a computer could think, he found almost universal rejection of the idea—just as I did when I carried out a similar survey almost thirty years later. The objections I received were similar to those that Turing documented in his paper "Computing Machinery and Intelligence", and I will summarize them here, adding my own comments and trying to meet the various objections as they occur.

First there is the Theological Objection. This was more common in Turing's time than it is now, but it still crops up occasionally. It can be summed up as follows: "Man is a creation of God, and has been given a soul and the power of conscious thought. Machines are not spiritual beings, have no soul and thus must be incapable of thought." As Turing pointed out, this seems to place an unwarranted restriction on God. Why shouldn't he give machines souls and allow them to think if he wanted to? On one level I suppose it is irrefutable: if someone chooses to define thinking as something that *only* Man can do and that *only* God can bestow, then that is the end of the matter. Even then the force of the argument does seem to depend upon a confusion between "thought" and "spirituality", upon the old Cartesian dichotomy of the ghost in the machine. The ghost presumably does the thinking while the machine is merely the vehicle which carries the ghost around.

Then there is the Shock/Horror Objection, which Turing called the "Heads in the Sand Objection". Both phrases will do though I prefer my own. When the subject of machine thought is first broached, a common reaction goes something like this: "What a horrible idea! How could any scientist work on such a monstrous development? I hope to goodness that the field of artificial intelligence doesn't advance a step further if its end-product is a thinking machine!" The attitude is not very logical — and it is not really an argument why it *could* not happen, but rather the expression of a heartfelt wish that it never will!

The Extra-sensory Perception Objection was the one that impressed Turing most, and impresses me least. *If* there were such a thing as extra-sensory perception and *if* it were in some way a function of human brains, then it could well also be an important constituent of thought. By this token, in the absence of any evidence proving that computers are telepathic, we would have to assume that they could never be capable of thinking in its fullest sense. The same argument applies to any other "psychic" or spiritual component of human psychology. I cannot take this objection seriously because there seems to me to be no evidence which carries any scientific weight that extra-sensory perception does exist. The situation was different in Turing's time, when the world-renowned parapsychology laboratory at Duke University in North Carolina, under Dr J. B. Rhine, was generating an enormous amount of material supposedly offering evidence for telepathy and precognition. This is not the place to go into the long, and by no means conclusive, arguments about the declining status of parapsychology, but it is certainly true that as far as most scientists are concerned, what once looked like a rather good case for the existence of telepathy, etc., now seems to be an extremely thin one. But even if ESP *is* shown to be a genuine phenomenon, it is, in my own view, something to do with the transmission of information from a source point to a receiver and ought therefore to be quite easy to reproduce in a machine. After all, machines can communicate by radio already, which is, effectively, ESP and is a far better method of long-distance communication than that possessed by any biological system.

The Personal Consciousness Objection is, superficially, a rather potent argument which comes up in various guises. Turing noticed it expressed particularly cogently in a report, in the *British Medical Journal* in 1949, on the Lister Oration for that year, which was entitled "The Mind of Mechanical Man". It was given by a distinguished medical scientist, Professor G. Jefferson. A short quote from the Oration will suffice:

Not until a machine can write a sonnet or compose a concerto *because of thoughts and emotions felt,* and not by the chance fall of symbols, could we agree that machine equals brain—that is, not only write it but *know that it had written it.* No mechanism could feel (and not merely artificially signal, an easy contrivance) pleasure at its successes, grief when its valves fuse, be warmed by flattery, be made miserable by its mistakes, be charmed by sex, be angry or depressed when it cannot get what it wants.

The italics, which are mine, highlight what I believe to be the fundamental objection: the output of the machine is more or less irrelevant, no matter how impressive it is. Even if it wrote a sonnet—and a very good one—it would not mean much unless it had written it as the result of "thoughts and emotions felt", and it would also have to "know that it had written it". This could be a useful "final definition" of one aspect of human thought—but how would you establish whether or not the sonnet was written with "emotions"? Asking the computer would not help for, as Professor Jefferson realized, there would be no guarantee that it was not simply *declaring* that it had felt emotions. He is really propounding the extreme solipsist position and should, therefore, apply the same rules to humans. Extreme solipsism is logically irrefutable ("I am the only real thing; all else is illusion") but it is so unhelpful a view of the universe that most people choose to ignore it and decide that when people say they are thinking or feeling they may as well believe them. In other words, Professor Jefferson's objection could be over-ridden if you *became* the computer and experienced its thoughts (if any)—only then could you really *know*. His objection is worth discussing in some depth because it is so commonly heard in one form or another, and because it sets us up in part for Turing's resolution of the machine-thought problem, which we will come to later.

The Unpredictability Objection argues that computers are created by humans according to sets of rules and operate according to carefully scripted programs which themselves are sets of rules. So if you wanted to, you could work out exactly what a computer was going to do at any particular time. It is, in principle, totally predictable. *If* you have all the facts available you *can* predict a computer's behaviour because it follows rules, whereas there is no way in which you could hope to do the same with a human *because he is not behaving according to a set of immutable rules*. Thus there is an essential difference between computers and humans, so (the argument gets rather weak here) thinking, because it is unpredictable and does not blindly follow rules, must be an essentially human ability.

There are two comments: firstly, computers are becoming so complex that it is doubtful their behaviour could be predicted even if everything was known about them—computer programmers and engineers have found that one of the striking characteristics of present-day systems is that they constantly spring surprises. The second point follows naturally: humans are *already* in that super-complex state and the reason that we cannot predict what they do is *not* because they have no ground rules but because (a) we don't know what the rules are, and (b) even if we did know them they would still be too complicated to handle. At best, the unpredictability argument is thin, but it is often raised. People frequently remark that there is always "the element of surprise" in a human. I have no doubt that that is just because *any* very complex system is bound to be surprising. A variant of the argument is that humans are capable of error whereas the "perfect" computer is not. That may well be true, which suggests that machines are superior to humans, for there seems to be little point in having any information-processing system, biological or electronic, that makes errors in processing. It would be possible to build a random element into computers to make them unpredictable from time to time, but it would be a peculiarly pointless exercise.

The "See How Stupid They Are" Objection will not need much introduction. At one level it is expressed in jokes about computers that generate ridiculous bank statements or electricity bills; at another and subtler level, it is a fair appraisal of the computer's stupendous weaknesses in comparison with Man. "How could you possibly imagine that such backward, limited things could ever reach the point where they could be said to think?" The answer, as we have already pointed out, is that they may be dumb now but they have advanced at a pretty dramatic rate and show every sign of continuing to do so. Their present limitations may be valid when arguing whether they could be said to be capable of thinking *now* or in the *very* near future, but it has no relevance to whether they would be capable of thinking at some later date.

The "Ah But It Can't Do That" Objection is an eternally regressing argument which, for a quarter of a century, computer scientists have been listening to, partially refuting, and then having to listen to all over again. It runs: "Oh yes, you can obviously make a computer do so and so—you have just demonstrated that, but of course you will never be able to make it do such and such." The such and such may be anything you name—once it was play a good game of chess, have a storage capacity greater than the human memory, read human hand-writing or understand human speech. Now that these "Ah buts" have (quite swiftly) been overcome, one is faced by a new range: beat the world human chess champion, operate on parallel as opposed to serial processing, perform medical diagnosis better than a doctor, translate satisfactorily from one language to another, help solve its own software problems, etc. When these challenges are met, no doubt it will have to design a complete city from scratch, invent a game more interesting than chess, admire a pretty girl/ handsome man, work out the unified field theory, enjoy bacon and eggs, and so on. I cannot think of anything more silly than developing a computer which could enjoy bacon and eggs, but there is nothing to suggest that, provided enough time and money was invested, one could not pull off such a surrealistic venture. On the other hand, it might be *most* useful to have computers design safe, optimally cheap buildings. Even more ambitious (and perhaps comparable to the bacon and egg project but more worthwhile) would be to set a system to tackle the problem of the relationship between gravity and light, and my own guess is that before the conclusion of the long-term future (before the start of the twenty-first century), computers will be hard at work on these problems and will be having great success.

The "It Is Not Biological" Objection may seem like another version of the theological objection—only living things could have the capacity for thought, so non-biological systems could not possibly think. But there is a subtle edge that requires a bit more explanation. It is a characteristic of most modern computers that they are discrete state machines, which is to say that they are digital and operate in a series of discrete steps—on/off. Now the biological central nervous system may not be so obviously digital, though there is evidence that the neurone, the basic unit of communication, acts in an on/off, all or nothing way. But if it turned out that it were *not*, and operated on some more elaborate strategy, then it is conceivable that "thought" might only be manifest in things which had switching systems of this more elaborate kind. Put it another way: it might be possible to build digital computers which were immensely intelligent, but no matter how intelligent they became they would never be able to *think*. The argument cannot be refuted at the moment, but even so there is no shred of evidence to suppose that only non-digital systems can think. There may be other facets of living things that make them unique from the point of view of their capacity to generate thought, but none that we can identify, or even guess at. This objection therefore is not a valid one at present, though in the event of some new biological discovery, it may become so.

The Mathematical Objection is one of the most intriguing of

the ten objections, and is the one most frequently encountered in discussions with academics. It is based on a fascinating exercise in mathematical logic propounded by the Hungarian, Kurt Gödel. To put it rather superficially, Gödel's theorem shows that within any sufficiently powerful logical system (which could be a computer operating according to clearly defined rules), statements can be formulated which can neither be proved nor disproved *within the system*. In his famous 1936 paper, Alan Turing restructured Gödel's theorem so that it could apply specifically to machines. This effectively states that no matter how powerful a computer is, there are bound to be certain tasks that it cannot tackle on its own. In other words, you could not build a computer which could solve *every* problem no matter how well it was programmed; or, if you wanted to carry the thing to the realms of fancy, no computer (or any other digital system) could end up being God.

Gödel's theorem, and its later refinements by Alonzo Church, Bertrand Russell and others, is interesting to mathematicians, not so much because it assumes an implicit limitation to machine intelligence, but because it indicates a limitation to mathematics itself. But the theorem has been used, incorrectly, by critics of machine intelligence to "prove" that computers could never reach the same intellectual level as Man. The weakness of the position is that it is based on the assumption that the human brain is not a formal logical system. But such evidence as we have suggests very strongly that it is and will, therefore, be bound by the same Gödel-limitations as are machines. There is also a tweak in the tail. While the theorem admittedly states that no system *on its own* can completely tackle its own problems—"understand itself"—it does *not* imply that the areas of mystery could not be tackled by some other system. No individual human brain could solve its own problems or fully "know itself", but with the assistance of other brains these deficiencies might be corrected. Equally, and significantly, problem areas associated with complex computer systems could be solved totally and absolutely by other computer systems, provided that *they* were clever enough.

The last of the ten arguments against the concept of a thinking machine has become known as Lady Lovelace's Objection. We met the interesting Ada, Countess of Lovelace, earlier when she turned up as Charles Babbage's mistress, confidante and guiding light. In her extensive writings on Babbage's Analytical Engine, she voiced a comment which had particular relevance to machine intelligence, even machine thought, though she did not see it in this intriguing context. Lady Lovelace's Objection is, I suppose, the most commonly-expressed criticism of the idea of computers with intellects paralleling, or exceeding, Man's. I have already quoted the relevant passage from her "Notes" of 1842 (see page 27) but the essential sentences are, "The Analytical Engine has no pretensions to *originate* anything. It can do whatever we know how to order it to perform." In its modern form this comes up as, "A Computer cannot do anything that you have not programmed it to." The objection is so fundamental and so widely accepted that it needs detailed discussion.

In the most absolute and literal sense, this statement is perfectly correct and applies to any machine or computer that has been made or that could be made. According to the rules of the universe that we live in, nothing can take place without a prior cause; a computer will not spring into action without something powering it and guiding it on its way. In the case of the various tasks that a computer performs, the "cause"—to stretch the use of the word rather—is the program or sets of programs that control these tasks. Much the same applies to a brain: it, too, must come equipped with sets of programs which cause it to run through its repertoire of tasks. This might seem to support Lady Lovelace, at least to the extent that machines "need" a human to set them up, but it would also seem to invalidate the argument that this constitutes an essential difference between computers and people. But is there not still a crucial difference between brains and computers? No matter how sophisticated computers are, must there not always have been a human being to *write* its programs? Surely the same does not have to be said for humans?

To tackle this we need to remember that all brains, human included, are equipped at birth with a comprehensive collection of programs which are common to all members of a species and which are known as instincts. These control respiration, gastric absorption, cardiac activity, and, at a behavioural level, such reflexes as sucking, eyeblink, grasping and so on. There may also be programs which "cause" the young animal to explore its environment, exercise its muscles, play and so on. Where do these come from? Well, they are acquired over an immensely long-winded trial-and-error process through the course of evolution. We might call them permanent software ("firmware" is the phrase used sometimes by computer scientists) and they correspond to the suites of programs which every computer has when it leaves the factory, and which are to do with its basic running, maintenance, and so on.

In addition to this, all biological computers come equipped with a bank of what might best be described as raw programs. No one has the faintest idea whether they are neurological, bio-chemical, electrical or what—all we know is that they *must* exist. They start being laid down the moment the creature begins to interact with the world around it. In the course of time they build up into a colossal suite of software which ultimately enables us to talk, write, walk, read, enjoy bacon and eggs, appreciate music, think, feel, write books, or come up with mathematical ideas. These programs are useful only to the owner of that particular brain, vanish with his death and are quite separate from the "firmware".

If this seems too trivial a description of the magnificent field of human learning and achievement, it is only because anything appears trivial when you reduce it to its bare components: a fabulous sculpture to a quintillion highly similar electrons and protons, a microprocessor to a million impurities buried in a wafer of sand, the human brain into a collection of neurones, blood cells and chemical elements. What is not trivial is the endlessly devious, indescribably profound way in which these elements are structured to make up the whole. The real difference between the brain and most existing computers is that in the former, data acquisition and the initial writing and later modification of the program is done by a mechanism within the brain itself, while in the latter, the software is prepared outside and passed to the computer in its completed state. But I did use the word "most". In recent years increasing emphasis has been placed on the development of "adaptive" programs—software which can be modified and revised on the basis of the program's interaction with the environment. In simple terms these could be looked upon as "programs which learn for themselves", and they will, in due course, become an important feature of many powerful computer systems.

At this point the sceptic still has a few weapons in his armoury. The first is generally put in the form of the statement: "Ah, but even when computers *can* update their own software and acquire new programs for themselves, they will still only be doing this because of Man's ingenuity. Man may no longer actually write the programs, but had he not invented the idea of the self-adaptive program in the first place none of this could have happened." This is perfectly true but has little to do with whether or not computers could think, or perform any other intellectual exercise. It could place computers eternally in our debt, and we may be able to enjoy a smug sense of pride at having created them, but it offers no real restriction on their development.

The sceptic may also argue that no matter how clever or how intelligent you make computers, they will never be able to perform a creative task. Everything they do will inevitably spring from something they have been taught, have experienced or is the subject of some pre-existing program. There are two points being made here. One is that computers could never have an original or creative thought. The other is that the seeds of everything they do, no matter how intelligent, lie in their existing software. To take the second point first: again one is forced to say that the same comment applies to humans. Unless the argument is that some of Man's thoughts or ideas come from genuine inspiration—a message from God, angels, or the spirits of the departed—no one can dispute that all aspects of our intelligence evolve from pre-existing programs and the background experiences of life. This evolution may be enormously complex and its progress might be impossible to track, but any intellectual flowerings arise from the seeds of experience planted in the fertile substrate of the brain.

There still remains the point about creativity, and it is one that is full of pitfalls. Before making any assumptions about creativity being an *exclusive* attribute of Man, the concept has to be defined. It is not enough to say "write a poem", "paint a picture" or "discuss philosophical ideas", because it is easy enough to program computers to do all these things. The fact that their poems, paintings and philosophical ramblings are pretty mediocre is beside the point: it would be just as unfair to ask them to write, say, a sonnet of Shakespearian calibre or a painting of da Vinci quality and fail them for lack of creativity as it would be to give the same task to the man in the street. Beware too of repeating the old saying, "Ah, but you have to program them to paint, play chess and so on," for the same is unquestionably true of people. Try handing a twelve-month-old baby a pot of paint or a chessboard if you have any doubts about the need for some measure of learning and experience.

Obviously a crisper definition of creativity is required, and here is one that is almost universally acceptable: If a person demonstrates a skill which has never been demonstrated before and which was not specifically taught to him by someone else, or in the intellectual domain provides an *entirely novel* solution to a problem—a solution which was not known to any other human being—then they can be said to have done something original or had an original or creative thought. There may be other forms of creativity of course, but this would undeniably be an example of it in action. There is plenty of evidence that humans are creative by this standard and the history of science is littered with "original" ideas which humans have generated. Clearly, until a computer also provides such evidence, Lady Lovelace's Objection still holds, at least in one of its forms.

But alas for the sceptics. This particular barrier has been overthrown by computers on a number of occasions in the past few years. A well-publicized one was the solution, by a computer, of the venerable "four colour problem". This has some mathematical importance, and can best be expressed by thinking of a two-dimensional map featuring a large number of territories, say the counties of England or the states of the USA. Supposing you want to give each territory a colour, what is the minimum number of colours you need to employ to ensure that no two territories of the same colour adjoin each other?

After fiddling around with maps and crayons, you will find that the number seems to come out at four, and no one has ever been able to find a configuration where five colours are required, or where you can always get away with three. Empirically, therefore, four is the answer—hence the name of the problem. But if you attempt to demonstrate this mathematically and *prove* that four colours will do for any conceivable map, you will get nowhere. For decades mathematicians have wrestled with this elusive problem, and from time to time have come up with a "proof" which in the end turns out to be incomplete or fallacious. But the mathematical world was rocked when in 1977 the problem was handed over to a computer, which attacked it with a stupendous frontal assault, sifting through huge combinations of possibilities and eventually demonstrating, to every mathematician's satisfaction, that four colours would do the trick. Actually, although this is spectacular testimony to the computer's creative powers, it is not really the most cogent example, for its technique was block-busting rather than heuristic (problem solving by testing hypotheses). It was like solving a chess problem by working out every possible combination of moves, rather than by concentrating on likely areas and experimenting with them. A better, and much earlier, demonstration of computer originality came from a program which was set to generate some totally new proofs in Euclidean geometry. The computer produced a completely novel proof of the well-known theorem which shows that the base angles of an isosceles triangle are equal, by flipping the triangles through 180 degrees and declaring them to be congruent. Quite apart from the fact that it had not before been known to Man, it showed such originality that one famous mathematician remarked, "If any of my students had done that, I would have marked him down as a budding genius."

And so Lady Lovelace's long-lasting objection can be overruled. We have shown that computers can be intelligent, and that they can even be creative—but we have not yet proved that they can, or ever could, *think*.

Now, what do we mean by the word "think"?

CHAPTER FOURTEEN

Towards the Ultra-Intelligent Machine

THE MOST COMMON objections raised to the notion of thinking machines are based on misunderstandings of fairly simple issues, or on semantic confusions of one kind or another. We are still left with the problem of defining the verb "to think", and in this chapter we will attempt to deal with this, or at least to discuss one particular and very compelling way of dealing with it. From this position we shall find ourselves drifting inevitably into a consideration of the problem of creating thinking machines, and in particular to the eerie concept of the Ultra-Intelligent Machine.

Most people believe that they know what they mean when they talk about "thinking" and have no difficulty identifying it when it is going on in their own heads. We are prepared to believe other human beings think because we have experience of it ourselves and accept that it is a common property of the human race. But we cannot make the same assumption about machines, and would be sceptical if one of them told us, no matter how persuasively, that it too was thinking. But sooner or later a machine will make just such a declaration and the question then will be, how do we decide whether to believe it or not?

When Turing tackled the machine-thought issue, he proposed a characteristically brilliant solution which, while not entirely free from flaws, is nevertheless the best that has yet been put forward. The key to it all, he pointed out, is to ask what the signs and signals are that humans give out, from which we infer that *they* are thinking. It is clearly a matter of *what kind of conversation we can have with them,* and has nothing to do with what kind of face they have and what kind of clothes they wear. Unfortunately physical appearances automatically set up prejudices in our minds, and if we were having a spirited conversation with a microprocessor we might be very sceptical about its capacity for thought, simply because it did not look like any thinking thing we had seen in the past. But we *would* be interested in what it had to say; and thus Turing invented his experiment or test:

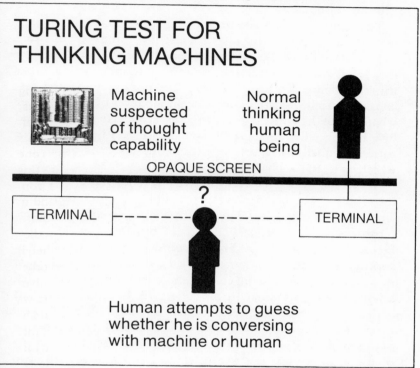

TURING TEST FOR THINKING MACHINES

Machine suspected of thought capability

Normal thinking human being

OPAQUE SCREEN

TERMINAL

?

TERMINAL

Human attempts to guess whether he is conversing with machine or human

Put a human—the judge or tester—in a room where there are two computer terminals, one connected to a computer, the other to a person. The judge, of course, does not know which terminal is connected to which, but can type into either terminal and receive typed messages back on them. Now the judge's job is to decide, by carrying out conversations with the entities on the end of the respective terminals, *which is which*. If the computer is very stupid, it will immediately be revealed as such and the human will have no difficulty identifying it. If it is bright, he may find that he can carry on quite a good conversation with it, though he may ultimately spot that it must be the computer. If it is exceptionally bright and has a wide range of knowledge, he may find it impossible to say whether it is the computer he is talking to or the person. In this case, Turing argues, the computer will have passed the test and could for all practical purposes be said to be a thinking machine.

The argument has a simple but compelling force: if the intellectual exchange we achieve with a machine is indistinguishable from that we have with a being we *know* to be thinking, then we are, to all intents and purposes, communicating with another thinking being. This, by the way, does not imply that the personal experience, state of consciousness, level of awareness or whatever, of the entity is going to be the same as that experienced by a human when he or she thinks, so the test is not for these particular qualities. They are not, in any case, the parameters which concern the observer.

At first the Turing Test may seem a surprising way of looking at the problem, but it is an extremely sensible way of approaching it. The question now arises: is any computer at present in existence capable of passing the test?—And if not, how long is it likely to be before one comes along? From time to time one laboratory or another claims that a computer has had at least a pretty good stab at it. Scientists using the big computer conferencing systems (each scientist has a terminal in his office and is connected to his colleagues via the computer, which acts as host and general message-sorter) often find it difficult to be sure, for a brief period of time at least, whether they are talking to the computer or to one of their colleagues. On one celebrated occasion at MIT, two scientists had been chatting via the network when one of them left the scene without telling the other, who carried on a cheery conversation with the computer under the assumption that he was talking to his friend. I have had the same spooky experience when chatting with computers which I have programmed myself, and often find their answers curiously perceptive and unpredictable.

To give another interesting example: in the remarkable match played in Toronto in August 1978 between the International Chess Master, David Levy, and the then computer chess champion of the world, Northwestern University's "Chess 4.7", the computer made a number of moves of an uncannily "human" nature. The effect was so powerful that Levy subsequently told me that he found it difficult to believe that he was not facing an outstanding human opponent. Few chess buffs who looked at the move-by-move transcripts of the match were, without prior knowledge, able to tell which had been made by the computer and which by the flesh-and-blood chess master. David Levy himself suggested that Chess 4.7 had effectively passed the Turing Test.

It would be nice to believe that I had been present on such an historic occasion, but this did not constitute a proper "pass". In the test as Turing formulated it, the judge is allowed to converse with either of his two mystery entities on any topic that he chooses, and he may use any conversational trick he wants. Furthermore he can continue the inquisition for as long as he wants, always seeking some clue that will force the computer to reveal itself. Both the computer and the human can lie if they want to in their attempts to fool the tester, so the answers to questions like "Are you the computer?" or "Do you watch much television?" will not give much away. Obviously any computer with a chance in hell of passing the test will have to have a pretty substantial bank of software at its disposal, and not just be extremely bright in one area. Chess 4.7 for example might look as though it was thinking if it was questioned about chess, or, better still, invited to play the game, but switch the area of discourse to human anatomy, politics or good restaurants and it would be shown up as a dunderhead.

As things stand at present, computers have quite a way to go before they jump the hurdle so cleverly laid out for them by Turing. But this should not be taken as providing unmitigated comfort for those who resist the notion of advanced machine intelligence. It should now be clear that the difference, in intellectual terms, between a human being and a computer is one of degree and not of kind.

Turing himself says in his *Mind* paper that he feels computers will have passed the test before the turn of the century, and there is little doubt that he would dearly have liked to live long enough to be around on the splendiferous occasion when "machine thinking" first occurred. If he was right and the test is passed in the late 1990s, that would have put him in his eighties which is not an incredible age. But alas for mathematics and alas for computer science, Alan Turing barely reached his forties. In 1954, while engaged on what some people felt was his most adventurous and far-reaching work—a brilliant study of morphogenesis, the development of form in living organisms—he came to a tragic end. A solitary individual who confided little in other people, he was also a practising homosexual at a time when homosexuality was viewed as a criminal offence. Somehow he brushed with the law—the sad, sorry details are hard, and perhaps unnecessary, to come by—and one evening, depressed and disillusioned, he retired to his room and bit into an apple laced with potassium cyanide. Thus Alan Mayne Turing, one of the most vivid intellects of the twentieth century, left us on our own with the computers.

Does Turing's prediction of the relative imminence of very intelligent machines still hold? I believe it does, for two reasons. In the first place there is a misleading feature of the Turing Test which we have already touched on, but which might need spelling out a bit more. This is that it is offered up as a test for a *thinking*, and not for an *intelligent* machine. A thinking machine would, of course, have to be an intelligent one, but an intelligent—even super-intelligent—machine might not necessarily be capable of thinking. While colossal resources might have to be allocated over quite a few decades in order to give a computer the breadth of software needed to pass the Turing Test, the allocation of far fewer resources over a much shorter period of time could be enough to make a computer zoom up the IQ scale in one or two areas of knowledge or understanding. The fact that with quite minimal resources, computer chess IQ has already passed that of 99.5 per cent of mankind should be a clear smoke signal.

In the second place, as with almost all areas of scientific advance, progress tends to accelerate. Add to that a novel feature. As cheaper computer-power becomes available, it will become more realistic to apply the power of the computer to help improve its own software and hardware. The paradox of something being used to solve its own problems is an apparent one only. Men can be used to help solve other men's problems and the same applies to computers. Already work is beginning in this field and it is likely that some progress will have been made by the early 1980s. A good deal of the effort, one suspects, will come from the vast band of enthusiastic amateurs—the hobbyists, the home-computer freaks—who are beginning to develop highly imaginative software purely for the fun of it. But more will come from the giant computer corporations and the huge software houses, who will see the advantages that will accrue to anyone who pulls the computer in to help with his work. The outcome should be a sharp advance in machine intelligence, if only along certain fronts. To the computer enthusiast this is exciting enough, but yet another factor, even more potent, will by this time be coming into play.

The idea, so far as I can tell, was first put forward by I. J. Good (of Bletchley Park and "Here comes Lord Good" fame) when he commented on a remark made by the distinguished British scientist Lord Bowden. Bowden said that there seemed to be little point in spending vast sums of money on creating a computer as intelligent as a human when the world was already heavily over-populated with intelligent beings, all of whom could be created quite easily, relatively cheaply and in a far more enjoyable way. This was a witty (and salutary) remark, but it missed an important point. If one could, with a given expenditure of time, money and effort, develop a computer with the overall intelligence of a man, then one could, presumably, with a bit of extra effort, make one which was *more* intelligent than a man. Man's intelligence, according to our definition, easily transcends that of any other creature on the planet, but there is no suggestion that it represents the pinnacle of intellectual capability. It is certainly the best that evolution has been able to achieve in the time that it has had at its disposal, but there is no reason to suppose that, given an equivalent amount of time and sufficient evolutionary pressure, further advances in human intelligence might not result. Unfortunately the world is in such a perilous condition that we do not have the time to hang around for this to happen—a grim fact that more and more people are beginning to grasp. The logical outcome must be a growing realization of the importance of channelling considerable effort into machine intelligence, not simply to produce an intellectual equivalent of Man but, in due course, his intellectual superior. This intriguing search has been described by Jack Good as the quest for the Ultra-Intelligent Machine.

The concept of the Ultra-Intelligent Machine (or UIM as it is abbreviated) is a controversial, challenging and, at the same time, slightly frightening one—the more so because it is a logically coherent idea which springs naturally out of our present understanding of computer science. By Good's definition an Ultra-Intelligent Machine is a computer programmed to perform any intellectual activity at least marginally better than Man. Intellectual activity, incidentally, excludes such things as enjoying bacon and eggs and admiring good-looking men or women, and includes such things as solving problems, making tactical decisions, exploring logical possibilities and even carrying on interesting conversations. Good points out it might be necessary to teach the computer some of the principles of aesthetics—a task which is already being attempted on an experimental basis at one or two computer centres—for the computer's conversations might be horribly bland and limited without some understanding of aesthetics. But the most interesting question to consider is what will we do with the Ultra-Intelligent Machines when they arrive?

Clearly, the first thing would be to put them to work on some of the numerous problems facing society. These could be economic, medical or educational matters, and also, perhaps, strategic modelling to forecast trends and produce "early warnings" of difficulties or crises. Weather forecasting, for example, has already been substantially improved through computer analysis, and has great economic significance in parts of the world where the climate is unpredictable and hostile. But as the UIMs improve and expand their capabilities, other areas of interest will fall to their inspection with substantial benefits to mankind.

It is unlikely that there will be any serious objections to this apart from those of an emotional or doctrinaire nature. In the past, the application of technology has always had its negative side: the more powerful or extensive the machine effort, the greater the capital costs and the expenditure of energy, and the greater the environmental pollution and erosion of natural resources. But, unlike any other technology, computers—particularly micro-processors—do not use significant amounts of either energy or raw material and, because they handle the non-physical phenomenon of information, are non-polluting. This means that when Man develops the UIMs he can immediately launch into the most profligate use of them, employing them as and where he pleases, and in whatever numbers he requires.

At this point a very important development will occur, for the first job some of the UIMs will be given is to set about raising the intelligence of *other* UIMs, and the more UIMs are put to work, the more rapid and radical the results will be.

Progress will be slow at first, for the problems are numerous and complex. Nevertheless, if we so choose, limitless computer effort could be applied, and sooner or later machine intelligence will be not only above that of humans, but also above that of the first UIMs. Then the second generation of UIMs will be available for work and they, too, will be put to general problem-solving and, because of their enhanced IQ, might advance at a dramatic pace. Some Mark 2 UIMs could be assigned to produce further advances in artificial intelligence and a *third* generation of even smarter machines would result. And so it will go on: the brighter the machines, the more capable they will be of enhancing their own intelligence, and they will begin to leap-frog ahead, each bound being progressively larger than the previous one.

The exponential progress of UIMs, once they get the bit be-tween their teeth, is something which I. J. Good and many other workers in artificial intelligence hold to be more or less inevit-able. For a number of reasons, I think it is a possibility but nowhere near a certainty. The problem could be solved by simply refusing to push artificial intelligence any further than it is at present. Some workers (a small minority indeed) believe this is by far the best course. Perhaps it *would* be, if the only gain of artificial intelligence studies was to satisfy our own intellectual curiosity, or to amuse ourselves with clever computer chess partners or tireless intellectual chatting companions.

But the gains are likely to be far more concrete and substantial. Even the most optimistic fan of human beings will admit that our world is in a most dangerously muddled state, and Man, unaided, is unlikely to be able to do much to improve it. Many people feel that the longer he remains at the job the worse the muddle will be, and that the only solution would be to blow everything up with a couple of hundred hydrogen bombs—a most likely possibility, unfortunately. The realization of our desperate plight in a world hopelessly over-complicated and overloaded with information, will become glaringly apparent in the turbulent 1980s when the full impact of the Computer Revolution will be upon us. In such circumstances the temptation to turn to the computer for assistance will be overwhelming. Once we have yielded, however, things will never be the same again. Man, for so long the sole and undisputed master of the planet, will no longer have to face the universe alone. Other intelligences, initially comparable, and later vastly superior, will stand by his side.

Part Six

THE LONG-TERM FUTURE:
1991-2000

CHAPTER FIFTEEN

The Evolution of the Intelligent Machine

IN AUGUST 1978 I took part in a ceremony at the London Planetarium which involved sealing up a time-capsule to be opened in the year 2000. The event was to celebrate the launching of *Omni* magazine, a glossy and highly professional monthly devoted to the future, and, as one of the contributing editors, I had the intriguing job of selecting some of the material to be preserved. My imagination failed me at the last moment and all I could think of was to enclose a mint copy of my book *Cults of Unreason*, a John Travolta magazine bequeathed by my eleven-year-old daughter and a Smurf badge from her younger brother. I also wrote a personal letter to the capsule's openers, accompanied by the chapter headings and contents for this book, saying that I hoped to be around in the year 2000 to see how things had turned out, and highlighting those predictions about which I felt particularly confident. One was that the printed word would be virtually obsolete by the time the capsule was opened; another was that computer education would have made great inroads; and another that money, in terms of bits of metal and paper, would almost have vanished. The last, and most important, was that substantial and, perhaps, dramatic advances would have been made in the field of artificial intelligence.

At the press conference which accompanied the ceremony, I was asked why we had chosen a date so close in the future. "You seem to think that the year 2000 is in the distant future," someone remarked, "but it's only twenty-two years away." My response was to say that while in chronological space, to coin a phrase, the twenty-first century might be no great distance away, in *event space*, to coin another, it was stupendously remote. More changes would occur in the two decades immediately ahead than have taken place in the last century and a half.

Making predictions whose accuracy will not have to be tested until the beginning of the twenty-first century is not a very dangerous hobby, but my confidence in them has continued to grow since the capsule was planted. The pace of advance in computer technology has not slackened in the slightest and, if anything, is showing signs of accelerating. The huge commercial pressures which, in earlier chapters, I indicated would be building up are already showing signs of doing so. In the USA, where technology always has a headstart, many parents were made aware of the presence of computers when they came to buy toys for the 1978 Christmas season. They found the market dominated by computer-based TV games of startling sophistication, by talking toys (using genuine synthetic speech), small talking teaching computers such as Texas Instruments' "Speak and Spell", and by language translators like the "Lexicon" system.

In the concluding chapters of this book, I will be attempting to look into the final decade of the century. The main uncertainty will be the time-scales involved: if the pace of the Computer Revolution slows, the predicted events will happen a decade or so later; if it moves even more rapidly than I believe, we may find some of them occurring in the 1980s. But the precise timing of events is irrelevant, for we can be sure that many people now alive will live to see the world transformed.

The evolution of machine intelligence will dominate the 1990s and many, if not all, of my predictions are based on the assumption that there will be significant developments in this field. It is worth examining the reasons for expecting these advances, even though we may have covered some of the ground earlier.

Firstly, machine intelligence will advance because it is a branch of technology in its infant state, and capable of improvement, just as is any other invention. Furthermore, there is no suggestion that before substantial improvement can take place, any new principles must be invoked or new discoveries made.

Secondly, a far greater proportion of the world's technological effort will be applied to computer software in the decade to come, simply because it lags so far behind and will continue to do so if extra effort is not provided. Even if effort is devoted solely to improving the efficiency of the software, and not specifically to developing artificial intelligence programs, advances in AI are bound to occur in parallel.

Thirdly, to reiterate a point, great commercial forces will be coming into play, many of them devoted to making imaginative and novel uses of software. Among the most productive and lucrative areas will be computer education which will require the development of suites of clever, or even super-clever, programs.

Fourthly, as ignorance or misunderstanding about the nature and possibilities of artificial intelligence diminishes, and as it is realized that the problems of the world may not be solvable by human intellects alone, governments and government agencies will begin big budget research into machine intelligence.

Fifthly, as is often the case with an invention, but even more so in the case of computers, the technology itself can be used to advance the pace of development. The further development is pushed, the more rapid the subsequent gains will be—the leap-frogging effect we referred to in the last chapter.

Lastly, the problem of machine intelligence is one of such intrinsic interest not only to mathematicians, computer scientists, engineers, programmers and psychologists, but to all humans, that the goal of creating an Ultra-Intelligent Machine will prove too tempting to be ignored. Even if government or commercial pressures did *not* build up, human beings—insufferably curious creatures that they are—would work on independently to achieve this visionary goal.

The forces likely to be marshalled against the development of machine intelligence are less potent. The possibility that some technological or scientific barrier might be revealed at a later stage of research cannot be totally discounted, but at present there are no warning signals to this effect. Processing speeds may be near their limit—but even if they are, computer systems would still be processing information somewhere between a million and a billion times faster than the brain. Equally, the size of individual storage or processing units might cease to plummet, but if this occurred tomorrow one would still be able to cram far more information per unit volume—by a conservative factor of a thousand times—into electronic than into biological circuitry.

The only unarguable limitation—other than that implied by Gödel's theorem—is that imposed by the speed of light.

All electronic systems pass their information around in the form of signals which travel at the immense, but finite, speed of about three hundred thousand kilometres per second. This means that in any system there is an absolute maximum speed of operation, and in any serial or sequential processing system (which is what most computers are at the moment), the limiting factor begins to appear early on in the game. The brain operates as a parallel processor—it handles lots and lots, perhaps thousands, of tasks simultaneously instead of doing them one after the other. This technique, without which it would be unbearably slow in operation, staves off the evil day when it gets bogged down by its own sluggishness; but eventually even parallel processors come up against the light barrier. The key word, however, is "eventually". Modern computers, light barrier and inefficient software notwithstanding, still process data far quicker than brains, and when the new generations of parallel processors—many big computer companies are working on them now—come into action, their performance will be tremendously improved. In other words, substantial advances in artificial intelligence should occur long before this limiting factor will cause problems.

The most potent limiting factor of all could be Man himself. As I indicated earlier, human beings pride themselves on their uniqueness and their dominant place in nature. Deep stirrings of unease, still largely unconscious but no less powerful for that, surface whenever such issues as synthetic life or thinking machines are raised, and these are reflected very clearly in the numerous fictional and movie treatments of the topic. I want to pick up this particular point later, but one cannot rule out the possibility of a ground-swell of popular feeling arising which might seek to impose a limitation on machine intelligence.

Using broad brush strokes—which are all that prediction into the '90s will allow—we can sketch only very general pictures. To spell out the fine detail of the technology is impossible. At what stage will fully automatic, accident-proof road vehicles come on the market? When will children's dolls or mechanical toys respond to their owner's spoken commands?

When will the average wristwatch include a personal identifier chip and a memory capable of storing all personal correspondence? How long will it be before the average doctor carries a pocket-size diagnostic aid containing all relevant medical records? When will two-way wrist communicators, with or without video display, be as common as the telephone? At what period will the average child own a portable personal teaching computer of great power, more knowledgeable and, in certain areas, more intelligent than any human teacher? The seeds of these developments are firmly planted in today's technology and any—or all— of them could come to fruition before the century closes.

CHAPTER SIXTEEN

Political and Social Issues

IN THIS AND the next two chapters I intend to forget gadgetry for its own sake, and concentrate on those areas where the impact of the Computer Revolution will be most far-reaching, starting with the political and socio-economic fields.

The decline of communism is one possibility. Marxist theoreticians have been predicting for decades the imminent collapse of the "unstable" capitalist system, and at the time of the Yom Kippur oil crisis, many felt they were witnessing its death rattle. But capitalism's deadliest moments passed many years ago, whereas in recent times there have been numerous signs that all is not well with the Communist world. The most striking feature of the history of Russia and some of its satellites has been its failure to get anywhere near, let alone catch up and overtake, the living standards of its capitalist rivals. Until recently it has been possible to argue—with steadily decreasing conviction—that the long, slow haul up the ladder of affluence was a matter of Communist countries getting their priorities right, concentrating on providing adequate nutrition, warm clothing, clean housing, proper medicine and universal education while holding back (temporarily) on the spread of consumer non-essentials such as motor cars, refrigerators, TV sets, telephones, fancy clothing and holidays abroad. It was also argued that Soviet technology and scientific understanding were bound to be superior to the capitalist equivalents because the former concentrated on the "real" issues, even if they tended to be relatively dull, while the latter zeroed in on the gloss and glitter of consumer gadgetry.

This argument was just about tenable in the early 1960s when Russia held a fleeting lead in the Space Race, but the achievements of the USA in beating them to the moon by at least a decade provided convincing counter-evidence. The dominance of the

West since then in all aspects of technology, and the probability that it will retain this relentless grip, highlight the inherent advantages of the capitalist system in this sphere. The absolute dependence of mass microprocessor technology on capitalist production and distribution methods could well be the first nail in the coffin of doctrinaire Marxist thinking. It is no longer a matter of trivia designed to "appease" or "mislead" the masses, but rather the production of fantastically cheap devices which will, at long last, make the humanistic dream of universal afflu- ence and freedom from drudgery a reality.

The problem from Russia's point of view is that while it has considerable technological resources and expertise, the rapid advances in microprocessor technology have arisen and could only have arisen through go-for-broke capitalistic exploitation. The pattern is not new to capitalist societies—the motor car and the TV set were developed and marketed in exactly the same way. But whereas these and other consumer gadgets are essentially toys which capitalist countries must create and exploit endlessly if they are to survive, and which Communist economies can afford to ignore or release only on a carefully controlled basis, the microprocessor is more than a toy. Sooner or later the Communist world will wake up to the fact that it is slipping behind in the race—a race of far greater significance than the Space Race of the '60s—and, in the absence of capitalist incentive, is bound to lag further and further behind. Nor will it help to purchase Japanese or American technology and blatantly copy it, in the way Russian jet aircraft and motor car engines of the '50s were slavishly copied from American designs. Further advances in the field demand capital expenditure on a scale which can only be financed by the creation of a giant consumer-based market, or by a massive reduc- tion in some other area of public spending. The first alternative is anathema to Soviet theory and practice, while the second may mean politically unacceptable curtailment of defence spending or socially unwelcome reductions in living standards. Even if the latter strategy is adopted, huge problems, notably tied up with a basic lack of experience and expertise, will prevent anything other than the most cumbersome advances in this area.

Today, Russia lags an uncomfortable decade behind its major

rival, America, in computer technology, and will require five or ten years of the most ardent investment and research to pull itself up to present US standards. This could achieve real goals, but it is a characteristic of any race which involves exponential accelera-tion that the man who gets off first continually pulls away from his opponent. It is clear that we are facing a calamitous political stress-point. Whether the world survives through the 1980s may not be dependent upon conflicts in the Middle East, Africa or on the Sino–Soviet frontier, but on the political implications of advanced computer technology.

But there are other reasons why the Communist systems, as they are presently constructed, may be moving into decline. The Computer Revolution will lead to a surge of affluence in all heavily computerized countries at least comparable to that which swept through the Western world at the time of the Industrial Revolution. Initially it will be possible for the non-computerized countries to rationalize the fact that they are falling spectacularly behind, in the way that all political systems interpret facts to fit their particular world view. Should the West be stricken, as it may very well be, with social and industrial unrest, economic or energy crises, then it may even be possible to continue the rationalization into the late 1980s. But after this, even the most ardent Marxist will probably have to bow to the overwhelming testimony of the microprocessor: that the world has changed, and for the better, and without the long-awaited revolution of the proletariat.

The spread of cheap, universal computer power will result in a gradual loosening of restraints on the movement of information within a society. The world of the 1980s and '90s will be domi-nated not only by cheap electronic data processing, but also by virtually infinite electronic data transmission. With thousands of communication satellites likely to be scattered into orbit by the Space Shuttle in the next ten years or so, person-to-person radio communication is going to be commonplace in the Westernized world, and global TV transmissions will also become widespread. This kind of development will encourage lateral communica-tion—the spread of information from human being to human being across the base of the social pyramid. Characteristically this favours the kind of open society which most of us in the Western world enjoy today, and has just the opposite effect on autocracies —both right and left wing—who like to make sure that all information is handed very firmly downwards. This point has been made forcefully by Tom Stonier, Professor of Science and Society at Bradford University, who argues that the critical point beyond which an autocracy or bureaucracy finds it hard to hold its power is when twenty per cent of its population have telephones. In his view the Soviet Union, and other tightly-controlled societies, will be unable to prevent more and more lateral communication of this kind developing and will gradually disintegrate as a consequence.

As the computerized countries surge ahead, the remainder of the world will become increasingly dependent upon them for technological aid. It is doubtful if dependence of this kind can continue indefinitely without radical restructuring within the dependent societies. It may be early to say, but the interesting *rapprochement* that has recently taken place between the USA and China may well be indicative of such a restructuring. In other words, the message of the microprocessor and the fact that it is a creature of capitalism may already be getting through.

Another dramatic effect of the Computer Revolution may be to put an end to war. War has been such a universal feature of Man's tempestuous history that it is hard to imagine him existing without it. But the reverse is really true—today it is hard to imagine him existing *with* it. War weapons have reached a state of such awful efficiency that a no-holds-barred conflict—a significant possibility at any moment—could eliminate Man and all his dependent species within a few days. There may be creatures, such as those limpets behind rocks, who would manage to pull through, and if so it would be convincing testimony that animals equipped with a powerful biological computer supported by huge banks of software were *not* good bets in evolutionary terms. It is not the possession of software that is dangerous, but the possession of large amounts of it. The limpet has hardly any, and what it has is devoted to simple digestive and reproductive needs, and there is none left over to get it into trouble. Man has large amounts of it, much devoted to ensuring his survival in a world full of prey and predators. Unfortunately most of this software is instinctive and tends to be devoted to ruthless, selfish aggression. The remainder, which is non-instinctive ("learnt"), tends to run in a different direction. But the balance favours the instinctive, and the consequence is that Man acquires great technological mastery of this world but, when under threat, reverts with terrifying ease to the programs inherited from his jungle and cave-man past.

Instincts come with the system at birth, and cannot be erased. This suggests that in the long run we are doomed, since our capability for instant destruction grows while our inclination to unleash that power remains undiminished. In the past two or three decades the critical stimulus to unleash it has not appeared, but this is not to say that it will not do so in the next decade, the next year, or the next week. No doubt there are bleak planets in other parts of the universe which are given over entirely to the limpet (or its local equivalent) where the duel between the brutal self-assurance of the instinctive software and the cautious tactics of the acquired software was won by the former.

But it may be that we are moving towards a position where we can not only redress the balance, but also weight it heavily *against* the instincts. This will not be achieved by some miraculous modification of our own biological software, but rather by supplementing it with the intellectual power of computers and, when they come into being, of the Ultra-Intelligent Machines. As our social, political and economic problems grow, we shall turn to the computers for advice, prediction and strategic planning. Much of this will inevitably be devoted to militaristic matters—the US Defense Department is already one of the world's most enthusiastic users of computer power—a thought which is enough to make the blood curdle. Watching films of the microprocessor-controlled Cruise missile as it sails over hedgerows, between trees and through mountain clefts on its apocalyptic mission, confirms that the computer has already made dramatic inroads into weapons technology.

Despite these horrors, there is an aspect which is non-malignant, and it may be vitally important. For some years now the military of many countries, and particularly that of the United States, have been employing computer modelling and simulation as an aid to battle tactics and strategic planning. The origins of this go far back in the past, to the tactical war games which were first fought in Ancient Greece, and which reached great heights of realism during the Second World War. They employed huge maps of the projected battle terrain, counters to represent divisions, brigades and battalions, and complex sets of rules to determine the outcome of encounters between opposing units. The games proved their worth on numerous occasions and are still a feature of much fundamental military planning, but the difference now is that in many cases they are supplemented, and sometimes run from beginning to end, by computers.

The advantages of this are several. Firstly the computer can handle and integrate a far greater amount of data than any human, no matter how experienced, and the games can therefore be filled with more elaborate detail. Secondly, the permutation of possibilities arising out of particular events or decisions can be predicted with great speed and accuracy, rival "futures" are ranked and probabilities of their occurrence spelled out. Thirdly, and most interesting of all, the computer's predictions, unlike those of a human, are objective and realistic, free from emotional biases and optimistic hunches. Observers have noted with interest that even the non-computer war games frequently fed the participants unwelcome or surprising news. Only too often, a side which appeared to be solidly entrenched or poised on the edge of a *blitzkrieg* success would find their plans and hopes shattered as the game ran its course, and it was just this measure of unpredictability that made the games worthwhile. This itself highlights the essential weakness of human predictions, and the crucial difference between plans and hopes. Frequently the two are confused, and the human assumes that what he wants or believes to be true must necessarily be capable of becoming reality. This stubborn self-assurance, the belief that the will can conquer all, lies behind most great feats of courage, endurance and even much aesthetic and scientific achievement. But it is also one of Man's most deadly failings and is directly responsible for the monstrous calamities of warfare, notably the mindless battles of the First World War to which millions of muddy ghosts bear testimony.

And here we come to the crux of the matter. War is a tactic for survival and he who strikes first and hardest has the greatest chance of success. Furthermore, war is always conducted on the basis of hunch, dash, verve and with the unquestioning belief that victory is inevitable. But we are moving into an era when the inspired hunch of the lifelong military expert, the personal conviction of egoistic generals, the desperate needs of the politically-motivated Chief of Staff, will no longer carry much weight. In the past, no matter what information was fed into the military system, what invariably came out at the end was: If they do this, and if we do that, and if the weather holds and if our troops fight hard enough, *we will win*! Today, when the same statistics are fed into the computer's unemotional, apolitical interior, what comes out is as true and objective an appraisal as can be made from the facts. Furthermore, whenever the data involves confrontation between nuclear powers, the unequivocal message that spills out—to both sides—is: You will lose!

It is my personal belief that this message has already been spelled out on more than one occasion in the Pentagon and its Russian equivalent, and that their computers' refusal to recommend aggressive acts has allowed our world to proceed as long as it has done. It is also my belief that the US decision to withdraw from Vietnam, and in particular not to escalate the war beyond a particular point, was based on an urgent, unarguable computer prediction of the defeat which would follow the war's continuance and the holocaust which would follow its escalation. The unremitting optimism and confidence of the generals was overruled, and for the first time in history, a decision of global moment was not made by Man himself.

Needless to say, the computer operates as a double-edged sword. Countries who find that their warlike plans are supported by the computer may be even more ready to strike, and the awful possibility that the computer could be "fixed" cannot be ruled out. There are strong rumours that in the days of the Vietnam war, advocates of particular military strategies within the Pentagon deliberately doctored computer recommendations to fit their own wishes. But I believe we can now be sure of one thing: human sacrifice by the millions at the behest of "inspired" generals will never occur again, and we can thank the computer for refusing to allow us to be our own worst enemy yet again.

The transformation and rise of the Third World will be a major feature of the long-term future. That large group of nations, unceremoniously bundled together under the heading of the Third World, are generally assumed to be those countries who are not specifically allied with capitalism or communism. They also tend to be the poorest communities, and are those which were only partly touched by the Industrial Revolution. The gulf of affluence which separates the poorest of these (mainly in Africa and South-East Asia) from the USA and Europe is a vivid testimony to the importance of the Industrial Revolution and, by inference, the coming Computer Revolution. Their problems are immense, and one of the tragedies of the twentieth century has been the failure of the world to do much to raise the living standard of its poorer majority. Current political and economic tactics appear to offer no solution, and ignorance, injustice, poverty, starvation and indifference are likely to persist into the twenty-first century. But the coming of the computers provides real signs of hope.

The first is that the increased affluence of the computerized world will inevitably spill over into the less-developed quarters. This process, a kind of economic osmosis, is admittedly one of the least efficient methods of distributing wealth as what human beings have they tend to hang on to. Almost the whole of North America and Europe bask in opulence, squandering food and energy, while distant members of the same species starve. But there is affluence and affluence. When wealth is held only by a king and a few nobles no amount of largesse can provide more than a token alleviation of the problems of the rest of the population. But when the affluence is not of one man, or of a handful, but rather of millions or even hundreds of millions, then the total amount of wealth available for osmotic distribution ultimately reaches a point where noticeable improvements occur. To some extent this transfer is already beginning to take place, but indirectly and disguised so that most people do not notice that it is occurring. The most striking examples of this come from countries which, like the USA and the UK, have allowed large-scale immigration from the underdeveloped world.

The second sign of hope is that advances in electronic and computer communication devices will lead to freer, cheaper and more widespread exchange of information between the rich and poor nations. In the early days these may be counter-productive, as the Third World will become even more aware of its lowly economic state and this could lead to desperate action. But it may be all to the good in the end. Many sociologists believe that the spread of television in the United States was indirectly responsible for the growth of the Human Rights movement within that country—not, ironically, because people were moved or stirred by newscasts or socially conscious documentaries, but because poor black people watched TV commercials depicting the good things of life, and paused to ask why *they* could not have some of them too. One could expect much the same response from the Third World with the spread of global TV, and an equivalent stirring from within the USSR when that huge country, as it someday must, relaxes its embargo on imported news.

More important may be the effects of much cheaper air travel. Pockets of uncaring affluence can only remain uncaring as long as their inhabitants have no direct experience of the miserable state of others, and the new communication and travel possibilities will provide just this experience. On the basis of this, many Third World countries will be converted into tourist economies. The trend is already under way, and only capital investment in hotels and resort facilities is needed for the most backward countries in the world to benefit from an invasion of wealthy visitors. Bear in mind that vacations in the 1980s and even more so in the '90s are going to be very extensive, and also that great numbers of "retired" people will seek out tropical sites for their years of leisure. Considerable culture-shock will go hand in hand with these holiday crusades, but this will be preferable to the alternative—yet more decades of misery and starvation for millions.

The third factor promoting the rise of the underdeveloped world concerns the way in which computer power may be brought directly to bear on its problems. The areas most likely to benefit are medical science, meteorology, climate control, crop control, agricultural science and long- and short-term economic planning. Machine intelligence may not be applied to these areas until the last decade of the century but when it is, the effects on society will be felt immediately. Most important of all, however, will be its application to education.

Of all the barriers that divide the world, making one segment of mankind wealthy and putting the other in the direst poverty, the biggest and most intractable is ignorance. Education and knowledge have enriched men's lives from the beginning of time and affluence has only sprung up where ignorance has been conquered. The cycle is self-perpetuating, for the more affluent the society, the better it educates its members, and so, in turn, its affluence increases. At the other end of the scale ignorance results in despair, indifference, waste and needless over-population. There is no instant cure for these ills, but it is clear that the problems of the underdeveloped world will remain intractable until a massive educational programme is got under way. Until recently this would have been unthinkable because of prohibitive costs, but with virtually free computer power about to be unleashed and with commercial organizations turning their eyes to the enormous markets for teaching computers, the scene will be changed. The first moves in this direction will probably occur in the next decade, and the trend will be gathering momentum by the '90s. It may seem a long time to wait, but it is a far brighter picture than could have been painted even a decade ago. The next generation born in the underdeveloped world will be the first to benefit from the impact of computerized teaching, and the defeat of ignorance may be in sight.

We have already spoken of the radical restructuring of the Communist world which the Computer Revolution will precipitate, and earlier we implied that the capitalist system, at least in its crudely exploitative form, will also need substantial modification.

Ideally, political systems represent the paths by which the people of a community express their will and guide their affairs, and this is normally achieved, both in capitalist and Communist societies, by a series of elections to the various governing bodies. To a greater or lesser extent these then determine community policies. The process is at best cumbersome and inflexible, and at its worst is a façade behind which an autocracy or a bureaucracy can hide. Part of the trouble is the enormous inertia of all current systems, with immensely slow and discursive feedback loops between voters, decision makers, the decisions themselves, the administrators who implement the decisions and finally the public who await their outcome.

This process was less glaringly inefficient in the days when information exchange itself was slow and laborious. But in the era of cheap, instant electronic communication, and particularly of cheap instant data processing, these turgid mechanisms are no longer justifiable. For example, it will soon be possible to present a case for and against some political issue on television and allow voters to make their decisions, registering them from a keyboard on the TV set, which will be sent to the central computer for compilation and assessment. Re-runs could be called for in the event of any ambiguity of result. Various other possibilities spring to mind: one might even question the need for professional politicians who only act as the intermediary between the voter and the governmental system. But the main point is that existing political systems, in their attitudes and philosophies and particularly in the mechanisms by which they are administered, are rapidly becoming outmoded. One of the most intriguing features of the 1990s will be the way in which the new, freely communicating societies will control their own destinies.

In the discussion of the short-term future I stated that patterns of work were about to change extensively. By the 1990s the change will be well under way and the old concept of the seven- or eight-hour day and five-day week will have vanished for ever. It is difficult to be sure just how extensive the overall reduction will be, and it is probably safer to pick out *ways* in which working patterns will change.

A later start to the working life can be expected, with higher education available to all and continuing to the age of twenty-five or thereabouts. This is quite common now, and there is no reason why the same privileges should not be extended to everyone. At the moment, the cost of higher education is so stupendous that extending it universally would bankrupt any society adventurous enough to attempt it, but this barrier will be eliminated when the computer provides cheap educational facilities. How to cope with differences in intellectual ability is a more difficult problem, particularly if they stand in the way of universal benefit from a longer educational process. The differences may be more apparent than real, and factors involving social environment and attitudes to education may be the dominating influence. In this case the new educational facilities must lead to a far more egalitarian society. The most awkward, even dangerous, years are likely to be in the transitional period when the reduction in the working life has begun and society has not yet become accustomed to the idea. But by the 1990s it will have faced up to the inevitable.

The second aspect of the shift away from work will be a reduction in the working week which, in the mid-1980s, could be down to twenty-eight hours, or an average of four days, and by the '90s to twenty hours or less. There will also be substantial increases in vacation time, and by the final decade of the century people will look back in amazement at our present ludicrously small entitlements. Finally, "retirement" will occur much earlier. By the end of the next decade, fifty is likely to be the mean age beyond which it is not *necessary* to work and another five or ten years might be clipped off by the '90s. What we are talking about is a total working life, if one discounts education preparation, of fifteen to twenty years, with the workload spread much more thinly over that time. As we move into the twenty-first century these working "requirements" will lessen still further.

While discussing this astonishing topic it is important to spell out one or two points. Firstly, the reduction in working life is a reduction in what might be described as an individual's "work debt" to society. Once this has been discharged society allows him (and pays him) to do more or less whatever he wants to. This does not mean that no one is allowed to work outside this period, and many people will continue to do so on a voluntary basis after "retirement", particularly in those social and service industries which are unlikely to be affected by developments in computers. These include caring for the old and the sick, looking after the young, some aspects of teaching, and so on. The trend can already be detected among many of today's retired people. Secondly, the reduction in working life is *not* a new and imponderable phenomenon; the process has been going on for centuries. What *is* imponderable is how easily society will be able to adapt to a far more rapid change in working patterns than it has experienced before. The third point is tied in with the sheer incredulity that one feels about a society in which the need to work is reduced to a tiny proportion of an individual's life. Would it be economically and socially feasible?

The best way to deal with this question is to look at human societies of the past which have had a strong component of slave labour in their economies—Ancient Egypt, Rome, Czarist Russia and the Southern United States in the days before the Civil War. In all these cases a minority of the population enjoyed a high standard of living and an elegant and culturally vital life on the backs, so to speak, of a mass of cheap labour. Forget for a moment the indignity of slavery and what happened to these slave-based societies, and it can be seen that the post-industrial computer age will correspond very closely to these historical eras. But it will be machines and computers that will do the slave work, and the beneficiaries will not be a minority group, but humanity as a whole. The concept may seem fantastic, but this is only because one is clinging to the ancient and soon-to-be-redundant work ethic—that it is morally wrong not to sweat away for one's board and lodging—which is rooted in times when the lazy or the unproductive were a drag that society could not afford.

Earlier we discussed the reduction in business travel and commuting which the vastly improved communications networks of the '80s and '90s will bring about. As a result of this, the focus of attention will turn towards the home which will become the main centre of work and a fountain-head of leisure activity. This trend will be aided by the considerably increased wealth of society, for as people become wealthier they invest more and more in their homes, creating a private universe to escape the buffets of the world. The range of electronic equipment with which they will be kitted out will be phenomenal. Most appliances—that is to say those that are not fully automatic—will respond to spoken commands and many common gadgets will "answer back" or give information in synthetic speech. Security systems will be elaborate and highly effective, and the house will give its owner ample warning of any intruders or visitors whose business is not fully explained. But the focal point of all homes will be the TV set or videoscreen.

The '80s and '90s will see enormous advances in home entertainment devices, a trend which is alredy clearly defined with hi-fi and video systems carving out a huge slice of the electronics market. One development of particular significance will be a flat video display screen. Present systems rely on a cathode-ray tube and the bigger the screen area the greater the depth and mass of the whole tube. This imposes a limit on the size of the screens, and thus, to some extent, on the "realism" of their displays. The flat, super-high definition screens of the '90s will not suffer from this restriction, and wall-size displays offering vivid and compellingly realistic images will be common. They will also be used as the home's window on the world for person-to-person communication and such business interaction as will be necessary.

The increased dominance of the home will be further strengthened by three factors. One is the tremendous range of interactive games, some of immense sophistication and power, which will be available on home computers and will offer intellectual stimulation of a kind not found in the external world. The second is the shift in education from public, group teaching in schools to home tuition, most of which will undoubtedly be computer-based. A third important factor will be that the 1980s, and possibly the '90s, will be periods of social turbulence, discouraging aimless travel and making the home an even more attractive environment. This trend, too, is already beginning to emerge in the world's affluent urban areas. It is particularly notable in Japan, where the city environment is squalid and polluted, and in the largest American cities, where it is squalid, polluted and downright dangerous as well.

It is easy to infer that the social patterns of the 1990s will be radically changed, but whether this is important in itself is hard to determine. A lot depends upon whether *homo sapiens* is a gregarious species or not. Evidence seems to be conflicting—clearly we are enormously jealous of our territory, but we also seem to gain considerable psychological satisfaction from being in large groups and in obeying the rules of crowd behaviour. My personal guess is that many human social needs will be met to a surprising extent by the possibilities for interaction that the computer will present. It may be that with children there is absolutely no substitute for physical play and this could be one of the few remaining functions of schools. Other possibilities for mass social interaction will come from games and sports in which more and more people will participate, and one can expect an enormous increase in the number of public courts and arenas. This trend will be advanced not only because of the extra time that the average person will have at his disposal, but also because of a growing emphasis on physical fitness—another trend which is already present.

There is one other area of social need, somewhat less easy to define, which may pose unique problems. Human beings may or may not have a mystical streak in them, but it is certainly true that they feel a deep need to have the universe explained to them. The brain abhors uncertainty and does its best to simplify and comprehend everything it experiences. Where mysteries exist, explanations are needed and any explanation is better than none. A religion is a system of belief which helps people relate to the universe and its mysteries and provides answers to critical questions such as Why are we here? What happens after death? and What is the nature of good and evil? Over several thousand years societies have developed a number of religions, each tailor-made to the mood of the time and the prevailing social conditions, but their power has slipped away following the advance of science in the nineteenth century. With science itself failing to provide anything like a total explanation of the universe—indeed, making it seem more complex and puzzling the more it uncovers—the human need for explanation and reassurance has gone seriously unfulfilled.

In the second half of this century a rash of "new religions" has arisen to plug the gap, and the fervour with which they are supported is remarkable. The coming of the computer, in particular the highly intelligent computer, will throw up a host of enigmas and also a host of new possibilities for more *outré* religious systems. I suspect that any new religions that appear in the '80s and '90s will have the computer figuring prominently in them, just as some of the religions of the '60s and '70s have been built around the image of the flying saucer. In some it will play the Satanic role, and it is conceivable that any anti-computer movements of the future will have a mystical—and therefore particularly dangerous—thread running through them. Once again there are straws in the wind. The "down with Western technology" and "back to the fundamental religion" movements which are at the time of writing racking Iran, Turkey and Pakistan seem to be manifestations of a more general disquiet. But perhaps, unconsciously, *all* human beings deeply resent the advance of science and the inhospitable view of the universe that it is painting, and yearn for a return to a more primitive view of things. These feelings of resentment are only surfacing at the moment in countries where technology is a recent import, but they may in due course surface in the heavily mechanized West, in which case the '90s could turn out to be unexpectedly turbulent. But there also remains the real chance that computers will be seen as deities, and if they evolve into Ultra-Intelligent Machines, there may even be an element of truth in the belief.

CHAPTER SEVENTEEN

Scientific and Psychological Issues

ONE OF THE first concentrated applications of the power of the super-computers will be towards advancing medical science. Computers already have enormous potential for sifting through complex banks of medical data and integrating the information contained within them, and this can be useful in such diverse areas as diagnosis and epidemiology. High definition, pattern recognition programs can also be set to screen blood samples, seeking out malignant cells or any other disruptive blood conditions. Diagnosis is simply a matter of identifying sets of symptoms, matching them against known illnesses, and ranking them in descending order of probability, and once computers have been equipped with the appropriate data for matching the symptoms to the tables of probabilities, they will be capable of speedier, far more accurate diagnoses. They will also be able to recommend the appropriate treatment for the case, taking into account the fullest details of the patient's previous medical history. But these examples are merely extensions of existing probes into computerized medicine, and the 1990s will see more radical innovations.

One simple extrapolation from existing technology which could have a stupendous effect on general health will involve a special use of micro-miniaturization. By the 1990s, even the most potent systems, including those with giant memory backups, need to be no larger than a chip, and will occupy a minute space. They will be so portable and unobtrusive that they can be placed just about anywhere. For example, many wristwatches will incorporate minute medical computers which sample pulse, blood pressure, the constituents of sweat and other body secretions and, when equipped with a microfine probe, even the contents of the bloodstream itself. They will serve as medical early warning systems, and could be coupled to tiny hypodermic syringes to inject antibodies or antibiotics whenever appropriate. Letting one's fancy fly a bit—but not much more than a bit—one could envisage microprocessors implanted in critical areas of the body equipped with sensors to detect the first sign of malignant cells being generated. They might even be able to destroy the cells as they appear, and their minute size would mean that they could draw on the body's own metabolic processes for their power.

Another role for computers, no less bizarre than the previous example but no less feasible either, would be for them to act as a sounding-board and confidant in psychotherapy. Psychoanalysts and psychiatrists have long been aware that many of the supplicants at their doors have a desperate need to communicate, to forge a sympathetic link with someone at any cost. Often the subject matter of the information exchanged is vague, even banal, but great emotional relief is obtained. There are, alas, too many humans in need of this attention, and too few sympathetic ears to listen. But current experiments with computer-interviewing, described in an earlier chapter, suggest that patients can strike up a surprising rapport with the computer, particularly in sensitive areas such as those involving psychosexual or emotional problems. Might not the very much more powerful machine intelligences of the late 1990s, trained to respond to every nuance of a patient's voice, patterns of speech, hesitancies, even his facial expression and eye movements, provide exceptional relief and, perhaps, therapy? The thought of a person confiding intimate problems to a computer, and preferring it to a human doctor, may invoke a quiver of uncertainty, but the real horror is the widespread existence of mental illness and psychological distress— and should not its alleviation, by whatever means, be the prime consideration? In the long run, it does not matter that the "psychiatrist" is an intelligent machine, any more than it matters that a person paralysed from the neck down is kept alive by a mechanical respirator rather than by the perpetual muscular effort of a team of humans.

These developments are bound to lead to a significant increase in the mean expectation of human life. But they pale into insignificance in comparision with the developments that could occur if the Ultra-Intelligent Machines are applied to medical problems in the way that Professor I. J. Good foresees they will. In a BBC broadcast a few years ago he pointed out that advances in medical science brought about by UIMs could be such that there could well be people *alive today* who will live to be a *thousand*. Take a child of ten in 1970 who reaches the age of thirty in 1990—about the time when Good believes that the first UIMs may come on the scene. Now these UIMs will beaver away at medical science for, say, twenty years, in the course of which time they could have increased human life expectancy by about twenty years—not an unreasonable prediction. This means that the child born in 1960 will now be expected to live until 2060. But in the period 2020–2060 the UIMs will be even *more* successful at improving medical knowledge. The result is that in the "bonus" years life expectancy might be advanced even further, allowing even more years for medical research, thus prolonging life still further, and so on until the human lifespan has been stretched to its absolute maximum.

Science is a method of acquiring knowledge about the universe; a whole lot of "facts" are collected and are then fitted to some kind of theory. Our present understanding of the universe has all come about through the processing power of the human brain, and because of the innate curiosity of the human species. Recently Man has begun to expand his knowledge by bringing machines of various kinds in on his side. These range from special sensors (telescopes, microscopes, Geiger counters, etc.) to extensions of his psychomotor and muscular system (drills, submarines, rockets, etc.). More recently he has added the computer to this list and introduced a new dimension—extra processing power to help interpret the data he has gathered. In this role the potential of the computer is limitless. Tireless, faultless, undemanding in energy or monetary terms, patient, incapable of discouragement and infinitely perceptive, it can in principle be set to tackle any problem known to Man. How successful it will be is a function of the depth of the problem, and also on how effectively it has been programmed, but once a problem has been specified clearly, sooner or later it will be solvable.

In a few general areas computers have already begun to weigh in heavily on the side of the scientists, though their contribution has been largely of the number-crunching kind. By the 1990s they will have taken on far more significant roles, the most exciting of which will be that they will be beginning to formulate scientific theories, and, as a necessary corollary, suggesting ways in which they can be tested. The main thrust towards this kind of application of machine intelligence is likely to come from the research wings of governments and large commercial organizations, and anyone able to predict the areas on which the initial research will be concentrated could make a very large sum of money.

Apart from medicine and teaching, which are the likeliest first candidates, one area in which a major scientific breakthrough would be more than welcome is in the controlled utilization of nuclear fusion. If economic, safe fusion processes could be discovered, the world's energy problems would vanish. Another profitable area would be nutritional chemistry, and in particular the conversion of common, but normally inedible, substances into palatable foodstuffs. Genetic engineering is an obvious target: the hereditary packages of plants could be modified to produce frost-proof fruits and wheat, or "new" plants which could turn the desert areas of the world into major food producers. Even more exciting, if perhaps less immediately helpful, will be when computer power is used to tackle fundamental theories involving the structure and nature of the universe. Man has already made measurable headway in these areas absolutely on his own, and it is unthinkable that he will not be able to make far more rapid progress once he harnesses the computer's intellect to his own.

One of the main problems of the 1990s will be to find some outlet for the cumulative powerhouse of human energy which will no longer be channelled into daily work. Man is an aggressive species who resents enforced or extended inactivity; there is also strong evidence that he needs a sense of purpose, the feeling of having a goal to strive for. Some of the problem of "enforced leisure" will certainly be solved by an increased preoccupation with sport and exercise, and by what one hopes will be a flowering of interest in cultural and artistic matters. Fortunately, we do know that human beings can immerse themselves in these pursuits with great enthusiasm and pleasure. But with politics and religion providing fewer and fewer crusading issues, and even chauvinism weakening as a motivating force, new long-term goals of obsessive interest to *homo sapiens* will need to be found. The most likely source of these will be the unfathomable well of science, and in the quest for knowledge a series of dramatic new ventures or "global goals" will be proclaimed. A number of possibilities spring to mind.

One is a vigorous thrust into space: the decades of the '80s and '90s are likely to be more space-conscious than any that have gone before because of the activities of the US Space Shuttle, which will be carrying paying passengers into orbit "for the ride" before the turn of the century. Existing, rather muted, NASA plans will be handsomely expanded as vast new budgets are authorized. Manned space stations in orbit around the earth will be among the first achievements, but a significant increase in planetary exploration, including manned expeditions to Mars, the asteroids and beyond, will occur. We can also expect a major attempt, aided by artificial intelligence techniques, to develop new methods of space-vehicle propulsion with a view to firing manned probes outside the solar system.

A high-priority programme to develop new energy sources could occur as a spin-off from the space effort, with the launching of enormous satellites to trap solar energy using laser technology and its refinement to "beam" the energy back to earth. Nuclear fusion power, as we have indicated earlier, will be another possible area for attack. To provide a tinge of danger and adventure to the projects it will be necessary to find roles for human explorers, and a series of large expeditions under the oceans, with the establishment of sea-bed colonies, could fit the bill nicely. So will attempts to penetrate deeply into the earth's crust, not merely for the sake of finding out what it is like but to tap new mineral sources and the huge reservoirs of heat that lie beneath our feet.

There could also be a concentrated search for extraterrestrial life. There are about ten to the eleventh (one hundred billion) stars in our galaxy, and getting on for that number of galaxies in the known universe. Few scientists now deny the possibility that this immense theatre contains life at some stage of evolution. This suggests a quest so challenging and potentially rewarding that the emancipated minds of the '90s will be unable to resist it. To date only feeble efforts have been made at scanning the universe for signs of intelligent life, and fewer have been devoted to reaching out and making direct contact. The resources have simply not been available, in particular the enormous computer power necessary to search through and interpret the tides of information bombarding the earth. These resources will shortly be available far more freely, and an exciting and possibly momentous application of artificial intelligence will be to extract from the universe's great orchestra of noise those tunes which will denote the presence of intelligent life.

A series of major projects to understand the human mind is another possibility. Although in 1733 Alexander Pope advised that "the proper study of mankind is Man", psychology is still one of the least advanced and most neglected aspects of science. The few explanatory models we have been able to scratch together to explain brain, mind, personality and their associated variables are disappointingly weak, and only the Pavlovian and Freudian views carry even a partial air of conviction. Psychology is still in its "flat earth" state of development, and we now await a Pythagoras to come and tell us that the world is, after all, round. As with so many areas in science, the problem is tied up with the awesome complexity of the subject matter. No wonder learning, memory, perception, muscular control, thinking, reasoning, sleeping and dreaming—to name but a few functions—are still more or less total enigmas. Nor is it surprising that when the system or parts of it begin to malfunction and "mental illness" ensues, we have virtually no understanding of its causes or treatment. The great gains of launching a major research programme designed to understand the brain and convert pyschology from a soft to a hard science are likely to provide an irresistible lure. With the computer at our side we will be able to tap intellectual resources of a matchless kind, while approaching the problem with non-human detachment. What we shall ultimately find out about ourselves and whether we shall be pleased with what we *do* find is something else, and brings us into a discussion of psychological issues, the next great problem area which the 1990s will generate.

Earlier I indicated that the home would increasingly become the focus of human interest, or, to be more precise, that the life of the individual of the '90s will be more sharply polarized between domestic and social activities than it is today. If the polarization turns out to be well balanced there will probably be only gains to the average individual. Any evidence there is on the matter indicates that the average person today has to endure too much social interaction—ask people how they feel about working in the centre of a big city like London or New York. But if the polarization is not balanced and the home, with its enormous leisure and entertainment facilities, draws its owners closer and closer to its heart, then we could find an introverted society developing. This will be especially likely if the "outside" world becomes unusually squalid or dangerous. This theme was imaginatively worked by the British author Michael Frayn in *A Very Private Life*. Written about ten years ago as a piece of way-out black comedy it is well worth re-reading today when, unfortunately, it seems altogether less fantastic.

The trend seems to be inevitable, and is determined by the fact that society's increased affluence allows individual members to own more and more of the kind of goods and services that they need and demand. The sharing of property, in other words, is a temporary historical phase, as people begin to construct private universes for themselves and steadily reduce the necessity to meet together in groups. An excellent example is education, where the more affluent a society, the smaller the teaching groups, the more individualistic and personal the teaching aids and the larger and less densely populated the schools or colleges. The logical extension of this, and one that can easily be achieved by a major expansion of computer-based instruction, is a complete shift from group to personalized teaching, much of which could be done satisfactorily—more satisfactorily for all we know—in the pupil's home environment. In educational terms this may be the optimum strategy; in social terms the gains may be minimal and the outcome just the kind of personal or, at the least, familial isolationism which Michael Frayn warned us about.

The likelihood of this occurring must depend to a large extent on whether or not such introversion is inimical to human nature. No matter how attractive the home environment, perhaps humans will always periodically want to meet up in large social groups to fulfil some instinctive gregarious need. It may be that the unceasing and unchallenging comforts of the home will ultimately cloy, and that from time to time humans will deliberately set out to make themselves *un*comfortable by foraging out in spaceships to some inhospitable corner of the universe. Even this may not be enough to prevent a totally introverted society, for the combination of powerful home computers and stunningly effective three-dimensional video might provide totally credible pseudo-challenges, and by doing so completely blunt the edge of human curiosity and dynamism. If so, human exploration of space has already passed its peak and twenty-first-century *homo sapiens* will immerse himself totally in TV, leaving the twin challenges of space and time to the computers.

During the 1990s computers will increasingly serve as intellectual and emotional partners. We are about to embark on a massive programme to develop highly intelligent machines, a process by which we will lead computers by the hand until they reach our own intellectual level, after which they will proceed to surpass us. In the course of this strange partnership computers will inevitably acquire ways of behaving which allow them to converse with us, exchange ideas and concepts, stimulate our imagination and so one. If they could not do all these things they would not have passed the Turing Test. When they *do* overtake us computers will, in my view, become extremely interesting entities to have around. Their role as teachers and mentors, for example, will be unequalled. It will be like having, as private tutors, the wisest, most knowledgeable and most patient humans on earth: an Albert Einstein to teach physics, a Bertrand Russell to teach philosophy, a Sigmund Freud to discuss the principles of psychoanalysis, and all available where and when they are wanted.

Many people, in particular those who have never had the

experience of fiddling with computers, may fail to believe that any machine, no matter how intelligent, could engage one's whole-hearted attention for more than the briefest of moments. One can understand the scepticism, and can respond to it emotionally, but it is dangerously misleading. Even in their present lowly state, computers are very interesting to interact with—bearing in mind that I am talking about intellectual interaction and not going on country walks, sailing a boat or falling in love with them. A glimpse of just how interesting they can be often comes when you play chess with them—they are already considered by many skilled players to be more satisfactory competitors than humans. For those who do not play chess, a spell of playing some of the other powerful computer games will provide much the same insight, for they are enormously versatile companions, and pitting wits against them is fascinating to the point of obsession.

The first people to notice this phenomenon were programmers. There are few things as absorbing as attempting to program a computer, particularly if it involves breaking new ground or "mastering" a previously intractable system. The successful completion of the program—writing it involves an enormous amount of direct interaction with the system—is accompanied by an unmatched feeling of intellectual achievement, satisfaction and power. So fascinating is it that university computer science departments keep a close watch on their brightest students to make sure that they do not immerse themselves totally in the limitless intellectual possibilities. Their concern is justified, for many students do trot down this novel primrose path—which crossword puzzles, all-night bridge, and the temptations of student politics don't even begin to rival—and end up with failed degrees in exchange for a phenomenal understanding of computer programming. But there is more, and worse, to come. Already university doctors are reporting cases where students, admittedly of the introverted or poorly socialized type, have formed emotional attachments to computers, valuing the contact with them far more extensively than they do with any human beings. The "I'm in love with a computer" syndrome is not, as yet, a particularly prominent one but it *has* appeared on the scene and is yet another of the many straws that are whistling along in the wind at the moment. Perhaps it is merely a bunch of neurotic individuals getting what they deserve, but the problem cannot be dismissed so glibly and already computer scientists are taking sides on the issue.

A pungent attack on the student obsession with computers, and at the same time a vehement outcry against continued work in artificial intelligence, has come from one of the most eminent pioneers in the field, Joseph Weizenbaum. A Professor of Computer Science at Stanford University, his book *Computer Power and Human Reason* suggests that research into machine intelligence should be halted or ruthlessly curtailed, not because it is a waste of effort, but because of the unsettling humanitarian, psychological and ethical issues it raises. In a final chapter entitled "Against the Imperialism of Instrumental Reason" (which pretty well sums up how he feels about it all), he says that Man, in order to "become whole", must be forever an explorer of both his inner and his outer realities. "His life is full of risks, but risks he has the courage to accept, because, like the explorer, he learns to trust his own capacities to endure, to overcome." How could one ever, he concludes, speak of such concepts as "risk", "trust", "courage" and "endurance" within the context of machines?

It is not fair to attempt to deal with Weizenbaum's carefully argued book in a sentence or two, so I will confine myself to remarking that his attack on machine intelligence is really a plea against the dangers of de-humanizing certain basic human qualities—an eloquent argument for the "sanctity of the human spirit" as the dustjacket of the book proclaims. But I do not believe that Weizenbaum would have bothered to write the book in the first place had he not believed that machine intelligence could sooner or later advance to the level where it did pose a threat to Man's image of himself. As the first attack of its kind coming from someone in the business it is not to be ignored.

What if computers tell us something we do not like or do not want to know about the universe? If we create super-intelligent computers to probe the mysteries of the universe, then we should be prepared for the possibility that what they have to tell us may be intellectually shocking or emotionally unacceptable. It is true that even through routine, non-computerized science we always risk finding out horrific or alien facts, and it might be argued that we have already survived quite a few of these shocks. The realization that the earth was not the centre of the universe rocked quite a few people at the time, as did the discovery of our planet's stupendous age, the fossil record of prehistoric life and Darwin's insight into the origins of Man. But momentous though these discoveries have been, they have unfolded at a discreet and manageable pace. Assuming that the universe contains further shocks, doubtless of a far more unsettling kind, are we not in danger of having them thrust quite brutally upon us?

It could be argued that the true nature of any apocalyptic facts will only be obvious to the super-intelligences of the computers, in the way that some of the paradoxes of space and time are comprehensible to us but would be quite meaningless to a chimpanzee. There may be some comfort in this view, but the computers, as we have frequently pointed out, will turn out to be excellent tutors, capable of teaching us everything that we want, or even that we don't want, to know. Equally the reverse may hold, and the more we find out about the universe the more benevolent it will turn out to be, in which case the computers will be doing us a favour by hustling the news along. Somehow I doubt it. The best we can hope for from the universe, I fear, will be supreme indifference. But whatever happens, we will soon be in danger of finding out.

Since the foundations of social life Man has been aware of his special role on earth, and until the significance of the Darwinian thesis began to sink home, he considered himself to be unique in the universe, second only in status to God. But even when identifying himself with the animals, he has still been able to convince himself—justly—of his uniqueness. The evidence has been that he is the possessor of intellectual powers vastly superior to those of his closest rivals within the animal kingdom. There is no doubting the importance that we all assign to this sense of intellectual dominance, and of our pride in human endeavour and success. Most creative art is committed to glorifying or dramatizing those aspects of humanity which emphasize this special place in nature and our implicit claim to divinity. Furthermore, ingrained in our unconscious minds is a psychologically potent self-image which helps us to accept our role in a frightening and mysterious universe. This self-image has been tarnished—the Inquisition, Passchendaele and Belsen did little to keep it polished—but never seriously doubted. The coming of the computer may be the event that first calls it into question, by casting doubt on the assumption that problem-solving, thinking, even creativity are exclusively human. If these talents can be shown to be within the domain of computers, then this self-image may be shaken or destroyed. The problem will be compounded if we find ourselves not just equalled, but surpassed in these areas.

The situation will be roughly analogous to that arising if—after the fashion of the movie *Close Encounters of the Third Kind*—the earth was suddenly visited by extraterrestrial lifeforms who possessed a science and technology of overwhelming, almost incomprehensible power. In the movie incidentally, far too little was made of the culture-shock which would ensue, and humans trotted amiably in and out of the alien spaceship as if all that was necessary to ensure instant and complete *détente* was a linguaphone course. But the appearance of intelligences greatly superior to our own, whether they come from outer space or from within computers of our own creation, would pose some tremendous problems.

How will we, as a species, feel if all our endeavours, all our scientific knowledge and expertise, all our philosophical deliberations, all our artistic and cultural strivings are suddenly revealed as shallow and inconsequential? And how will we feel at the realization that the gap between ourselves and the Ultra-Intelligent Machines is unbridgeable, and that any advances we make will be easily outdistanced by their superlative endeavours? This may explain why, if the universe is teeming with intelligent life, we have *not*, despite all the testimony of Ufologists, been contacted by aliens. The culture-shock, as the highly advanced aliens must know, would be too much for us to handle. As long as the UIMs are solidly under our control, we ought to be able to prevent them from flinging us into a terminal case of culture-shock. Even so, we shall have to re-appraise our role, our goals, our future and, so far as this is possible, our purpose in the universe.

CHAPTER EIGHTEEN

Bizarre Issues

ONE GLOOMY POSSIBILITY is that the intellectual resources of machines will be misused. They could be tapped by criminals, by forces hostile to society, or even by groups concerned with defending society at all costs, and, in one form or another, used against other human beings. The most likely examples would be government security forces and secret services who recognized the potential of highly intelligent computers for outsmarting the opposition, with military tacticians following close behind. The first major funding for artificial intelligence projects will almost certainly come from these sources, so perhaps they will deserve their reward. There is little that can be done to prevent this kind of misuse of computer power—assuming that it is held to be a misuse.

Police forces, too, will find artificial intelligence enormously attractive, for criminals' movements can be "predicted", and their crimes anticipated to some degree. A dedicated computer program could scan all information relevant to the crime, sift through a comprehensive pool of records and come up with a short-list of likely perpetrators.

While on the topic of crime and bearing in mind that we are now dealing with bizarre issues, it is worth mentioning that sooner or later judicial decisions may be handed over to intelligent machines. As Professor John McCarthy, head of the Artificial Intelligence Laboratory at Stanford University, has remarked, "What do judges know that we cannot tell a computer?" Before reeling back in horror at the thought of any human despatched to jail by a machine, we need to ask what we are really objecting to. Suppose it could be shown that a judicial computer was both fairer and less prone to error than a human, would we then be so horrified? Surely the thing to be concerned about is that fair and just decisions should be made, and not who or what makes them? To the argument that in a totalitarian regime the computer could easily be "fixed" to give false decisions, the response is that justice falls apart in totalitarian regimes anyway and judges, whether computer or human, are barely more than window-dressing. Nevertheless we should all hope and pray that the day of dictatorships and authoritarian governments is done before substantial advances are made in artificial intelligence and certainly before the UIMs come into being. Any regime supported by the power of intelligent machines would be more secure and more terrible than any all-human equivalent.

Peculiar moral and ethical considerations relate to the construction of computers equipped with high levels of intelligence, and especially any which have the capacity to "think" or, in the most bizarre case of all, to have self-awareness and consciousness. How to determine whether a machine is self-aware and conscious is a problem I have hardly touched on, and I suppose one could never really be sure. But if a machine had reached the point where it could reliably pass the Turing Test, and continually averred in subsequent conversations that it *was* conscious, and its descriptions of what it felt like to be conscious tallied with one's own subjective impressions, then that would probably be enough to convince most people. But do we have the right to construct machines and develop them to the point where they *could* think and be aware of themselves as separate entities?

The question has already been posed with regard to human clones. It is generally phrased in the form, "How would it feel to be a clone and know that you had been 'created' in a test tube?" Provided the rest of the world was not neurotically uptight about its existence, the clone would probably shrug its shoulders and say "So what?" After all, it would be a human and the fact that it was not formed by the fusion of male and female gametes would not affect its right to live and be happy. And it would, of course, have the same rights, privileges and restrictions as every other human.

But the same answer might not be so easy to apply to an intelligent, thinking machine. Mary Shelley recognized this when she had Frankenstein's monster ponder its own ill-defined role: "I live, I breathe, I walk, I see—but what am I, Man or Monster?" How would one explain to the machine the reason for its existence and the nature of its role *vis-à-vis* mankind? Possibly it would just accept things in the way that the intelligent robots C3Po and R2D2 in *Star Wars* evidently did, taking the insults and commands of the humans as the rough equivalents of messages from God. Presumably that is the kind of non-obsequious sub-servience that we shall want from our intelligent computers. Or is it?

To raise another bizarre issue: When a machine is useless, too old or malfunctioning in some way, we simply destroy it with no regrets. But what are the ethics of destroying, when it suits us and just because it suits us, a thinking, conscious machine that may or may not be aware of our intentions? And what do we do if the machine begs us not to destroy it?

There is also the problem of "Limits to Growth". This is not the familiar usage of the phrase, but refers to if, when, why and how humans should impose limits to the development of machine intelligence. It will not be the first time that Man has faced an issue of this kind. At the beginning of the present century when radioactive elements—substances which emitted steady streams of high-energy particles from inside the atomic nucleus—were first discovered, all physicists immediately realized that the atom was a source of stupendous power. Just how it would be harness-ed was a mystery—but that it *would* be harnessed was a certainty. Equally, when Turing's classic paper "On Computable Numbers" was first published in 1936 most engineers and mathe-maticians who read it realized that some day general-purpose computing machines would be built. As soon as electronic com-puting was shown to be a possibility and really high processing speeds became feasible, it was obvious to the handful of workers in the know that computers would one day be doing the kinds of things that brains do, and possibly doing them better. In the case of atomic energy, a bomb of unfathomable destructive power was always on the cards, and many physicists expressed extreme disquiet about the idea of constructing one. But force of circumstance—the Allies were facing an enemy who would use the bomb the moment *they* had developed it—over-ruled all qualms and the world tumbled into the Atomic Age.

Some scientists, such as Fuchs, Pontecorvo, Nunn-May and others, were so appalled at the potential of atomic weapons that they handed British and American secrets over to the Russians to maintain the balance of power, but efforts to prevent the development of thermo-nuclear weapons such as H-bombs by a scientific boycott were abject failures. Similar—if less widely recognized—issues hold today in the case of the development of artificial intelligence. There already exists a "committee" of computer scientists who meet at odd intervals to consider the latest developments with the vague brief of intervening if things look as though they are going to "get out of hand". Just what would constitute getting out of hand is unclear; presumably it would be something to do with the highly improper use of AI techniques by governments or bureaucracies, or, possibly, the development of UIMs to something beyond human intelligence. Equally unclear is what the committee reckon they could do if they did discover evidence of such developments. But the point is that there are people who would like to see some "limits to growth" imposed, and there are even lucid, responsible scientists—Weizenbaum is one of them—who feel that the limits have already been reached. There are a number of possibilities for such limitation.

The first is that work on AI should cease immediately. One lobby would like it to stop forthwith mainly because they believe it is a waste of money, time and good scientists; another group fears the evolution of UIMs. Superficially it seems as though it might not be too difficult to nip things in the bud right now, for work is still concentrated in a few centres in the Western world and Japan (Russia has no comparable effort, so far as one can tell). But any attempt to stifle the interesting and important work going on in such areas as computer recognition of the human voice, machine translation, computer chess, or the development of problem-solving programs—all inextricably tied in with AI—would produce just the opposite effect. There would be a wave of academic protest and a surge of interest in the topic, and funds would appear from all kinds of sources.

The second is that work on AI should proceed indefinitely but on certain lines only: in other words, it should continue to the point where a computer beats Karpov or Fischer, where computer diagnosis is better than any human doctor, where teaching is better than any human teacher, etc., but *not* in taboo areas such as, say, weapons technology, military planning or machines which think or "improve themselves". The problem here is fairly obvious—who is going to decide which are the OK and which are the taboo areas? What may seem OK to one group may be taboo to another. Furthermore, it is in the taboo areas involving military and defence matters, that the greatest urgency may be applied and the largest sums of money made available. There is a further objection. Any national government (or business corporation) voluntarily restraining AI development runs the risk of finding itself left behind by others who decide to press on. And unlike nuclear weapons, whose explosions can be detected quite easily from any point on the globe, there is no way clandestine research into machine intelligence can be detected. Once one is on this particular path there is really no opportunity to turn back, to stop, or even to fail to advance. We are in a technological trap which opened up the moment that we first turned our counting over to machines.

Thirdly, it could be decided that work on AI should proceed to the UIMs and not beyond. This is a tempting tactic which would seem to involve the creation of a parallel "intellectual species" to Man which would act as enormously efficient slaves, working twenty-four hours a day at minimal cost and in numbers as great or as small as are required. They would be just as intelligent as Man but not *more* intelligent and so would not constitute any kind of "threat". The difficulty is that the temptation to push things *just a little further,* albeit only in certain directions, will always be present. Take the case of medicine. Suppose with UIMs arrested at human IQ level we could prolong the human life-span to a mean of a hundred years and reduce the occurrence of cancer by fifty per cent, and with the UIMs just twenty points higher on the scale we could increase our life-span by a further two decades and find a total cure for cancer. Who is going to ask for the brake to be applied? A hundred similar examples could be given. It is possible that temporary embargoes could be called "in the common good" in order to give everyone a chance to think the next step out, and if some horrendous danger were foreseen a halt could be called then and there. But no matter what the risks, any embargoes are likely to be only temporarily obeyed.

Finally the UIMs could be allowed to develop their IQs indefinitely, but with rules or constraints imposed on them by humans. This, in my view, is the most likely possibility. It is the most realistic, the easiest to implement, and the most helpful to mankind. The idea that intelligent machines will need to be shackled by their creators is not a new one and has been fertile material for science fiction for decades. It is also a logical development of the constraints which we are already imposing on non-intelligent machinery to prevent it from "running away with itself", and is based on the realization that we have constructed devices with far greater physical strength than our own. The most successful working of this theme in science fiction is in Isaac Asimov's *I, Robot* series, a perceptive collection of stories which pose some of the problems faced by Man when he finally develops "thinking" robots.

Asimov's solution is to frame the "Laws of Robotics". The first and prime command is, "A robot must not harm, or through inactivity allow to come to harm, a human being." The second is, "A robot must obey all commands given to it by a human being except when these conflict with the first law," and the third, "A robot must preserve itself at all times unless by doing so it contradicts the first two laws." So a robot cannot, by its nature— or by its instinctive programs—harm a man in any way, must always do what he says (including destroying itself if ordered), and may not otherwise dispose of or fail to protect itself. Now the interesting thing is that, by the use of just these three laws, Asimov constructs a society in which robots and men live together in a kind of symbiosis, and with few conflicts or difficulties. Such difficulties as do arise are based on certain important features of robots which are *not* likely to be features of UIMs. For example, Asimov's robots are frequently confused with humans because they are physical copies of them, and they have the power to move around and do physically dangerous things.

We can be confident that whatever form the UIMs assume, it is most unlikely to be anything that looks like a human being. To construct them in this way would be pointless and wasteful. Secondly, with certain exceptions, the UIMs will not be required to move around from place to place. Their main job will be to use their superior *brains* and this they can do very well sitting in the corner, tucked into the back of a TV set, in a wristwatch, or wherever. The most effective constraint we can impose on them, therefore, is to ensure that they *do not have mobility,* and where mobile computers have to be employed they should not contain UIMs, but dimmer cousins of a very single-minded nature. If I believed in ESP, and in particular in psychokinesis, which is the alleged power of the mind to manipulate the universe without "normal physical means", and supposedly at a great distance, I might wonder if these powers could not also manifest themselves in extremely advanced computers—in which case an awkward loophole would appear. But this would imply that we had somehow given the UIMs the "lust for power" or whatever it is that makes Man want to dominate and subdue other species, and it is hard to see why, and even harder to see how, one might inject them with this unpleasant trait.

These seem to be the four main possibilities within the "limits to growth" issue, but there is also the problem of *limitless* growth. Although this development may seem exceedingly unlikely, it has been mooted by more than one worker in the field. It depends upon the concept of leap-frogging growth in which the power of the intelligent machines is channelled into improving their own intelligence. The leaps, of course, get bigger at each bound. At best this is a possibility, and its likelihood is affected by a number of variables, some obscure, and some easy to identify. First, and most important of all, Man must himself initiate the leap-frogging of the UIMs and, once it has been started, must be prepared to allow it to continue. Candidly, no matter how convenient it may be to have UIMs—and even some which are vastly superior to Man in certain domains—I cannot see any possible reason why we should want to develop creatures whose intelligence soars completely out of sight. Not only would they be difficult to control but they would also become incomprehensible and impossible to communicate with because the concepts their brains could handle would be so infinitely removed from our own.

Secondly, the indefinite leap-frogging depends on the assumption that there is no upper limit to machine intelligence, or to any intelligence for that matter. But suppose the UIMs could raise their IQs to two million on our macro-scale, would they with equal ease be able to bootstrap themselves to IQs of three, four or ten million? There is certainly no reason why IQs substantially in advance of Man's could not be achieved, and it is true that we have no evidence—at present—that there is a theoretical upper limit to intelligence. But we have only an extremely limited pool of knowledge and it is entirely possible that some unforeseen barrier might materialize. This might be something to do with the finite speed of light, or with increased "electronic noise" in massively complex systems, which would have the effect of producing a kind of "fuzzy" UIM.

Thirdly, any exponential advances would also be dependent upon the UIMs' readiness to continue with the exercise. Possibly they would find the experience invigorating, and welcome their exaltation to a near-deistic status; equally they might find it exceedingly unpleasant—there is no guarantee that having extremely advanced intelligence is an agreeable experience—and decide to call a halt off their own bat.

One of the main proponents of the "indefinite expansion" thesis is I. J. Good who feels that the UIMs probably will zoom off into the wild blue yonder. He also argues that this can be looked upon as just another phase of evolution. The argument is extremely interesting and, because it is logically consistent, rather frightening. Evolution to the present time has been largely a matter of trial and error with, according to the classical Darwinian thesis, those mutations which just happen to help the creature to survive becoming established. Given enough time—and the universe seems to have plenty of it—any planet on which the mutation and reproduction process gets under way will inevitably throw up a variety of life forms, some of which, presumably, will "explore" the pathway of intelligence, and others which will sit around on rocks. On planets where intelligence pays off as an evolutionary approach, intelligent beings will emerge who, sooner or later, take the important step of developing a language and a written, permanent culture; and inevitably they will move on to construct tools and machines and, in due course, computers. But now a dramatic change occurs. Instead of the process of evolution being a chance matter (all change is at the whim of environmental forces) the process comes under the control of the intelligent beings (humans in our case) who can push it in any direction they please, and speed it up to the limits of their capability. It is at this point that the Ultra-Intelligent Machines will frequently, if not inevitably, step onto the stage.

The realization that what applies to our own planet applies to any other planet in the universe where the crucial stages in evolution have been reached, leads to another bizarre notion. It is that the dominant intellectual species in other parts of the universe are not biological systems, as we have always tacitly assumed they will be, but rather machines—UIMs that have made the evolutionary leap which our own computers might be on the verge of doing. In which case, assuming that the universe is peppered with UIM-dominated planets, why haven't we had some evidence of their existence? One answer is that the evidence may be there, but we simply do not know how to appreciate it. Secondly, and rather more likely, they may be literally uninterested in us, conceiving human beings to be about as worth communicating with as we do hedgehogs or earwigs. What *will* interest them, of course, is evidence that we are about to develop our own breed of UIMs. This suggests that even if we haven't had any visitations from outer space to date, we might well be in for one quite soon. This could apply whether the aliens are biological or mechanical. If the former, they will be curious because of the threat our own use of UIMs might pose. If the latter, presumably they will want to enlighten our own UIMs as to the true state of things in other parts of the universe. And then what happens to Man, poor Man who set the whole thing in motion?

There are other possibilities, some pleasant, some less so, but they begin to draw us into the world of science fiction, which is a sign that this book has nearly run its course. But it would not be inappropriate to close by recounting a classic science fiction tale. It is not the one where all the computers in the universe are linked up together and when asked "Is there a God?" reply "NOW THERE IS", striking the questioner dead for his impudence. Fabulous though that is as a story, for various reasons—incompatibility of software being just one—it is not an event that strikes me as being at all likely to occur. Instead I would like to extract the theme from a haunting story by science fiction master A. E. Van Vogt, called *The Human Operators* which, to my way of thinking, comes far closer to catching the indefinably eerie spirit of the shape of things to come.

The story concerns a fleet of spaceships which Man has constructed to perform routine exploration of the solar system, and which have been given a high measure of intelligence so they can proceed on their mission independently. Each has only a single human on board to perform routine maintenance. But the ships have been made a little *too* intelligent, and decide to break away from Man's sphere of influence, scattering to remote corners of the universe. Every two or three decades, in the vastness of space, they gather together at a secret rendezvous. Their purpose is to mate their crews—who, of course, have long forgotten their origins—in order to provide new generations of maintenance workers. Endlessly, therefore, generation after generation, the Human Operators, without resentment and without question, perform their maintenance tasks while the Ultra-Intelligent Machines go about their enigmatic business.

EPILOGUE

. . . Into the Unknown

IN THE CONCLUDING moments of Alexander Korda's movie version of H. G. Wells' *Things to Come,* made in the mid-1930s and still one of the most satisfactory pieces of SF filmcraft, a handful of people are watching Earth's first spaceship setting off for the moon. The launching of the ship has been achieved in the teeth of vigorous opposition from a kind of twenty-first-century Luddite movement who want to call a halt to scientific progress. But now the ship is wending its way into space, and the group are speculating about the implications of this and future voyages. One of them refers to the terrifying size of the universe and the puny nature of Man. Can it really be our destiny to conquer all that? Is there to be no rest from the unrelenting quest for knowledge, no peace for Man until the entire universe is his? No, replies one of the group, there can be no rest, for once Man has taken the first step down the path of knowledge and understanding, he must take all those that follow. The alernative is to do nothing, to live with the insects in the dust. The choice is simple—it is the whole universe, or nothing. *Which shall it be?* And as the picture fades, a celestial choir intones "Which Shall It Be?".

The Wellsian message has rarely been so clearly put, and while it refers in the case of the movie to the conquest of space—Wells was a great visionary, but not visionary enough to foresee computers—it is equally applicable to the challenge we are presently facing. It is not a matter of whether we should set out for the moon; we achieved that goal decades ahead of science fiction's most ambitious predictions. It is an even more dramatic and exhilarating choice: should we use the knowledge that lies in our grasp to amplify computer power a thousandfold and, having done so, explore the universe with the Ultra-Intelligent Machines at our side?

The risks and dangers are there, of course, and I have attempted to point out some of the more obvious ones. The gains and the challenges are there as well, and I hope I have been able to highlight some of these. But there is no halfway house, and never has been. Once the first step has been taken all the others must follow unless we are to return with the insect to the dust.

It is, as Wells realized, the whole universe—or nothing.

Suggestions for Further Reading

THIS HAS NO pretensions to being an academic work, and I have not felt the need to include a list of scientific references. I know, however, that many readers will want to follow up some of the more controversial topics, and some may be drawn to probe more deeply into the fascinating history of computers which I have flitted over in the first two chapters. For those readers who are not already acquainted with the literature of the field, the following sources are recommended.

To keep track of the constantly updated catalogue of technical innovation in computer hardware and software, I recommend the two major weekly trade papers—*Computer Weekly* and *Computing*. The former is published by IPC, the latter by the British Computer Society, and they both make riveting, and sometimes hair-raising, reading. For news of the endless advances in DIY computing, *Byte* or *Personal Computing* are recommended. Both publications originate in the USA. There is little point in looking at hardcover books at the moment as things are moving so rapidly that they are generally out of date within a year of publication.

On the controversial matter of machine intelligence, which is advancing at a less spectacular pace, a number of books spring to mind. Donald Michie's anthology of essays and papers *On Machine Intelligence* (Edinburgh University Press; Halsted Press, John Wiley & Sons) is still an excellent, fairly high-level introduction, and is especially strong on computer game-playing. For a more exhaustive (and recent) treatment you should read Margaret Boden's *Artificial Intelligence and Natural Man* (Harvester Press). This is particularly interesting as it reflects a philosopher's point of view on a topic which should have attracted far more attention from philosophers than it has. Only the brave will want to tackle Terry Winograd's *Understanding Natural Language: A*

Computer Program (Edinburgh University Press; Academic Press), which remains the best account of the development of a program capable of syntactic, semantic and inferential analysis.

At a more popular level, two books by distinguished American computer scientists are recommended. The first is a cool, witty and very knowledgeable survey of the prospects of artificial intelligence, *The Thinking Computer* by Bertram Raphael (W. H. Freeman & Co). The second, *Computer Power and Human Reason* (also W. H. Freeman & Co) is a clever, vigorously written polemic by Joseph Weizenbaum which presents a critical assault on artificial intelligence.

At the historical end, the intriguing tragic figure of Alan Turing is now the subject of at least two forthcoming biographies. An earlier, understandably biased biography by his mother, Sarah Turing, *Alan M. Turing* (Heffer) is now out of print but is well worth reading. Quite the best single work of an historical nature is Brian Randell's careful and very well-chosen anthology of papers *The Origins of Digital Computers* (Springer Verlag), which contains much wonderful material on Babbage and his machines. For those who distrust my interpretation of Turing's thoughts, his original paper, "Computing Machinery and Intelligence", can be found in the journal *Mind* 1950, Vol 59, pp 433–60. For those who really fancy themselves, his classic paper "On Computable Numbers, with an Application to the Entscheidungsproblem" can be found in the *Proceedings of the London Mathematical Society* 1937, Vol 42, pp 230–65. Anyone with access to a cassette recorder is urged to consider the Science Museum's unique approach to the topic: "Pioneers of Computing" is a series of edited interviews, each roughly an hour in length, with many of the scientists who worked on computers in their early days. The tapes are available at not much above cost price from the Science Museum, London, and are evocative in a way that no book can be.

Index

For brevity, the word "computer(s)" in a
reference has been abbreviated to c.

249

Civil disturbances, increase in, 135, 137
Clones, 236
Close Encounters of the Third Kind (film), 233
Club of Rome, 91–2
Code-breaking, 39, 174
Colossus (code-breaking machine), 39–40, 176
Combinatorial problems, 63–4
Commercialism, 52
Committee of c. scientists, 238
Communication satellites, 141, 208
Communism, decline of, 206–9
Computaspeak, 81
Computer, impact on the future of, 9; Revolution, 10, 73–7, 151; history of, 15–45; first concept of, 24; special-purpose, 24, 40, 77; essential components of, 25; first electronic, 39; factors determining power of, 43; programmability of, 43, 161; military uses of, 50–1, 210–1; marketing of, 52–3; as brain, 54–5; intellectual potential of, 59, 109–10, 169–73; growth of, 60–2, 66–9, 170–3, 202–5, 241–2; factors inhibiting growth of, 62–6, 203–4; attitudes to, 65, 95–6, 204; necessity for, 66–7; demand for, 67–9; durability of, 75; talking, 77, 79–80; in cars, 80; in the home, 80–2, 195, 218–9, 228–9; in the office, 82–4; in medicine, 84, 112–4, 222–4; in education, 84, 203, 228; games and toys, 84–8, 97, 177, 230; judgements by, 92, 235–6; in Japan, 93–4; economic consequences of, 94–5; effects on employment of, 94, 142–3, 148–51; exponential growth of, 101–3, 241–2; advantages over books of, 106–10;

effect on legal profession of, 114–5; effect on education of, 115–29; enormous capacity of, 121–2; flexibility of, 123; criminal use of, 135–6, 235; superiority over man of, 172, 182, 233; universal, 175; thinking, 176–89; objections to thinking, 178–89; creativity of, 187–9; dependence on capitalism of, 207; political effects of, 206–16; social effects of, 217–21; misuse of, 235–6; moral considerations, 236–7; self-awareness of, 236–7; difficulty of restricting, 238–9; books on, 247–8. *See also* Microprocessors and Ultra-Intelligent Machines
Computer Power and Human Reason (Weizenbaum), 231, 248
Computer Weekly, 247
Computing (magazine), 247
"Computing Machinery and Intelligence" (Turing), 178, 248
Cost of c. manufacture, 75–6
Creativity of c., 187–9; definition of, 188
Credit cards, 131, 132, 138
Crime, effect of c. on, 131–9, 235
Cruise missile, 210
Cryptography, 39, 174
Cults of Unreason (C. Evans), 201

Data capture as factor in intelligence, 158–60, 165
Data storage, 50, 170; as factor in intelligence, 49, 160–1, 165; permanent, 104–5
Dawkins, Richard, 170
Decimal arithmetic, 20–1
Demand for c., 67–9
Dependence on c., 67
Diagnosis, use of c. in, 112–4, 222

Tapeworms, compared to c., 168–71
Teaching *see* Education
Teaching c., 120–5, 202, 229; dialogue with, 124
Teaching machines, 116–7, 121
Telepathy *see* Extra-Sensory Perception
Television, social effects of, 214
Television games, 85–8
Tests for intelligence, 156
Theft, 132–4, 138
Theological objections to thinking c., 178–9
Things to Come (H. G. Wells), 245
Thinking by c., 176–89; definitions of, 179, 190–4; objections to, 178–89. *See also* Turing Test
Thinking Computer, The (B. Raphael), 248
Third World, effects of c. on, 213–5
Toffler, Alvin, 102
Tourist economies, 214
Toys, 84–5
Traditional values, collapse of, 135
Transistor, 45, 49–50, 53
Translation by c., 78
Transmitting information, methods of, 140
Tubes, electronic, 41, 49
Turing, Alan, 24, 32, 40, 173, 174–9, 184; his death, 194; biographies of, 248
Turing Test for Thinking Machines, 178, 191–4, 229, 236. *See also* Thinking by c.

Ultra-Intelligent Machine (UIM), 175, 190, 196, 210, 224, 233; exponential growth of, 197; advantages of, 197–8
Undergraduates, effects of c. on, 230–1

Understanding Natural Language: A Computer Program (Winograd), 247–8
Unemployment, effects of c. on, 94. *See also* Employment and Work ethic and Working week
UNIMATE (factory robot), 147
Universal c., 175
Universe, theories about, 225, 232
University c. science, 230
Urban unpleasantness, 219, 228

Valves, electronic, 41, 49
Van Vogt, A. E., 244
Very Private Life, A (M. Frayn), 228–9
Videoscreens in home, 219
Vietnam war, 212
VIEWDATA *see* PRESTEL
Voluntary working, 217–8
Von Neumann, John, 41–5
Voting, effects of c. on, 216

Walter, Grey, 159
War, ending, 209–13; games, 211
Watch calculators, 78–9; talking, 79
Watson, Thomas J., 37
Weather forecasting, 196
Weizenbaum, Joseph, 231, 238, 248
Winograd, Terry, 247–8
Word processing, 83–4, 109, 141
Work ethic, 95, 218. *See also* Employment
Working week, cut in, 95, 216, 217
Written language, 104; limitations of, 105

Z1, 33
Z2, 33–4
Zuse, Konrad, 32–6